RELIGION
IN
CHINA TODAY

By Foster Stockwell

NEW WORLD PRESS   BEIJING, CHINA

First Edition 1993

ISBN 7-80005-184-6

Published by
NEW WORLD PRESS
24 Baiwanzhuang Road, Beijing 100037, China

Distributed by
CHINA INTERNATIONAL BOOK TRADING CORPORATION
35 Chegongzhuang Xilu, Beijing 100044, China
P.O. Box 399, Beijing, China

Printed in the People's Republic of China

CONTENTS

INTRODUCTION

This book presents a panorama of religious life today in China. It is based on many interviews with Chinese religious leaders and other investigations conducted at the invitation of the editorial board of the New World Press in Beijing. The book is designed primarily for persons in the West who may be planning a visit to China or who have an interest in world religions. For this reason, I have attempted to present the most up-to-date and accurate information about the status of religion in China today.

My own interest in China's religions stretches back to my childhood. I spent the early years of my life in China — in Chengdu, Sichuan Province. My father was one of the many Methodist missionaries who worked in that country before 1949. My family lived there for more than twenty years. I remember as a boy often visiting Buddhist and Taoist temples — even staying over night in some of them during family travels. I met Tibetan Buddhists who were assisting my mother, a professional musician, in her studies of ethnic music, and I watched from a distance with deep fascination groups of Taoist and Buddhist worshipers on special religious festival days.

In recent years I have had the opportunity to visit China many times on business or for personal pleasure. Again the variety and development of religious life there has afforded one focus for my interests. It has been helpful to be able to view current developments from the perspective of my memories of pre-revolutionary China. Perhaps it is the lack of such a perspective that fuels much of the misinformation that circulates in the Western press about religion in this country.

Some persons in the West view religious life in China as

a highly secret process, with religious groups barely able to keep their heads above water in the sea of atheism. Such a view is a perversion of reality. Religious life in China is quite as vibrant as it is in most other parts of the world. And the religious leaders of China are making remarkable and independent contributions to religious thinking throughout the world. The Buddhists, for example, are developing the concept of "worldly Buddhism" that may eventually revitalize Buddhist understandings all over the world. And some of the analyses of "liberation theology" that are coming from Protestant circles are adding a healthy re-evaluation to this theological development in Protestant and Catholic circles outside of China.

Visitors from the West may find it strange to discover that the Chinese view Catholicism and Protestantism as two different religions, since in the West they are seen as having the same roots. The differences in China are partially the result of a long rivalry between Catholic and Protestant missionaries from the West before the 1949 revolution. They also reflect different ways that these missionaries translated the word "God" and other Biblical concepts into the Chinese language after they began to work in China.

Before you begin to read this book, I need to enter a word of caution about the statistics I have used. They are based on the information I was given, and are likely true for the fall of 1991. But every day, every week, every month these figures change. One needs to remember that new churches and other religious sites are being opened each month in China and the religious population is growing rapidly in some places. So a more recent visitor may not receive the same statistics I was given.

This book could not have been written without the help of many persons, but most of all my wife, Rhoda. She helped to design the itinerary and series of questions, traveled with me, managed the tape recording of all the interview sessions, and provided critical advice and editorial skills to the project.

I would also like to express appreciation to my able

2

translator, Shi Jicai, who is a member of the editorial staff of the New World Press and the executive editor of this book, and Lin Wusun, the director of the Foreign Languages Publishing and Distribution Administration in Beijing. The various staffs of the many Religious Affairs Bureaus that we visited were most helpful and cooperative as were the many persons in all the religious institutions we interviewed and all the Cultural Bureaus who arranged the interviews. The many persons who should be thanked are too numerous to list here.

A few of these include: Master Taoist Min Zhiting, Deputy Director and Associate Secretary-General of the Chinese Taoist Association, and Master Taoist Huang Xinyang, Associate Secretary-General of the Chinese Taoist Association; Zhou Shaoliang, Vice-Chairman of the Chinese Buddhist Association, Shi Nengxing, Director of the Fayuan Temple in Beijing, Wang Yongping, Secretary-General of the Shanghai Buddhist Association, Zhen Chan, President of the Shanghai Buddhist Association and Abbot of the Shanghai Jade Buddha Temple, and Jiamyang Tubudan, Deputy Director of the Yonghe Lamasery in Beijing; Haji Shen Xiaxi and Ahung An Shiwei, Chairman and Vice-Chairman of the Chinese Islamic Association, and Abdola Huang Qiurun, President of the Islamic Association of Fujian Province.

Also Bishop Zong Huaide, President of the Chinese Patriotic Catholic Association and Acting President of the Administrative Commission of the Catholic Church in China, Bishop Fu Tieshan, Vice-Chairman of the Chinese Patriotic Catholic Association, and Zhu Shichang, General Secretary of the Chinese Patriotic Catholic Association; Bishop Ding Guangxun, Chairman of the Chinese Protestant Three-Self Patriotic Movement and Chairman of the China Christian Council, Bishop Sun Yanli, Chairman of the Shanghai Christian Council, Ding Yanren, Associate General Secretary of the Amity Foundation, Shi Ruzhang, Associate General Secretary of the YWCA, Li Shoubao, General Secretary of the YMCA, and Li Yaping, Associate General Secretary of the YMCA; Professors Wang Weifan, Luo Zhenfang, and Li

3

Yading of the Jinling Union Theological Seminary, and Zhu Shipu, head of the Chinese Orthodox Church in Harbin.

It is my hope that after reading this book you will not only want to visit these sites for yourself, but you will also have acquired a deeper appreciation for the diversity and breadth of religious experience in China, not only as practiced today but throughout history.

OVERVIEW:

Marco Polo, Religion, and Marxism

The starting point for any survey of religion in China, ancient or modern, should be Quanzhou.* This bustling city on the southern coast of Fujian Province is absent from most tourist agendas. It is scarcely known outside China. You can find it in history books only as the place from which Marco Polo returned to Italy in 1292.

Then it was called the City of Tung (Zaitung). It rivaled Alexandria in Egypt as the largest trading center in the world. According to Marco Polo's *Description of the World*, "The magnificent and beautiful City of Tung is one of the biggest ports in the world. It is unimaginable that so many merchants converge here, and the merchandise is piled up skyhigh."

Marco Polo apparently didn't realize that Quanzhou was unique among cities in one other way — in religion. It was a center not only for Chinese religions but also for religions from many parts of the world. Records show that believers in at least ten major and minor religions worshipped there, coexisting in relative harmony.

The archaeological and historical evidence shows there were Chinese Taoist, Buddhist, and Ma Zhu temples. There were several Arabian mosques. There were Indian Hindu, Brahman, and Jain worship places. There were Persian Zoroastrians and Manichaens. There was at least one Syrian Christian church founded by members of the Nestorian sect.

---

* The *pin yin* system of transliteration common in China today is used herein for all Chinese words, with the exception of terms such as "Taoism" (the *pin yin* form is "Daoism") that are so commonly spelled this way that to use the *pin yin* would only cause confusion.

And, because this was a center for trade, there were probably some Jews, although archaeological evidence for this group has yet to be found at Quanzhou.

Some of these religions have disappeared, others are no longer found in China. But at least four of them — Taoism, Buddhism, Islam, and Christianity still thrive in many parts of the country.

Marco Polo shows no particular interest in the religions of China. From the pages of his book one would never know that the countryside was peppered with Taoist and Buddhist temples. Nor would one know that the Emperor, Kublai Khan, was himself a devotee of Buddhism, while the Emperor's mother was a Nestorian Christian. Marco Polo only tells us that the Emperor commanded a special palace ceremony for the Christians in his entourage. The Emperor had just learned it was their Easter holiday. The traveler then adds that Kublai observed the festivals of the Jews, Muslims and Buddhists in the same way.

The neglect of religions in China by Marco Polo accords with the commonly held belief that this country is, and always has been, non-religious. The Chinese language doesn't even have a term for the concept "religion," in the occidental sense of the word — a fact that underlines this belief. The Chinese instead use expressions such as "school" or "teachings."

ETHICAL FOUNDATIONS

Scholars both in China and the West will tell you that Chinese society derives from an ethical system rather than a religious one. China has never had a state religion, as Japan has with Shintoism. And China was never divided into a checkerboard pattern of religious states, as one finds in India. There have been times in China when certain emperors tried to impose their religious preferences on the rest of the country, but such attempts were short lived and always ended in failure. Thus the country has been free from the religious wars and strife that shaped much of the history of Europe, the Middle East, and the Americas.

At least from the Tang Dynasty (618-907) onward, according to historical reports, the various governments of China have been relatively tolerant toward all religious beliefs and traditions. That is, so long as they weren't a threat to state authority or to the well-ordering of society. In cases where religious believers presented such a threat, they would be ruthlessly persecuted. Even the common people were of the opinion that threats to state authority would undermine the foundations of the state. Such threats might lead to anarchy and immorality.

The Chinese people have always had a tradition of ancestry worship and acceptance of destiny. But these traditional practices never constituted an organized religion. Instead, the Chinese have taken a rather pragmatic view toward all religions, believing in one or another when beset by life's problems and disposing of that belief when the problems disappear.

To keep the record straight, there are a few geographical areas in China — Tibet is the prime example — where competing religions were never permitted. The Tibetan Buddhist leaders, or Lamas, have jealously protected their religious homeland, keeping all other sects out. When Portuguese Catholic missionaries tried to set up a base in Tibet, in 1624, they were slaughtered for their attempts by a Lama-led mob. And, as recently as 1939, Tibetan fanatics chased YMCA workers from this area after they tried to set up a hostel there.

Although the Dalai Lama, from his exile home in India, claims there is no longer freedom to practice religion in Tibet, in fact it was only after 1949, when the Communist government came to power in China, that Tibetan Lamas finally had to conform to state laws that guarantee freedom of religion. In other words, only recently has it been even conceivable for any non-Buddhist worshipers to practice their religion in Tibet without facing repression. Yet there are still no Taoist, Islam, or Christian worship sites in this area. Chinese government proclamations state, and all Chinese

Buddhists that I talked with agree, that the Dalai Lama's aims are political and not religious.

There have been times in China when local governors and warlords imposed their own religious beliefs on populations under their control. However such restrictions were local in nature and not the policy of any national government.

The ethical basis for Chinese society stems from the writings of the philosopher Confucius (Kong Fuzi) rather than from religious teachings. These have provided working rules for Chinese society ever since the reign of Emperor Wudi of the Han Dynasty (206 B.C.-A.D. 220). They form a system of ethical precepts for the proper management of society. Confucianism views man as a social creature bound to his fellows through five relations — sovereign and subject, parent and child, elder and younger brother, husband and wife, and friend and friend. The most strongly emphasized is the filial relation. Confucianism advocates engagement, action, and duties in human relationships. Correct conduct proceeds not through compulsion, but through a sense of virtue achieved by observing suitable models of deportment.

These Confucian precepts certainly were not all original to Confucius himself. Some of the mores and customs he espoused must have existed long before him in some parts of China. But after his teachings became widely known they, in turn, affected and reshaped the mores and customs of the Chinese people as a whole.

Even today one can see a correspondence between the moral values of Confucianism and those of socialism. Both emphasize collective interests and community welfare. Both emphasize the educational or remolding process an individual goes through in serving the common welfare. These shared features separate both Confucianism and socialism from the individualism and self-centered morality of most Western societies dominated by a capitalist system.

Confucius is, and always has been, honored as a great educator. Before his time (c. 551-479? B.C.) there were only schools of archery in China. He was the first to state clearly that in education there should be no class distinctions. He required no qualifications of birth for his own students, who he trained in the administrative and diplomatic arts. In fact one of the legacies of his educational teaching is the bureaucratic system of government in which anyone who is trainable and ambitious can become a scholar and serve as an official, no matter what his family's social position might have been.

Throughout China and other parts of Southeast Asia there are many temples erected to the memory of Confucius. Usually these consist of a series of courtyards, surrounded by buildings in beautiful Chinese style. Some of these buildings contain inscribed stone tablets; others are empty rooms in which visiting scholars once lived during times when they studied Confucian documents and teachings. There are also gardens and many fine old trees. Some of the temples are among the most beautiful and awe-inspiring structures in China. Scholars and officials manage them rather than priests.

Many people say that Confucianism is a religion because of these temples and because there are believers who treat the memory of this teacher with great reverence. On Confucius' traditional birthday local scholars and officials sometimes assemble to make sacrifices, read liturgical essays, and listen to speeches. The officials are not asked if they believe in the rituals or not. What is important is that they perform them.

And there have been times in Chinese history when Confucianism was treated almost like an official religion. This was the case between the 8th and 16th centuries, when images of his disciples stood in the temples and were worshipped by followers. The feudal rulers of that time made great efforts to deify Confucius. They tried to sanctify the classical Confucian texts and transform Confucianism into a theology by assimilating Buddhist and Taoist religious concepts. The images were later replaced by carved and gilded tablets bearing only the names of the disciples.

But Confucianism has no clergy leadership and it does not teach reverence for a god or gods. As Confucius reportedly said: "Respect ghosts and gods, but stand aloof

9

from them." Nor does Confucianism hold to any belief in the existence of a life after death. One can find religious worshipers of Confucius in some of the temples of Hong Kong and other parts of Southeast Asia. However, the Confucian temples in China today are treated as historical rather than religious sites, and one seldom, if ever, finds worshipers there. Confucianism is viewed as a moral teaching and ethical humanism rather than as a religion.

Of course, whether a system of belief is a religion or not depends on how you define the word "religion." If your definition is broad enough to include anything that provides a sense of the holy, or "numen," then Confucianism would likely fall into this category. But if your definition includes only those beliefs that encompass a power greater than human understanding, then you must rule out Confucianism.

For this study of religion in China today, I have decided to accept the evaluation of the Chinese themselves__ that Confucianism is not a religion. For much the same reason I am excluding various local folk practices that occasionally have ceremonies that resemble religious rites. Some authorities list these as Chinese folk religions. A few of these folk practices have been incorporated into Taoism. The others, like Chinese ancestor worship, lack many of the normal elements of an established religion.

RELIGION ALWAYS SIGNIFICANT

Religions have played as significant a role in the life and culture of the Chinese people as they have in any other civilization. The country is the birthplace of Taoism. And Buddhism, which began in India, has always had more followers in China than anywhere else in the world.

Even today in this supposedly non-religious country, according to official government statistics, there are about 100 million religious believers. This includes believers in Taoism, Buddhism, Islam, and Christianity, in both its Catholic and Protestant forms. And there are about 225,000 full-time religious professionals. Admittedly 100 million is less than ten percent of the total population of China — 1.1 billion (1990 census). But it is a great many worshipers no less.

The evidence for the impact of religion on China's history is everywhere. Pagodas and other cultural sites of former religious significance dot the countryside. Announcements come daily about new religious artifacts discovered in tombs and other archaeological excavations. And there are plenty of temples, mosques, and churches that are still in use, most of them filled to capacity on holy days.

Religion has not only made its impression on China but China has affected religions that came from elsewhere. Zen Buddhism is the most striking example. Known in China as Chan Buddhism, it developed out of an intermixture of otherworldly Indian concepts with the pragmatic and down-to-earth Chinese way of viewing life.

Taoism and the various Chinese forms of Buddhism have also taken root elsewhere in the world, particularly in Japan, Indonesia, and other parts of Southeast Asia. The Muslims of Brunei trace their roots to China, specifically to Quanzhou. Proof of these Chinese origins is shown by the many pilgrimages made by members of these groups to China to visit the temples, monasteries, and mosques that gave their sects birth.

In this book I will describe what is happening to religion in China today. I will look at each of the established religious groups, consider its leadership and numbers of followers, and describe some of the special religious sites that an interested visitor might wish to see during a tour of China. I also will provide some historical material about the Jews of China, although they no longer exist as a religious community. I include the Jews because of the wide interest in this subject among Americans and Europeans.

The book does not cover two minor religions that exist in China today — Shamanism and Dongba. Only a few ethnic groups still practice these religions, and they are apparently abandoning such beliefs as they adapt to modern living conditions. Some of the believers eventually may even convert to one of the other religions, as the Manchu ethnic minority did

11

during the 17th and 18th centuries. Before that, the Manchus believed in Shamanism. Now they are Tibetan Buddhists.

Members of the Xibo, Oroqen, Ewenki, Daur, and Hezhe ethnic minorities still practice Shamanism. Their numbers are few. The Hezhe minority has a population of only 1,489. Most of these minorities are nomadic and forest people. The Oroqens, for example, live much like the American Iroquoi Indians did in the 1700s.

Shamanism holds that invisible forces or spirits pervade the world and affect people's lives. The role of the shaman, or medium, is to shield human beings from these spirits by contacting the mysterious spirit world and making its destructive powers harmless.

Dongba is a religion exclusively practiced by the Naxis, an ethnic minority found in Yunnan Province in Southwest China. The religion has its roots in Bon, a now-extinct, pre-Buddhist religion of Tibet. The Dongba belief includes a multitude of demons and mini-deities that must be exorcised by specially designated persons. The rituals are highly specialized and the number of trained exorcists is diminishing. Some of the Naxis have adopted Tibetan Buddhism as their religion, and it is likely that more will do so in the future.

COMMUNIST ATTITUDES TOWARD RELIGION

After decades of cold-war conditioning, one often hears people in the West say that religion is suppressed by the government in China. Or they will say there are no longer any "real" religions in this country because the state doesn't permit "honest" worship. Such people argue that this is proven by the fact that the country has a Communist government. After all, "everyone knows that Communists are atheists."

The argument arose from a simplistic, two-sided view of the world in which things related to the "communist camp" are bad and things related to the "free world," good. It is not only erroneous, but represents a modern example of

seeing China through misplaced Western concepts and preju-
dices.

It is faulty because it assumes that all Communist governments are similar to the one established by the Bolsheviks
of Russia in 1917. But China's history is not at all like
Russia's. The Russian workers revolted against the Czar and
the state religion that provided moral support for his
outmoded political system. Some historians believe that the
success of the Russian revolution required suppression of the
established Russian Orthodox Church. At least the church
had to be severed from its role as supporter of the Czarist
state.

In China there never was such a state religion. And,
though most religious leaders in China tried to remain aloof
from the political turmoil that ended in the Communist victory of 1949, some of them took an active role in opposing the
former Nationalist government. Unlike Russian Marxists,
who until recently viewed all religions as counterrevolutionary, Chinese Marxists have united with various
religious groups to further the aims of the revolution.

Communist Party directives do not show high regard for
religion. They view religious beliefs in much the same way as
do Communists in other countries. But they give the matter
of opposing religion low priority. The political position of the
Chinese Communist Party is that it is of minor importance if
some people cherish religious beliefs. The Communist Party
leaders are far more interested in seeing that China becomes
prosperous and that people's lives are improved. They realize that, to do this, religious faiths must be tolerated and
respected.

Each of the constitutions written and adopted by the
Chinese government since the Communists came to power includes an article on religious freedom. The first constitution
was adopted in 1954, the second in 1975, and the third in
1978, after the Cultural Revolution. Its Article 46 reads:
"Citizens enjoy freedom to believe in religion and freedom
not to believe in religion and to propagate atheism."

In the opinion of many religious leaders, the clause

13

about atheism is discriminatory. They requested the government to remove this clause because it is undemocratic to permit the propagation of atheism without also permitting the propagation of religion.

The government agreed, and the clause was removed. When the constitution was rewritten and adopted by the Fifth Session of the Fifth National People's Congress on December 4, 1982, it had a new section on religious freedom (Article 36) that reads: "Citizens of the People's Republic of China enjoy freedom of religious belief. No state organ, public organization or individual may compel citizens to believe in, or not to believe in, any religion; nor may they discriminate against any citizens who believe in, or do not believe in, any religion. The state protects normal religious activities. No one may make use of religion to engage in activities that disrupt public order, impair the health of citizens, or interfere with the educational system of the state. Religious bodies and religious affairs are not subject to any foreign domination."

Those who assume that all Communists are atheists because Karl Marx once said, "religion is the opiate of the people" don't know about the heated discussions that sometimes take place in Marxist circles over this issue. In Russia, atheist societies were once actively promoted by the Communist Party, but not elsewhere. Consider, for example, the membership of the Communist Party of Italy, the largest such party in Western Europe. Reportedly, many of its members are also members of the Catholic Church. And many Communists in the countries of South and Central America maintain active church ties. The Cuban Communist Party, as of October 1990, declared that religious people could join the Party.

It is true, of course, that the Chinese Communist Party expects its members to be atheists and not to take part in religious activities. But this rule is generally ignored for Communist members of some Chinese ethnic minorities. The Party wants its members to be close to the people. To be a member of a Muslim ethnic minority and not be a practicing Muslim, for example, would so isolate the Party member from others within the community — families, friends, and political contacts — that the individual would be ineffective as a Party member.

Also, since the Third Plenum of the Eleventh Communist Party Central Committee meeting (December 1978) there has been much discussion within Chinese Communist circles over whether or not religion should be characterized as an "opiate of the people." Many Chinese Marxist scholars have pointed out that both Marx and Engels characterized religion differently when discussing the matter in other contexts. Engels, for example, showed that religion clearly functioned to mobilize and unify the people for revolutionary struggle during the German peasant wars. Thus, only a few Marxist scholars in China still speak of the "opiate nature of religion."

The argument that the Chinese Communists suppress religion shows no recognition of the Chinese Communist Party's desire to unite all Chinese people in the cause of building their socialist system. It is the method by which they seek to enlist the support of non-Communists. As Marx wrote in *The Communist Manifesto*: "Communists ... labor everywhere for the union and agreement of the democratic parties of all countries."

For the Chinese Communists the task of building this unity became the paramount process by which they would win their revolution and build a socialist society. The Party members tried many approaches to create the necessary climate of unity, sometimes failing but eventually succeeding in this difficult task. As a result, the Chinese Communists gave this process substance not found elsewhere in the Communist movements of the world.

The Chinese Communist Party was founded in 1921, and as early as 1923, at their Third Party Congress, the Communists approved a method of work that placed members directly within the leadership bodies of the Guomindang (Kuomintang), or Nationalist Party. They operated there as a "left block" within the leadership, forming a "united

15

front'' from above. This ended in failure. It was followed by the White Terror and a campaign of annihilation directed against Communist revolutionary bases by Chiang Kai-shek and forces of the Nationalist army.

The Communist revolutionaries, under the leadership of Mao Zedong, reconsolidated only after their famous and tortuous Long March that took them to the revolutionary base at Yan'an. There the Party initiated a second United Front (1937-45) involving Communist and Guomindang cooperation in the War of Resistance Against Japan. Having learned from the mistakes of the first try at forming such a "united front" from above, they took care to build this one from below.

DYNAMICS OF THE UNITED FRONT

The principle that correct leadership "flows from the masses to the masses" is a cornerstone of the united front policy as developed in China. It encourages popular participation from below and a style of leadership in which everyone's opinion has some weight. It is the direct opposite of the elitist forms of leadership that ruled China for more than 2,000 years. Its implementation in this society, where peasants traditionally had nothing to say about the actions of government, has gained the Communist Party and its Communist government widespread support among the people, especially those in the rural areas.

The Chinese Communist Party says that it views its role as one of continually trying to represent the masses by listening to their ideas, concentrating these in a systematic form, and then going back to the people to propagate, explain, and test the ideas in everyday practice. They call this the mass line.

It means that Communists must be open to learning from others while they are setting an example for others through their actions and behavior. Especially prominent in Chinese discussions of the united front are certain kinds of behavior. These include the admonition that Communist Party members recognize situations in which they lack expertise and experience. In such cases, they should rely on non-Communists to instruct them. The Party members must be aware of their own shortcomings and mistakes. They should exercise leadership as if it were a collective enterprise. And no Communists should allow themselves to act in any way that might lead to accusations of dictatorial behavior.

As anyone can see, such learning from non-Communists implies that Party members themselves may experience changes through participation in the united front. Mao Zedong recognized this possibility and discussed it in an article titled "The Role of the Chinese Communist Party in the National War." There he says bluntly: "It is entirely wrong to think that we alone are good and no one else is any good."

BUILDING A UNITED FRONT

During the War of Resistance Against Japan, the Chinese Communists sought aid from every patriotic anti-Japanese organization within Chinese society, including the religious ones. Several noted religious leaders joined in this struggle against Japan. The Buddhist Yuan Yin organized monks into an ambulance corps and visited Buddhist centers in Southeast Asia to solicit aid. Ma Xiangbo, a Catholic leader, participated with Communists in the Shanghai resistance movement. Y. T. Wu (Wu Yaozong), a well-known Protestant leader, solicited medical supplies for the Communist Eighth Route Army and New Fourth Army. Patriotic Taoist and Muslim believers even joined army detachments during the war.

As Chairman Mao Zedong summed up the experience in his *On Coalition Government*, written in 1945, what China needed most was a new democratic state, "a united front democratic alliance based on the overwhelming majority of the people, under the leadership of the working class." The abbot of the Jade Buddha Temple in Shanghai, Zhen Chan, told me that Chairman Mao also said, in another context, "if there is only one religious person in China, we should

17

still respect him.''

China's War of Resistance Against Japan ended in 1945. Chiang Kai-shek was in no mood to engage in any further cooperation with the Communists. He turned his Guomindang troops around to attack them and try again to annihilate all of them. Despite a lavish supply of arms and money from the West, Chiang's army lost battle after battle. By 1949, the Communist Party took power in China, and Chiang, with his demoralized and diminishing army, fled to Taiwan.

The new Communist government continued to pursue its policy of building a united front after it came to power. It took pains to see that every sector of society — farmers, factory workers, intellectuals — was represented in the new government and included in its decision-making bodies. When one looks in detail at each of China's religions, one will see that they still have elected representatives in the consultative branches of the Chinese government. They have them at the local levels as well as at the national level.

Wherever one goes today in China one finds religious leaders speaking of their task as one of teaching followers "to love their religion and to love their country." Before 1949 one seldom, if ever, heard such a formulation from these Chinese leaders. It is one of the legacies of the united front, and it would be wrong to view this patriotism as just a reaction to pressures from the state. It is a genuine response on the part of religious leaders to the way the government acts to protect their rights and to include their views in discussions of government policy.

Unfortunately, individual Party members often fail to live up to the principles and expectations of the united front. And during the notorious ten-year period of the Cultural Revolution the very concept was under criticism. Radicals argued that the united front is a capitulationist and revisionist approach that only subverts and delays revolutionary change.

CHINA AFTER 1949

The history of China since 1949 can be divided into four stages, each of which had its effect on the various religious communities. The first (1949-56) is one of consolidation after winning the revolution. The second (1957-65) is a period of intensified political and class struggles aimed at greater economic development. The third (1966-76) is the Cultural Revolution. The fourth (1977-the present) is a return to economic development and an opening to the outside world.

In September 1949, the Chinese Communists announced the formation of their government. The land was severely devastated by war, the people mired in abysmal poverty and suffering. Transportation and communication systems were in a shambles. Factories no longer operated, and farmland lay untilled. But the new government could claim that the power of imperialism was broken. The various imperial powers that claimed land and special rights in this country, starting as early as the Opium War in 1840 and lasting until the defeat of the Japanese in 1945, were now gone.

Mao Zedong announced to the world on the eve of the founding of the new People's Republic: "China must be independent, China must be liberated, China's affairs must be decided and run by the Chinese themselves, and no further interference, not even the slightest, will be tolerated from any imperialist country" (*Address to the Preparatory Committee of the New Political Consultative Conference*).

The country immediately entered an era of rapid change and progress. The Qinghai-Tibet Highway, the Lanzhou-Xinjiang and Chengdu-Chongqing rail lines, the Yangtze River Bridge at Wuhan, the first batch of Chinese-made motor vehicles from an assembly line at Changchun, the maiden flight of the first Chinese-made airplane are but a few examples of the achievements under the new government.

The most important change was land reform, virtually completed all over the country by 1952. This smashed, once and for all, the harsh feudal system of landlord dominance over peasants that had endured in China since the 5th century B.C. A total of 450 million peasants took part in this struggle for a fair distribution of land. Old land deeds, usurers' receipts, receipts for children sold, were thrown into the flames.

By the end of 1952, the total output value of both industry and agriculture reached the highest peak in Chinese history. During the First Five-Year Plan (1953-57), the industrial output value increased by an average of 18 percent a year, and agricultural output value increased by an average 4.5 percent a year. As Professor Maurice Meisner wrote in *Mao's China: A History of the People's Republic*, "In the first three years of the People's Republic, the Communists wrought more fundamental changes in the social structure of China than had occurred in the previous 2,000 years."

For the religious organizations this was a period of discovering a Chinese national consciousness. Imperialist powers of the West could no longer operate in China, and soon the missionaries of the Catholic, Protestant, and Russian Orthodox churches left China, either by their own desire or because they were expelled by the new government. Patriotic organizations were formed by some of the religious groups. The Chinese Protestants established a Three-Self Patriotic Movement — advocating self-administration, self-support, and self-propagation — in 1954. The Catholics formed the Chinese Patriotic Catholic Association in 1957. A similar group gathered members of the Chinese Orthodox Church, previously called the Russian Orthodox Church, in 1956. The Buddhists (1953), Muslims (1953), and Taoists (1957) also established national organizations all under the watchful eye of the Communist Party.

The period was beset with much controversy within society as a whole and within the religious communities. The Communist Party hoped that religion would wither away as people's living conditions improved. They initiated a series of campaigns to root out "old evils" and to consolidate their rule. These included: the Suppression of Evil Landlords (1950-53); the Suppression of Spies and Counterrevolutionaries (1950-51); the Suppression of Heterodox Sects (1951-55); and the Elimination of Counterrevolutionaries (1955).

Each of these campaigns, and particularly the last one, found targets within the religious sectors of society. Some Buddhists were attacked as landlords, some Catholics and Protestants as spies and counterrevolutionaries. But the vast majority of worshipers continued to support the government in its efforts to improve the economic life of the people.

In April 1957, Mao Zedong put forward the policy of "Letting a hundred flowers blossom and a hundred schools of thought contend." This policy gave rise to a lively atmosphere of discussion among intellectuals and in society as a whole. In September, the Chinese Communist Party declared at its Eighth National Congress that stormy, large-scale class struggles were a thing of the past. Rather, the main tasks of the country, from now on, would be to develop production, achieve industrialization, and raise the material and cultural living standards of the people.

Nevertheless, two months later a fierce struggle swept the country against "anti-Party and anti-socialist bourgeois Rightists." By the end of this movement, in the summer of 1958, more than 500,000 people had been labeled "Rightists," including many of the leading intellectuals and some religious leaders. It would be more than twenty years before all of them were fully rehabilitated. Years later, the consequences were officially summed up in the following words:

"The scope of the anti-Rightist struggle was made far too broad.... As a result, a large number of people were wrongly labeled 'Rightists.' This harmed many good comrades and cadres and friends who have cooperated with the Party over a long period of time, including many talented intellectuals. For many years, they had to bear the wrong verdicts, the repression and misfortunes, unable to do their part for the socialist cause. This is a loss not only to them as individuals but to the country as a whole" (annotations to the *Resolution on CPC History, 1949-81*).

Even before the Anti-Rightist Movement ended, the

Great Leap Forward began, in early 1958. It represented more revolutionary enthusiasm than reality. The enthusiasm produced incredible reports of grain production rising to eighteen tons per *mu* (one-fifteenth of a hectare); of places that provided free meals for all; of successful smelting of iron and steel in backyards; and of drives to set up universities in every county and to discover poets in every village.

At the same time, another movement started in the countryside — the universal establishing of people's communes. This campaign began in the summer of 1958. Within a few months, more than 120 million rural households (some 99 percent of the rural population) were organized into 26,000 communes. These large units combined grassroots government bodies and economic organizations. Within their territory, the communes managed everything from agriculture, industry, and commerce to education and military affairs. They became the basic-level administrative unit in the rural areas, with highly concentrated powers.

The Great Leap Forward and the rashly begun people's commune movement seriously disrupted the national economy. To add to the economic problems, at the end of the decade, the Soviet Union withdrew all its aid and technical help because of ideological disagreements between the Russian and Chinese Communist parties. On top of that, a series of natural disasters occurred that damaged harvests in many areas. The years 1959-61 were hard everywhere, and in some rural districts there was famine. "Serious cases of dropsy or even the deaths of men and animals from hunger occurred in quite a few areas" (annotations to the *Resolution on CPC History, 1949-81*).

Yet, despite these setbacks, industrial fixed assets reportedly quadrupled between 1956 and 1966. In 1965 the newly set up petroleum industry reported output topping 10 million tons, ending China's dependence on imported oil. New petrochemical plants supplied the market with ever more chemical fibers, chemical fertilizers, and plastic goods. The pressing demand for cotton, once the only cheap source of raw material for clothing the country's huge population

(720 million by 1965), visibly relaxed. The watch and bicycle industries, which formerly could assemble only imported parts, were now in mass production. And the emergence of an electronics industry made available low-cost transistor radios.

For many religious leaders, particularly Christians, this was a period of uncertainty and fear. The anti-Rightist struggle led to widespread attacks against individual church leaders because of their former associations with foreign missionaries and because of Communist statements about the backward nature of religion. Some religious leaders arrested at this time were indeed involved in open and covert attacks on the Communist government, but most were mistakenly charged with such crimes.

THE CULTURAL REVOLUTION

Even as the country pressed ahead economically with increased momentum, there was talk of class struggle. This escalated ominously. One call after another was issued: "Never forget class struggle," "One must talk about class struggle yearly, monthly, daily," "Once you grasp class struggle, everything will fall into place."

Thus the Cultural Revolution began in 1966. With the full support of Mao Zedong, Red Guards and "rebel" groups emerged. Their first action was to "do away with the four olds." They smashed Buddhist statues in temples, cut women's long hair to make it short and in "revolutionary" style, and "struggled against" men and women of letters for allegedly spreading the "old culture." They stopped at nothing to "sweep away all demons and monsters."

People said that the reason the "four olds" could exist and spread was that they had the protection of "capitalist-roaders in authority." This led to the conclusion that the Cultural Revolution was a "great political revolution." Because the basic issue in any political revolution is the seizure of political power, "rebel" groups in every facto-

23

ry and work place moved to seize power from the so-called capitalist-roaders. They replaced the old ruling structure with newborn "revolutionary committees."

The Cultural Revolution turned social values upside down. It lauded violence and mayhem, as well as the looting and burning of public and private property, as "revolutionary actions." It excused brutality or even admired it as an expression of intense class hatred. And, while it regarded civility as bourgeois hypocrisy, it admired rudeness as proletarian style. In retrospect, many of the events of this period were pure insanity.

Religious activities came to a standstill. The government authorities closed all the temples, mosques, and churches and turned their properties over to schools and factories. Some were destroyed and most were severely damaged. The authorities also sent full-time religious workers to re-education schools. Many of these religious staff members were then put to work on farms and in the factories. Some lost their homes. Their congregations became scattered.

"The general estimation," according again to the annotations to the *Resolution on CPC History, 1949-81*, "is that during the ten years' turmoil, more than 100 million people were affected because of trumped-up or blown-up charges, or because someone else in the family had been victimized on such charges." Many people died unredressed, from the Chairman of the People's Republic, Liu Shaoqi, to a Beijing night-soil collector, Shi Chuanxiang. The national economy was on the brink of collapse.

The Cultural Revolution ended with the arrest of the Gang of Four in 1976. This was the ultra-Left group that was trying to seize power in the name of the Cultural Revolution. Celebrations in the streets greeted their downfall. In Shanghai, the wine shops sold out all their stock in a matter of hours. That same year Chairman Mao Zedong died as did Premier Zhou Enlai, the other best-known figure of the Chinese Communist revolution. So did Zhu De, perhaps the most famous general of the Chinese Communist army. The Party and its government began the difficult process of returning the country to its course of economic development.

STAGE OF REFORM

In December 1978, the Eleventh Central Committee of the Chinese Communist Party called on all its members to break free from the bonds of dogmatism and "to seek truth from facts." It also proclaimed that the national focus should shift from class struggle to socialist modernization. This, and other decisions introducing drastic changes in national policy, made that meeting a landmark in the history of the People's Republic of China.

The first stage of the reform started in the countryside and affected the lives of some 800 million people. The large-scale communes were dismantled and the practice of rigid egalitarianism — "eating from the communal pot" — was abolished. Though some well-run collectives have continued to operate, most farm areas have adopted a contract responsibility system based on individual households. Each household is responsible for a certain amount of land and contracts to sell set quantities of produce to the state. Each household can dispose of the remainder of its produce as it wishes, usually by selling it in the free market.

Diversification of crops and sideline activities is encouraged, and state purchase prices of farm products have risen significantly. These measures have spurred the farmers' initiative. Between 1978 and 1984, national grain output rose from 300 million to 400 million tons. Constantly increasing supplies of non-staple foods — meat, poultry, eggs, and vegetables — have flooded into the emerging free markets in the cities.

With their increased earnings, farmers have begun to set up collectively or privately owned small enterprises known as "township enterprises." These include industry, commerce, transport, building, and the service trades. The once-banned individual economy, or private enterprises (most of them small in scale), have reappeared as a supplement to publicly owned enterprises.

The guiding principle since 1978 has been one of establishing a planned commodity economy on the basis of public ownership. (For a long time in the past, commodity economy was regarded as a feature unique to capitalism.) The goal is to change from a system marked by overcentralization to one in which market regulation plays an active role.

Beginning in 1979, China officially introduced the policy of opening to the outside world. As Deng Xiaoping, the architect of China's reform and open policy, said:

"Isolation prevents any country's development. We suffered from this and so did our forefathers.... Isolation lasted more than 300 years, from the middle of the Ming Dynasty (1368-1644) to the Opium War (1840).... As a result, China fell into poverty and ignorance."

From 1980 to 1990, coal output increased from 620 million to 1.08 billion tons; crude oil from 106 million to 138 million tons; electricity from 300.6 billion to 618.0 kwh; steel from 37.12 million to 66.04 million tons; and cement from 80 million to 213 million tons. Consumer goods, before in short supply, are now plentiful and in great variety.

Economic and trade relations have grown apace. The total trade volume in 1990 reached 115.4 billion U.S. dollars. Trade relations now exist between China and more than 180 countries and regions. Hong Kong, Japan, and the United States are the largest trade partners, while business transactions with other countries are also increasing. China used to be a seller of primary products, but now manufactured goods occupy more than 70% of its exports.

The closed churches, mosques, and temples are once again open or are under repair. Religious personnel are back at their posts, and the number of worshipers increases daily. The Protestant Church alone is now more than five times its size in 1949, with two churches being opened throughout the country, on average, every week.

Hostility between the Chinese in Taiwan who support the Nationalists and those on the mainland has diminished in recent years. Many tourists today travel from Taiwan to China to visit their relatives and ancestral home towns. Quite a few of them visit the temples, churches, and mosques of China. There are apparently no major differences separating the Taoists and Buddhists of Taiwan from those of China. There are differences, however, for the Catholics and Protestants of these two lands.

The Vatican has maintained relations with the Nationalist government on Taiwan since 1949, and has no official relationships with China. Thus the Catholics of Taiwan are separated from the independent Catholics of the mainland by their adherence to the policies of Rome. And the Protestants of Taiwan are still divided into the numerous denominations that Western Christians brought to Asia. The Taiwan Baptists, Presbyterians, Methodists, and Seventh Day Adventists find it difficult to comprehend the united post-denominational Protestants of China.

When Hong Kong (separated from China by the British after the Opium War) is again united with the mainland in 1997, strains will undoubtedly surface between the Hong Kong Protestants and Catholics and those of the mainland because of some of these same differences. Yet the Chinese insist that they will allow Hong Kong to keep its present economy and institutions. Undoubtedly after 1997 there will be two different Chinese Catholic churches existing side by side, one under the rules of Rome and the other independent. And most likely there will be a Chinese Protestant Church on the mainland and many Protestant denominations on the island of Hong Kong.

One final event of recent history needs mentioning — the demonstrations at Tiananmen Square. These began, in 1989, on April 15 and ended with the government imposing martial law on June 3 and 4, in a bloody incident that attracted worldwide attention.

The demonstrations started when university students went to Tiananmen Square, in the center of Beijing, to mourn the death of the former Communist Party general secretary, Hu Yaobang. But soon many big-and small-character posters appeared on university campuses that had nothing to do with this mourning. Some of them called for more democracy. Others openly agitated for the overthrow of the government and ending the socialist system.

Soon, many college students in Beijing took to the streets. The most commonly used slogans in the demonstrations were the ones easiest for the public to accept: "More democracy!" "Down with corruption!" "Punish the official profiteers!" Similar demonstrations took place in Shanghai, Nanjing, and other large cities. Among the students participating in the demonstrations were those from some of the Protestant seminaries as well as students belonging to other religious groups. In Xi'an and Changsha, non-student toughs took advantage of the situation to loot downtown areas.

In May, several thousand university students staged a hunger strike in Tiananmen Square. Many people from Beijing and from out of town thronged the streets and the square to voice their support for the strikers. Some came just to see what was happening. It was an explosive situation.

The Beijing demonstrations were quickly put down by the use of military force on the night of June 3. There were arrests and reportedly a number of executions of persons accused of killing army personnel and destroying property. On June 24, the Communist Party Central Committee elected Jiang Zemin general secretary, to head the Party's third-generation of leadership, after Deng Xiaoping retired. (The first generation was centered around Mao Zedong, the second around Deng Xiaoping.) The situation in Beijing and the rest of the country gradually calmed down.

But the effects of the Tiananmen incident were evident in many ways. There was an immediate decline in the number of tourists entering China from the West. The government began a series of mandatory education sessions for office and factory leaders on the subject of the demonstrations, and there were reports of a tightening-up of surveillance by the security branches of the government. And many people throughout China were heard to express their concern that stability needed to be maintained.

Perhaps because of overriding interest in the Tiananmen

uddhist monks from Wutai Mountain perform a medley of ancient music.

argest Taoist statue of Laozi in China was carved from a single ock during the Song Dynasty. It tands near Quanzhou.

Catholic Bishop Fu Tieshan, surrounded by priests and nuns, consecrated the reopening, in 1955, of the Church of Our Savior in Beijing.

Buddhist worshipers crowd Kaiyuan Temple in Quanzhou on one of the many special festival days.

The Catholic Church of Our Savior in Beijing is always crowded for Sunday Mass.

Protestant choir in Beijing performs on Christmas Eve.

Two disciples of Mohammed were set to China by the Prophet around 620 A.D. Their graves are the focal point of the Sacred Muslim Graveyard near Quanzhou.

Many visitors enter the Grand Buddha Hall of the Kaiyuan Temple, in Quanzhou, on any day of the week.

One of the many ancient graves located in the Sacred Muslim Graveyard on Lingshan Hill, near Quanzhou.

Muslims kneel at prayer at the Niujie Mosque in Beijing.

This Muslim mosque in Beijing serves as both a place of worship and as a training school for future religious leaders.

Beautifully maintained gardens flank the walkway to the front door of the Protestant Theological Seminary in Nanjing.

Zixiao Temple is one of the many temples and other Taoist points of interest on Wudang Mountain in Hubei Province.

Taoists at the White Cloud Temple in Beijing conduct a special ceremony in honor of the founder of Taoism, Laozi.

Two Taoist priests practice martial arts at their monastery on Laoshan Mountain in Shandong Province.

Ting Yenren, Education Director for the Amity Foundation, greets a visitor at the entrance to the offices of this Christian initiated service organization.

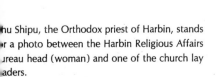

Zhu Shipu, the Orthodox priest of Harbin, stands for a photo between the Harbin Religious Affairs Bureau head (woman) and one of the church lay leaders.

St. Paul's Protestant Church in Nanjing is a former Anglican structure.

The Orthodox Church in Harbin, though n[ ] small, once hosted a Russian Orthodox traini[ ] school.

A Muslim family in the Xinjiang Uygur Autonomous Region celebrates Corban.

Tibet's Tashilhunpo Monastery is justly famous for its beauty and long history as a center for Lamaism.

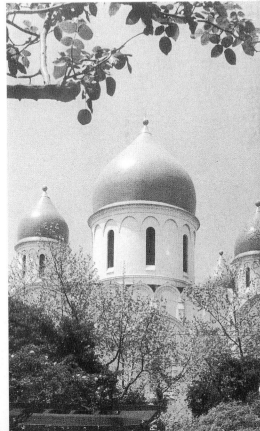

The beautiful Orthodox Church on Xinle Road in Shanghai has Byzantine towers of blue and gold.

The Ruili Monastery in Yunnan Province is a fine example of the architecture found in Pali Buddhism.

Hundreds of Buddhist carvings and statues dot the walls of the Jinge Temple, erected in 770 A.D., on the sacred Buddhist mountain called Wutai.

Small shrine by the side of the road in Fujian Province was erected to a local god said to protect the fields. Many such local gods have been incorporated into the Taoist religion.

Entrance to Cao'an Temple near Quanzhou, built on the site of a former Manichean temple. It contains a stone replica of Mani, one of the few remnants of this religion in the world.

The Cao'an Temple is now a Buddhist nunnery, where orphaned children are cared for. The replica of Mani in this temple has become a Buddhist worship symbol.

This wooden pagoda, erected by Buddhist monks in 1056 A.D., is still standing in Yingxian County, Shanxi Province.

The Xuankong Buddhist Temple in Shanxi Province hangs from the side of a cliff face. It was built between 471 and 523 A.D.

demonstrations, the world press failed to take note of the fact that Muslim students in Beijing were staging a major demonstration of their own at that same time to protest what they considered an affront to the Muslims of China. To the Muslims this was a much more important event than the demonstrations at Tiananmen. But we will hold those details for the chapter about the Muslims of China.

The Tiananmen events, followed by the rapid changes in Eastern Europe and the fall of the Soviet Union, have turned the search light of the Western media on China and its human rights record. Many books and articles have been published describing and analysing these events. Within China, however, the first desire of most people is an improvement in their living standards. After all, the country has the world's largest population but only a small acreage of arable land. Most Chinese agree with the writer in a recent issue of the *Beijing Review*, who wrote that once their country reaches a certain level of subsistence there will certainly be "greater progress in the promotion and protection of human rights."

Since the Tiananmen demonstrations, the government has taken great pains to reaffirm its policy of reform and opening to the outside world. It has also taken measures to correct some of the imbalances that had developed in people's incomes due to the rapidity of economic growth. And efforts have been intensified to educate the public in collectivism and socialism.

The next chapter will deal with one of the special government institutions — the Religious Affairs Bureau. It is important to know about this organ of government because it monitors all the religious groups in China, and every religious institution must relate to it in some way.

In closing this overview, it is interesting to note the status of religion in China today. Here is what some people call a non-religious country governed by an avowedly atheist Communist Party. This country only recently went through a ten-year period when all religious activities were curtailed and all churches, mosques, and temples closed. Yet today, almost every religion in China is experiencing membership growth far beyond what existed before this government came to power.

RELIGION AND THE GOVERNMENT

The very name "Religious Affairs Bureau" evokes suspicion on the part of Westerners hearing for the first time about this government agency in China. The Westerner assumes it must be an agency set up to control and interfere with the religious life of the Chinese people. No such government agency exists in America or the countries of Western Europe.

The immediate questions asked are, "What does the Religious Affairs Bureau do?" and "Why does there need to be one?" When a Chinese person explains there is not just one Religious Affairs Bureau but many, the questioner naturally concludes that this is a giant network of bureaucracies designed to restrict religious freedom. There are Religious Affairs Bureaus at the national level, provincial level, county level, and, in some cases, at the city district level.

It was with great curiosity, therefore, that I approached my first interview with members of the Religious Affairs Bureau of China's State Council. This agency is directly under the State Council. Its offices are in the nation's capital, Beijing. My prepared list of questions was long and many of these questions were directed to the issue of religious freedom in China.

Before I say anything about this interview, however, we should look briefly at the general concept of freedom. Freedom is something everyone favors, and something most governments claim they have. But the concept is closely bound to cultural factors, so much so that what is considered freedom by one person living in one set of circumstances may be just the opposite for another person in a different set of circumstances.

31

Most worshipers in China view the various Religious Affairs Bureaus as agencies to protect their religious rights, not as agencies that limit their freedom to worship. Although, we did learn there are wide variations in behavior and administration among the various Religious Affairs Bureaus of the different provinces and counties. Some do a great deal to help religious workers solve their problems. Others do not. Some of the personnel in these bureaus are sensitive to the needs of the religious community. Others put barriers in their way. None of the personnel of these bureaus have much working experience in the field of religion, because they do not themselves belong to any worshipping communities. Their role is to represent the government in the implementation of its religious policy.

The car in which I was taken to the offices of the Religious Affairs Bureau of the State Council wound its way through a series of narrow streets in the north central part of the city. It was early in the morning and the streets were crowded with bicyclers going to work. Sometimes we had to stop and wait until the traffic jam ahead cleared. We drove past the long wall that stands beside the Chinese Communist Party headquarters. We also went past two primary schools and a hospital. Eventually, we arrived at the gate to a compound of nondescript office buildings. The Religious Affairs Bureau shares quarters with several other state agencies in Beijing.

Mr. Wang, a man in his early thirties, met us at the door. He is the Deputy Chief of the bureau's Department of Policy Research and Legislation. We followed him into the building and up a wide staircase to the third floor, where we were ushered into a large sitting room.

After the obligatory filling of tea cups, we were joined by Mr. Duan, Chief of the bureau's Department of Policy Research and Legislation, and Mr. Zhao, Deputy Director of the Center for Religious Research. I took out my notebook and, with permission, turned on the tape recorder.

My first question was, "What is the function of the Religious Affairs Bureau?

Mr. Duan told us that their job is "to implement the policy of freedom of religious belief; examine and promote the implementation of religious policy and relevant rules and regulations; support the patriotic religious groups to independently conduct work according to their respective characteristics and within the scope of the Constitution and laws; to ensure democratic consultation and effective cooperation between the government and religious groups; to coordinate relations between religious and non-religious believers; to support the religious groups in their friendly exchanges with foreign religious groups in accordance with the principle of independence and self-reliance; to fight against permeation of hostile overseas religious forces; to educate religious believers in patriotism and socialism; to consolidate and develop the patriotic unity with religious groups, and to unite all people in religious groups of all nationalities so as to promote the socialist material and cultural civilization.''

The answer was hardly enlightening. There were many high-sounding phrases, but nothing that gave me a concrete picture of what the bureau does. I probed the matter further, pushing for examples and looking at the answers from my own American understanding of religious freedom.

By the end of the two-hour interview, I had only a vague idea of the bureau's role. It was not until after I had met with a number of other Religious Affairs Bureaus at all levels that I could pull together a picture of what these units actually do and who their personnel are. Therefore, rather than continue with the transcription of this one interview, I will summarize the findings from all the meetings.

REGAINING PROPERTY

To my surprise, the various Religious Affairs Bureaus, particularly the ones at the county level, spend most of their time negotiating matters of property. The job of returning temples, mosques, and churches to their rightful owners still needs to be completed. The Cultural Revolution ended with most of the property once owned by religious organizations being used for secular purposes and in the hands of other institutions. Many temples were occupied by primary and middle schools. Most churches were used as factories and warehouses. The living quarters of mosques were turned into business offices and workers' apartments.

At the end of the Cultural Revolution, in 1976, the government decided that the property of religious organizations should be returned to its original owners. But accomplishing this transfer is no easy task. Time and again I heard about how a local Religious Affairs Bureau was working to find new locations for schools, factories, and office buildings so the religious institutions could reoccupy their sites. In some cases this has meant constructing new buildings for the factories. The Religious Affairs Bureau provides government loans, if needed, so the factory or office complex can construct the new facilities at another location. Sometimes the bureau can find empty facilities as temporary quarters for the secular enterprise so the worship site can be renovated and reused for religious purposes.

In Shanghai, the Catholic Church wanted to reopen its convent in Songjiang County (within the city limits). The site is one of some beauty because it is at the foot of a small mountain. For this reason, the county government decided that the interests of Shanghai might better be served by building a hotel and other tourist facilities there. The county, in fact, put funds into planting trees in the area and otherwise preparing the land for this eventual tourist use. They certainly didn't want to lose their investment and the potential of this site as a money-making venture for Shanghai.

The Catholics themselves had little power to get this land back, and so they turned to the Religious Affairs Bureau. The bureau intervened on behalf of the Catholics. After months of negotiations, the bureau finally got the county to agree to relinquish the land and return it to the Catholics. The convent is now the largest such Catholic institution in China. It is training many novices for future life work in the church.

Occasionally the bureau has to mediate property disputes

between different religious groups. In the case of the Catholic convent property, the land included a small temple that the Buddhists wanted to reopen. The Religious Affairs Bureau negotiated with the Buddhists and was able to convince them that they could use their other temples more wisely. The bureau pointed out that the Catholics didn't have such an option. So the Buddhists agreed to abandon that site and turn it over to the convent.

We found many churches and temples that are still partially occupied by factories or offices, the religious services taking place in just one section of the complex. The secular institution remains because, as yet, it has found nowhere else to move. While occupying this property, the secular institution pays rent to the religious organization. In such cases, the Religious Affairs Bureaus are working diligently with both the secular and religious units to find ways for the factories and offices to vacate all the property so it can once again be used solely for religious purposes.

The government provides large sums of money for renovating temples, mosques, and churches damaged during the Cultural Revolution. And the religious institutions themselves have collected large amounts for maintenance and rebuilding. By the end of 1990, more than 30,000 temples, mosques, and churches were renovated or rebuilt. There were also some 20,000 other types of meeting places open for worship. The result is that more worship sites are now open than before the Cultural Revolution, but not as many as existed before 1949. It is estimated there were 100,000 temples, mosques, and churches then.

With the continuing increase in number of believers in China, more religious sites will need to be opened in the future. And even now, in some areas, more worship places need to be constructed. Money for all this comes from contributions from worshipers, rent paid to the religious organizations by occupiers of their property, and from government loans secured through the Religious Affairs Bureau.

Finally, the government earmarks some money every year for the repair of temples, mosques, and churches of par-

Religions of China

(100 Million Worshippers)

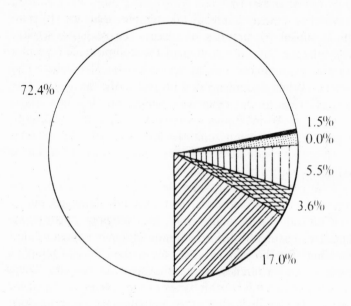

72.4%

1.5%
0.0%

5.5%

3.6%

17.0%

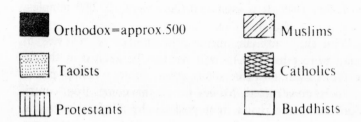

■ Orthodox=approx.500		▨ Muslims	
⣿ Taoists		▧ Catholics	
⫿ Protestants		☐ Buddhists	

ticular historical significance. Quite a number of these are listed for protection as key national or local historical sites. For example, in 1963 the government designated 163 temples and other religious structures as national relics.

Some religious buildings not so designated are still protected by the government because they someday may be. Such is the situation with a particularly beautiful Orthodox Church in Shanghai that was constructed shortly before 1949. The interior of this church was destroyed during the Cultural Revolution, and it now stands unused because there are too few Orthodox believers in Shanghai to constitute a congregation. The original congregation of Russians and East Europeans long ago departed from this city. The government takes care of the exterior, periodically painting its striking blue roof. If the interior is ever restored, it will undoubtedly become a tourist attraction.

UPHOLDING THE LAW

Now let us turn to the legal matters that concern the various Religious Affairs Bureaus. The Chinese Constitution guarantees the right to believe in any religion. Yet discrimination against religious believers does occur. There are many people in China who, because of their prejudice, can't see any positive role that religion can play. They minimize or even negate the way religion is manifested in Chinese philosophy, culture, and art.

When religious personnel complain that some governmental official or other individual is acting to limit religious freedom, that complaint goes to the Religious Affairs Bureau of that local area. It is the bureau's duty to investigate the charge and deal with the individual(s) involved.

The bureau representatives usually act by first explaining the government's policy to the offending individual and counseling that person so the problem will not recur. If this doesn't work, the bureau representatives then may publicly criticize the offender. And, if necessary, they may bring the matter to the attention of the local police authorities.

According to Article 147 of the Criminal Law of the People's Republic of China, "State personnel who are charged with unlawfully depriving citizens of their freedom to believe in religion or who seriously violate the customs of the ethnic minorities may be sentenced to imprisonment or detention for up to two years' time."

The bureau also deals with the other side of religious freedom — the right of individuals not to believe. In areas where religious worshipers live in compact communities, such as in some of the Muslim ethnic minority areas, discrimination against non-believers sometimes occurs. It may take the form of forcing others to participate in worship against their will. The Religious Affairs Bureaus in such areas, when told of this problem, act to protect the non-believers' rights.

The bureau also investigates law-breaking and criminal behavior conducted in the name of religion. This includes practices that may injure the lives and property of people. All persons pretending to be gods and ghosts and spreading fallacies to deceive and harm people by cheating them out of their money are severely punished according to the law. A recent example is a person in southern China who traveled from village to village declaring himself to be the living Jesus Christ and collecting large sums of money from villagers by telling them he would intercede on their behalf in heaven. The man confessed to this crime after he was arrested by the security police, and he was sentenced to four years in prison.

There are reportedly cases of unscrupulous men who exploit women in the name of religion. Women make up the majority of believers in China, as they do in most countries. Such men have been able to seduce women by playing on their religious affections. In some cases, these men have been accused of raping the women. For example, You Shengji, a self-proclaimed preacher from Sixian County in Anhui Province, was arrested for seducing 16 women in this way, 12 of them young girls.

The government deems it a criminal offense for sects or sorcerers to perform fortune telling, divination, exorcism of evil spirits, planchette writings, or holding demonstrations to pray for rain or magic cures. Individuals in the privacy of their own homes can, of course, keep up these old practices since the authorities make a distinction between "the masses" who take part in such "superstitious" activities and "the sorcerers and witches who spread fallacies to deceive people and harm them." But all who make their living by phrenology, fortune telling, geomancy, dispersal of ghosts from sick people, and performing magic to produce rainfall are admonished, educated, and helped to find other means for earning a living.

The government makes a distinction between normal religious activities and what they call superstitious activities. This is why the government has adopted different policies toward each of these. It is the Religious Affairs Bureau that takes pains to delineate these differences.

The various Religious Affairs Bureaus sometimes monitor and investigate reports of anti-government political activities conducted under the cloak of religion. Some foreign powers hostile to China have used this kind of cover to try to undermine the normal social order of the country. Where the evidence for such political activities is irrefutable, the bureaus turn this information over to the police for prosecution.

According to the resolution of the Sixth Plenary Session of the 11th Central Committee of the Chinese Communist Party, held in June 1981, "religious believers ... must not engage in propaganda against Marxism-Leninism and Mao Zedong Thought and ... must not interfere with politics and education in their religious activities."

Of course, this reference to education means public education. Training within the various religious academies is a matter left to the schools themselves. The religious groups sponsor their own educational institutions, select their own administrators, and appoint teachers for such schools. They set their own curriculum. They can invite teachers and lecturers from abroad, if they wish. And they can stock their library shelves with books on religion donated by religious groups from abroad, if these books are used exclusively within the school. The Religious Affairs Bureaus only take interest in

39

these religious schools if their policies and regulations come into conflict with the state.

There are now about 3,000 students attending such religious training schools that are maintained by the various religious groups. Eight of these are institutes at the national level. There are more than 40 such schools that operate at the regional level. Several of them were built and opened with Religious Affairs Bureau support. The personnel of the bureau recognizes the urgency for the need to train younger religious workers to take the place of those trained before 1949, persons now past retirement age.

In the few cases where these religious schools hire teachers from foreign countries to give lectures or handle special classes, they make sure that these teachers do not preach outside the schools or use their position for any kind of anti-government or anti-Party propaganda. The government forbids this and its Religious Affairs Bureaus watch to be sure that such unacceptable behavior does not take place. Also, most of the schools themselves make this prohibition part of their hiring contract.

The problem of foreign teachers using their position to promote religion is real in the area of public education, if not in religious education. Some of those hired to teach English in Chinese universities, particularly teachers from America, arrive in China with the full intention of using their post to promote their own religious commitment. Protestant fundamentalists, Mormons, and some Catholic lay workers have been eager to accept the relatively low salaries paid to foreign teachers in China so they can act as "missionaries" to the Chinese students. Such teachers then use their position to "educate" their Chinese students on the values of religion. They turn private English-tutoring sessions into conversations about the Bible, and try to implant their own religious beliefs on the students.

The Religious Affairs Bureau has nothing to do with teachers hired by the public universities. These are the responsibility of the State Education Commission. Nor does the Religious Affairs Bureau have jurisdiction regarding the distribution of pamphlets, Bibles, or books smuggled into China from abroad by foreign religious groups. This problem is handled by Customs agents. Books and religious materials that are sent or brought to China and go through the proper Customs procedures are usually accepted unless they blatantly undermine the government.

The Chinese laws forbid any religious pressure being put on children and they forbid the recruitment of children by the monasteries and nunneries. Buddhist monasteries in the past often recruited boys six or seven years old as students for the priesthood. The Chinese point out that such pressures reduce a child's freedom of choice for or against religion when that child becomes old enough to make their own decision.

One other legal matter needs to be mentioned. This is the protection of religious grave sites, another concern for the Religious Affairs Bureaus. In this country where farmland is scarce, it takes constant vigilance to keep farmers from encroaching on land that may appear to be fallow and yet is set aside by one or another religious group for use as a burial site.

INTERNATIONAL RELATIONS

When Chinese religious groups set up contacts with religious groups outside China they notify the Religious Affairs Bureau. Thus, for instance, when Muslims decide to go on a pilgrimage to Mecca, they first seek the approval of the Religious Affairs Bureau. This is not just a matter of the bureau keeping tabs on religious activities, it is also needed because the bureau arranges for transportation, procures Chinese passports, applies for foreign visas, and buys the tickets, no small task in China as any tourist will testify.

Relations between Chinese religious groups and their foreign counterparts can be initiated by any of the groups or by their foreign contacts. The government says it welcomes such relations, although they must not lead to domination by the foreign agency over the Chinese religious body. Many of the Taoist, Buddhist, Muslim, and Christian leaders travel

41

abroad to attend international conferences and visit foreign religious institutions. And many religious persons from elsewhere come to China to meet with religious leaders, climb China's sacred mountains, and visit the significant temples, mosques, and churches.

The Religious Affairs Bureau has helped religious groups by assisting in negotiations with the government to purchase printing equipment, paper, and other supplies for the printing of Christian Bibles, Buddhist Sutras, and other types of religious classics. For example, in 1980 the bureau helped the Protestant Three-Self Patriotic Movement arrange for the purchase of eighty-two tons of paper with which to print Bibles. More than six million copies of the Bible have been printed in recent years.

The Religious Affairs Bureau takes an active role in the drafting of laws that apply in the religious field, and it makes sure that all the religious bodies are consulted before any such law is approved. Suggestions submitted by religious bodies to the government about such laws go to the central authorities through this bureau.

With the expansion of religious activities and the perfection of China's legal system, it is acknowledged by numerous religious leaders that the state now needs a comprehensive religious law that would deal with all relations between the state and religious believers and non-believers. Preparatory work on this is now going on. Religious delegates to the Standing Committee of the National People's Congress have submitted a tentative draft for such a comprehensive religious law. Members of the Religious Affairs Bureau of the State Council are working on another one.

When completed, this comprehensive religious law is expected to specify legislatively the state's policy in handling religious issues, protect the legitimate rights and interests of religious organizations, and establish the proper relationship between believers and non-believers and between religious organizations and other social groups. It is also expected to put an end to the use of religion as a pretext to commit crimes. It is anticipated that this law will help strengthen the unity between the religious and non-religious people of China in their efforts to build a modern socialist country.

Before such a law will be passed, it will be circulated to religious groups in all provinces, autonomous regions, and municipalities. Opinions from all concerned departments will be solicited. Then the Law Committee of the National People's Congress will bring it before the Congress for their discussion and approval. It is not known when this process will be completed.

In Quanzhou, we discovered one more thing that the Religious Affairs Bureaus can accomplish — Chinese interfaith cooperation. The man in charge of the Religious Affairs Bureau in that city brought together a group of religious leaders so that I might interview them all at the same time. The bureau leader introduced them one at a time and asked each to give an overview of what is happening in their religious community within the Quanzhou area.

At the table were the local leaders of the Protestant Christian Council, Chinese Islamic Association, Buddhist Association, Taoist Association, and Chinese Patriotic Catholic Association. They were quite different in terms of training, background, and the particular aspects of religion on which they focused. The Muslim smoked heavily, as did the bureau leader and the Taoist. No one else in the room did. It rather surprised me that the Taoist smoked. It indicated that he is part of the Southern Chinese Taoist tradition rather than the Northern. Taoists in the north are much stricter in their adherence to dietary and general health laws.

After the overviews were completed, I directed my first question to the group as a whole. I pointed out that it was quite unusual for me to find so many different religious representatives around a single table. I thought it would be difficult to arrange this kind of a meeting in most countries of the West. I told them that I was honored that they had been willing to gather in this way on my behalf. I then asked if this was the first time such a gathering had occurred.

Several members of the group laughed, probably at me and my suggestion that they came together only on my be-

43

half. They told me that they met in this way once or twice a month. The process had been started by the Religious Affairs Bureau, but they now often met on their own because they found value in the cross fertilization of ideas and discussion of common problems.

They said that China's united front policy naturally leads to such meetings. They gather to discuss common suggestions they wish to make to the county and national government. None of them interferes in the religious beliefs of the others. They said it is their common love for the country that binds them together.

Perhaps Quanzhou is unique. After all, this city from which Marco Polo departed has a long history of many religions living at relative peace with one another. I did not hear about any other monthly interfaith meetings such as this in other cities of China.

I do know that the various religious groups in China joined in prayers for peace in 1986, during the Year of World Peace. And in 1985, the religious organizations jointly sponsored a painting and calligraphy exhibition, giving more than 300 works to the China Welfare Fund for the Handicapped. This past year the religious groups cooperated in the campaign to gather flood-relief supplies for China's flood victims. And undoubtedly they have joined in other activities of public interest, but I don't have more data on this.

ORGANIZATION OF THE BUREAU

The Religious Affairs Bureaus are a natural outgrowth of the united front policy developed by the Chinese Communists during their Long March. The Communists early realized that achieving consensus among the people required that they favor religious freedom. Thus freedom of religion became one of the basic principles of the united front.

The Religious Affairs Bureau of the State Council was not formally established until November 1954, when nineteen other governmental departments were created. At first it was headed by He Chengxiang. He was succeeded by Xiao Xianfa in 1961. Qiao Liansheng took the post in 1981, and the present director is Ren Wuzhi. This state bureau, as well as all the subsidiary provincial and local Religious Affairs Bureaus, was shut down during the Cultural Revolution.

In a sense, having a Religious Affairs Bureau is nothing new in China. Various emperors throughout history had their own agencies of this sort. During the Yuan Dynasty (1206-1368), for example, the government centered its religious affairs department for the southern coast provinces of China at Quanzhou.

The Religious Affairs Bureau of the State Council is today divided into two departments. The first handles the daily affairs related to the various religious organizations. The second is in charge of drafting religious policy. The representatives we met with in Beijing were members of this second department.

The Religious Affairs Bureaus I met with on the local level are not divided in this way. Instead, they work together in one department and assign specific individuals within that department to deal with each of the different religions. In this way, the assigned individual can become familiar with a specific religion, get to know the various local staff representatives of that religion, and develop ties that are essential to good working relations between the government and the religious group.

None of these Religious Affairs Bureau persons had much understanding of religion before they came to work for the bureau. They learn about religion on the job through short courses that are given within the bureau and through contacts with the religious groups. The Religious Affairs Bureau in Shanghai holds such short courses on a regular basis. They last for ten days to two months time. And the Shanghai bureau has recently developed, in cooperation with Fudan University, a two-year course on religion for new employees of the bureau.

The bureau in Shanghai has more than 40 employees who average 30 to 40 years in age, half of whom are women. It also supervises the religious bureaus of the several counties that make up the city and suburbs of Shanghai, and each of these have their own staff.

The bureau of Jiangsu Province, located in Nanjing, has a staff of 32, only five of whom are women. One of these women was not there when we interviewed members of the bureau because she was attending a university overseas, studying English. This bureau is also in charge of ethnic minority affairs for the province. Such a combining of these two government agencies also occurs in many other provinces. Within Jiangsu Province there are also many county Religious Affairs Bureaus that together have more than 300 staff members.

A woman heads the Religious Affairs Bureau in Heilongjiang Province, located in Harbin. It is a small department with only six staff members. She is not a college graduate and previously worked in a factory. She told us that she has had to learn most of what she knows from studying government policy documents on religion and from her contacts with members of the religious groups. When she was first assigned to the job, she told us, she felt that she had to tread very carefully so as not to step on any religious taboos.

No member of the Religious Affairs Bureaus, as far as I could find out, is a member of any religious community, with one lone exception. This is the Deputy Director of the Religious Affairs Bureau in Qinghai Province. This province is a sparsely populated one in China's northwest, an area with many Tibetan Buddhists. This Deputy Director is a Buddhist and was formerly a director of the Chinese Buddhist Association in Beijing.

Many of the bureau members are members of the Chinese Communist Party, since this is a government position. They are assigned to this job by higher government agencies and may or may not have any university training. The Shanghai Bureau takes pride in the fact that all its staff members are college graduates. They come to the bureau either directly from graduation or they are assigned there from other government agencies. Most of them majored in the liberal arts while in college — particularly in philosophy and history.

Perhaps the career backgrounds of the three bureau members we met with in Beijing will give a better picture of the staffing of these bureaus. Mr. Duan was a 1964 graduate of the Northwest Institute of Laws and State Politics. He was appointed to the bureau because of his expertise in legal matters not because of any interest in religion. Mr. Zhao graduated from the History Department of Beijing University in 1962, then taught history for a time at the Institute of Buddhist Studies in Beijing before he was assigned to the bureau. He now specializes in research on religions for this bureau. Mr. Wang is a 1983 graduate of Department of Philosophy at Nanjing University. He worked for a time for the United Front Work Department in Beijing, and then was assigned to this bureau.

Generally when new employees are assigned to these bureaus they arrive with no understanding of religion or its practice. Some admitted to me that they tended to view all religious believers with suspicion at first. They came with an inadequate understanding of how China's united front policies relate to believers and religious groups. Only after these staff members worked within the bureau for some time and got to know various persons in the religious community did they develop more tolerant attitudes.

In some counties, I was told, Leftist tendencies continue to be a barrier to the government's implementation of its religious policies. Here the Religious Affairs Bureaus interfere with, rather than aid, the daily workings of the religious organizations. The bureau personnel in such counties think that because they aided in the return of property to the churches, temples, and mosques they now have the right to control the activities that go on within these structures.

After the June 4, 1989, Tiananmen incident, the government instituted a number of economic and social reforms in China, and it took steps to better ascertain public opinion. A Communist Party document, issued February 5, 1991, called on the Religious Affairs Bureaus to "stop undesirable elements from using religion ... to create chaos, ... resist infiltration by outside hostile forces,'' and to register all places of worship. Some religious leaders have expressed concern over this directive because it potentially could be misused. They remember how such directives were abused during the Cultural Revolution and anti-Rightist campaigns of the past.

The registration is probably just a bureaucratic procedure, but in the counties where Leftist tendencies prevail it has already been used to limit religious activities. In one county, for example, all the existing Protestant churches and meeting points filled out the necessary registration papers. Out of 91 such applications only 20 were accepted by the bureau as legitimate churches. Some were turned down because their geographical location was too close to that of another registered site. This is clearly a case of the bureau interfering with the right of religious groups to worship as they wish, i.e. to determine for themselves what is a church and what is not.

THE CPPCC

Religious leaders participate directly in deliberations toward forming government policy at meetings of the various people's congresses and the Chinese People's Political Consultative Congress (CPPCC). There are altogether about 10,000 representatives of religious groups who are delegates to these people's congresses and CPPCC meetings at the national, provincial, and local levels.

Because more religious leaders are delegates to the CPPCC meetings than to the people's congresses, we will look at this body first. All religious associations are represented at some level of the CPPCC — national, provincial, or local. There are about 2,000 different religious associations in China, eight at the national level, 160 at the provincial level, and the rest at the county level.

The CPPCC is an organization that consists of the Chinese Communist Party, various independent democratic parties, non-party democrats, people's organizations, religious groups, members of ethnic minorities, and personages who attend by special invitation. It was first called together, in 1948, during the Chinese People's Liberation War.

At that time, on May 1, the Communist Party proposed that all democratic parties, people's organizations, and other prominent people convene a new political consultative conference to set up a coalition government that would establish a new China. This proposal won an immediate, appreciative response from many elements of the Chinese society. Preparations for the conference took place at Harbin on November 25, and on June 19, 1949, the first preparatory session was held. The delegates decided to call the organization the Chinese People's Political Consultative Conference.

Altogether 662 representatives from 45 units on special invitation took part in the congress. There were eight Buddhist, Muslim, and Christian delegates. Because the war was still going on, nationwide universal suffrage was impossible, and the time was not yet ripe for convening a National People's Congress. The CPPCC, in fact, exercised the functions and powers of a National People's Congress.

The session adopted the "Common Program" of the CPPCC, a document that included an article on religious freedom and served as the country's provisional constitution. It also adopted the Rules of Organization of the CPPCC and the Rules of Organization of the Central People's Government of the People's Republic of China. It furthermore proclaimed the founding of the People's Republic of China.

The CPPCC decided on Beijing (formerly called Beiping) as the capital, the five-starred flag as the national flag, and the *March of the Volunteers* as the national anthem. It decided that the Christian era rather than the old Chinese lunar calendar was to be the way of numbering years. It also elected a chairman, vice-chairmen, and members of the Central People's Government, and named the First National Committee of the CPPCC.

The religious composition at the Second CPPCC included twelve Buddhist, Muslim, and Christian delegates, eighteen who attended the Third, and sixteen who attended the Fourth. After the start of the Cultural Revolution, the activities of the CPPCC stopped until 1977, when it resumed its normal work.

The purpose of the CPPCC is to hold political consultations and aid the state organizations in implementing structural reforms to improve their work, raise their efficiency, get rid of bureaucratic practices, struggle against corruption, and supervise the implementation of the Constitution, laws, principles, and policies. It also coordinates relations among various parts of society and strengthens the unity and cooperation among the different parties.

The CPPCC holds plenary sessions at various levels, meetings of the standing committee at various levels, meetings of the chairmen of the CPPCC at various levels, meetings on special subjects of interest to the standing members, and meetings of special committees. It discusses important principles, policies, and plans of the state; hears reports on the work of the government, national budget, and plan for economic and social development; and makes recommendations about policies and principles of foreign affairs, internal affairs, and development of the patriotic united front.

The present National Committee of the CPPCC has 66 members who officially represent religious organizations. Of these, 20 are also members of the CPPCC's special Religion Committee, one of the CPPCC's 14 special committees. Lay Buddhist Zhao Puchu, vice-chairman of the National Committee of the CPPCC, chairman of the Chinese Buddhist Association and President of the Chinese Institute of Buddhist Studies, serves as the chairman of the Religion Committee.

Since 1984, the CPPCC's Religion Committee has annually organized all its members to investigate the religious situation in various provinces and municipalities. In doing so, contacts between different religions are strengthened and the government's policies on religion are further implemented. In September 1989, this Religion Committee and the Chinese Taoist Association sponsored a joint meeting to commemorate the 20th anniversary of the death of noted scholar Chen Yingning, the former chairman of the Chinese Taoist Association.

The CPPCC's Religion Committee recently organized a series of lectures to help journalists become more familiar with what religion is all about. The lectures were given by leaders of the five major religions: Buddhism, Islam, Taoism, Catholicism, and Protestantism. This public education effort was conducted because many articles offensive to religious people have been published by the Chinese news media in recent years.

From almost the beginning, the CPPCC decided to set up local committees in key cities, important districts, and provincial capitals. These developed rapidly. By 1966, there were more than 1,000 such local committees. In 1982 the CPPCC decided to extend this structure further. They then set up local committees in provinces, autonomous regions, and centrally administered municipalities. If conditions permitted it, they were also to be set up in autonomous prefectures, cities divided into districts, counties, autonomous counties, cities not divided into districts, and municipal districts.

At the annual meetings of the national and local CPPCCs, members from the religious groups often make proposals and put forward suggestions about the government's work. They also report on their followers' wishes and demands. Some of these suggestions have received positive attention and have been adopted. When Article 147 of the Criminal Law, cited above, was formulated and approved by the National CPPCC, this took place only after a period of consideration and discussion by the religious representatives to that body.

THE PEOPLE'S CONGRESS

The National People's Congress of the People's Republic of China is the highest organ of state power. It makes the laws and determines the political direction for the country. There are members of this body at both the national and local levels who are leaders in the religious communities, but they are not so elected. Instead, these persons are elected as

51

individuals to represent their local districts. No statistics are available, therefore, as to how many members of the various People's Congresses also have religious affiliations.

The National People's Congress is composed of deputies elected by the provinces, autonomous regions, and centrally administered municipalities, and by the armed forces. The deputies include representatives from various democratic parties, people's organizations, various nationalities, and different classes and strata. The National People's Congress is considered to be broadly representative.

It has the power to amend the Constitution and supervise its enforcement, and to enact or amend basic statutes concerning criminal offenses, civil affairs, the state organs, and other matters. It also can elect, or recall from office, the President and Vice-Presidents of the People's Republic of China; decide the choice of the Premier and Vice-Premiers of the State Council, State Councilors, Ministers in charge of ministries or commissions, the Auditor-General, and the Secretary-General of the State Council; elect the Chairman of the Central Military Commission and decide the choice of Vice-Chairmen and all other members of the Central Military Commission; and elect and remove, or recall from office, the President of the Supreme People's Court and the Procurator-General of the Supreme People's Procuratorate.

This body examines and approves the plan for national economic and social development and reports on its implementation. It decides questions of war and peace, and alters or annuls inappropriate decisions of the Standing Committee of the National People's Congress. Finally, it exercises such other functions and powers as the highest organ of state power should exercise.

The National People's Congress is elected for a term of five years, and usually meets in session once a year. Of the 2,970 deputies to the Eighth National People's Congress held in 1988, 684 were workers and peasants making up 23% of the total; 697 were intellectuals, or 23.5%; 733 were cadres, or 24.7%; 540 were representatives of the various democratic parties and those with no party affiliation, or

18.2%; 267 were deputies from the People's Liberation Army, or 9%; and 49 were returned overseas Chinese, or 1.6%. There were 634 women, or 21.3%, and 445 representatives of minority nationalities, or 15%.

Before the National People's Congress formally opens, it meets in a preparatory session to elect the Presidium and the Secretary-General and to adopt the agenda of the formal session. Sessions of the National People's Congress are presided over by the Presidium, which appoints several members to serve as Executive Chairmen.

Bills put forward by the National People's Congress, its Presidium, its Standing Committee and various special committees, the State Council, the Central Military Commission, the Supreme People's Court, and the Supreme People's Procuratorate are submitted by the President to delegations for examination. These are composed of deputies from the provinces, autonomous regions, and centrally administered municipalities, and the People's Liberation Army. Relevant special committees of the National People's Congress also examine proposed bills and make a report. Voting is usually carried out by secret ballot or a show of hands.

The permanent organ of the National People's Congress is its Standing Committee, responsible to the National People's Congress and reports on its work to the Congress. It functions as the highest organ of state power. The Standing Committee is composed of a Chairman, Vice-Chairmen, and other members elected by the National People's Congress.

The Standing Committee does the work of the National People's Congress when it is not in session. It interprets the Constitution and supervises its enforcement; examines and approves partial adjustments to the plan for national economic and social development; and supervises the work of the State Council, the Central Military Commission, the Supreme People's Court, and the Supreme People's Procuratorate.

Special committees, both permanent and provisional, also exist within the National People's Congress. The permanent committees include the Nationalities Committee, Law Committee, Financial and Economic Committee, Foreign Af-

53

fairs Committee, Overseas Chinese Committee, and other special committees as are necessary.

THE UNITED FRONT WORK DEPARTMENT

One other government structure that needs consideration because of its links to the religious community is the United Front Work Department. This is a Communist Party organ whose task is to relate to important forces of society outside the Communist Party, including the democratic parties, religious organizations, ethnic minorities, and overseas Chinese.

In the days before the People's Republic of China was founded, the United Front Work Department was crucial in establishing links between the government and the people. However, during the Cultural Revolution this organization was criticized for being "capitulationist" and closed down. It was not revived until the Third Plenary Session of the 11th Central Committee of the Chinese Communist Party, held in December 1978. Its present director is Yan Mingfu, the son of a man who was once a staff member of the YMCA in Chongqing, Sichuan Province.

Whereas the CPPCC is a forum for the discussion of government policies, the United Front Work Department is a working group that implements all government policies that relate to political, social, and religious organizations outside the Communist Party. It has a hierarchy of its own, and it functions at national, provincial, and local levels. Its work sometimes overlaps that of the Religious Affairs Bureaus, although specifically its job is to coordinate the united front and not to deal with the day-to-day needs and activities of the religious groups.

With these government organizations in mind, we can now turn in the next chapters to the individual religions themselves. We will start with the one that is native to China, the Taoists.

TAOISTS:

Preserving the Ancient Wisdom

Taoism is the only major religion that came exclusively from Chinese roots and grew to maturity in Chinese soil. In ancient times, Taoist monks made the most important contributions to Chinese science, art, literature, and medicine. Many of the temples and monasteries they built are monuments to Chinese architecture. Their ways of keeping healthy are hailed today by practitioners all over the world.

In China, most people now view the Taoists as contributors to past culture and preservers of that culture in today's world. However, this has not always been so. The various feudal governments of China were loath to recognize the contributions of Taoism. The powerful Confucian philosophers disparaged this religion as a series of hopeless folk tales and mystical incantations. The more dominant religion, Buddhism, took every opportunity to cast verbal stones at its rival. Only rarely were the Taoists acknowledged for their part in the totality of Chinese culture.

One of the many ancient Taoist legends says that the founder of the Northern Song Dynasty (960-1127), Zhao Kuangyin, played chess with a Taoist monk on one of the five peaks of Mount Huashan, located east of the city of Xi'an. The future emperor lost the game to the monk, named Chen Tuan. So the mountain became the exclusive property of Taoists. Feudal emperors of later dynasties never demanded tribute from the Mount Huashan Taoists. The mountain was theirs and off limits to tax collectors. In the hearts of the devout, this mountain became sacred.

Many visitors have written poems and articles about their journeys to Mount Huashan. Some have left calligraphic inscriptions on the mountain rocks, thus enriching its beauty.

The site of the famous chess match is preserved and, until early in this century, contained a chess board with the pieces placed as they were at the end of this famous competition.

To be realistic, the emperor didn't lose much in surrendering this chess game. The mountain is all but impossible to climb. If it has any mineral deposits, they are yet to be found. And the rocks and crags leave little room for growing vegetables. A small weather station, located inside the temple on Huashan's west peak, is the only thing of much use to the government today.

I climbed Mount Huashan in 1983, one of the most difficult tasks I have ever accomplished. The mountain has only one way to its top. This is by steps cut into a slanting cliff face. The steps are lined with iron chains on both sides to aid the climber who must use two hands to move upward carefully. At one particularly difficult ascent there are 260 steps so narrow only one person can climb or descend at a time. The steps are cut in a breach between two facing stone cliffs. As you climb, you can't see anything but the surrounding rock faces.

Looking downward from the top of this narrow breach is like looking into a deep well with stairs down its side. The entry hole at the top is so small it could be covered with an iron plate that would then prevent all others from mounting higher.

Just when the climber thinks the route might improve and become level for a distance, one arrives at a series of stone steps mounting the cliff face at nearly a 90 degree angle. This section is called the "Hundred-Foot Gorge." Beyond this is the "Two Immortals Bridge," the "Monkey's Frown," the "Sky Ladder," and the "Black Dragon Ridge." Each has its own difficulties and hazards.

How the ancient Taoist construction workers cut this path into the mountainside is a matter of mystery. They must have dangled from the rocks by ropes to chisel away at the cliff face. And how difficult it must have been for them to carry up building materials for the many temples they erected

56

on the five peaks. Some of the special corner stones must have been dragged up the cliff face by monks holding on to chains, ropes, and even vines to crawl forward.

During the Cultural Revolution, Red Guards tried to ascend Mount Huashan to destroy all its temples and ancient Taoist artifacts. They apparently found the climb too difficult, for only the lower temples suffered any damage.

It is probable that Taoists are the only ones who could create the temples and other structures that make this sacred mountain so magnificent. Taoists thrive on hardship. They spend their lives in rigid physical and mental practices directed toward perfection. Others falter before their kind of self-disciplined regimen of exercise and diet. This fear of hardship may even explain why the number of Taoist practitioners has declined since the end of the Qing Dynasty (1911).

The Religious Affairs Bureau of the State Council says there are 60 to 70 million Taoist and Buddhist worshipers in China today. They combine the number of worshipers for the two religions because many Chinese pray and leave gifts at both Taoist and Buddhist temples to be sure that all good and evil spirits are satisfied. An old Chinese saying has it that the vast majority of people "wear a Confucian crown, a Taoist robe, and a pair of Buddhist sandals."

Certainly there are many more Buddhists than Taoists in China. The Taoist temples and shrines are never filled to capacity, as are the Buddhist ones. And there are fewer Taoist temples and shrines, even though the Chinese Taoist Association says, with the exception of Tibetans, there are Taoists among all the 56 ethnic groups that make up China's population. My own guess as to the number of Taoist worshipers in China today, and I think it is a reasonable estimate, is about 1.5 million.

The number who give their whole lives to Taoist practices — the Taoist priests and nuns — can be estimated more accurately. Here the Taoist Association says there are approximately 6,000 to 7,000 full-time religious workers living in the various Taoist temples and monasteries of China. This includes both priests and nuns. Others put the figure as low as 2,600, but again no one knows for sure. Taoists are individualists and don't like to be counted. The Taoist Association says there also may be as many as 30,000 unknown and part time Taoist monks who have no temple affiliations and who are scattered throughout the countryside.

Taoism took form in the late period of the Eastern Han Dynasty (the 2nd century A.D.), after a long gestation period. Its beliefs grew out of the crude animism, sorcery, and witchcraft practiced in ancient China. From the beginning, Taoism has had a belief in spirits, both good and evil, and has occasionally appended local folk gods to its polytheistic religion.

Even today the Taoists are willing to incorporate local village deities and bits of folk religion. For example, within the past decade the Chairman of the Chinese Taoist Association, Li Yuhang, added the goddess Ma Zhu to the Taoist list of deities. Ma Zhu is a folk goddess said to protect sailors and fishermen. She was first worshipped in Fujian Province during the Southern Song Dynasty (1127-1279). A cult of followers, particularly persons who made their living from the sea, grew up around this goddess. Temples to her honor now stand in Hong Kong, Taiwan, and some other parts of Southeast Asia. For many centuries the Taoist canons excluded worship of this goddess, Ma Zhu. But now Taoists are free to add her to their prayers.

LAOZI

Taoist believers look on Laozi, who lived sometime before 400 B.C., as their great teacher. They take his *Dao De Jing* (*The Classic of the Tao and Its Virtue*) as their central religious text. In this work, Laozi says the basic principle is: first, be benevolent; second, be pure; and, third, do not act in advance of other people. Being benevolent means assuming an amiable attitude toward everything in the universe and maintaining universal harmony. Being pure means getting rid of extravagant hopes and being plain in mind and body. Not daring to act in advance of other people means being modest, and holding the self in check, instead of assuming an attitude of strength and dominance.

The word "Tao," translates as "the way." In its broadest sense, the Tao is the way the universe functions, the path taken by all natural events. The Tao is nature's way, expressed in effortless action. Taoists often use the image of water to illustrate such effortless action. Water always settles to the lowest level and yet can wear away even the hardest of substances.

According to Taoism, the cosmos is a magnitude of harmony and order. It is active, not static. Its state is one of change and variation, perpetually becoming and fading away, contracting and expanding. The Tao guides its function as an ordering principle. Within the Tao, the two elementary powers, *yin* and *yang*, function by reciprocal action. *Yin* and *yang* are the two polar opposites into which all things can be classified. Thus dark and light, life and death, male and female, good and evil, strong and weak are all manifestations of *yin* and *yang*.

Taoism places value on individualism and mystic experience. Taoists strive to become one with nature through effortless action. Their goal is a life in harmony with the cosmos. Through various health and exercise disciplines, Taoists try to achieve a long life and eventually even physical immortality.

Believing that human beings can actually attain immortality, Taoists have built their doctrines on rigid physical and mental practices directed toward this ultimate aim. There is no parallel in any other religion of the world. Taoists claim that at least eight persons, the Eight Immortals, have attained union with Tao and achieved this goal. One was a humorist and song writer, another a scholar, another a poet, another a calligrapher, and another a great traveler. One was a woman who vowed to remain a virgin all her life. Still another might be called a gardener because of his ability to make flowers grow at command. And one spent most of his days as a crippled beggar. These eight came from different classes of society and lived in different centuries. Some are verifiable persons in history.

Near the top of Mount Huashan, I came across an inscription on a rock that said "anyone who passes this point will become half an Immortal." I laboriously climbed beyond. However, I doubt if I will ever have the strength or courage to climb Mount Huashan again to see if I can immortalize my other half.

The Director of the White Cloud Temple in Beijing told us that he began to go to a Taoist temple at about age twelve, after friends and neighbors in his village told him that the Taoists could improve his health. He said he was a particularly sickly child and easily succumbed to diseases. He listened to the Taoist teachings and, at first, practiced their health routines secretly because he was still in school and did not dare face the embarrassment of doing religious activities publicly. His health gradually improved and he became stronger. Eventually, he decided to become a Taoist priest in the county temple near his hometown. During the Cultural Revolution, he again had to pursue his exercises in secret. He joined the White Cloud Temple in 1983, and then was assigned elsewhere to take advanced courses in the philosophy of Taoism. After graduation, he was elected to be the White Cloud Temple's manager in 1986. He is also the director of the temple orchestra and Deputy Secretary of the Chinese Taoist Association.

The religion, in many ways, is diametrically opposed to Confucianism. The Taoists condemn Confucius for advocating excessive government and for his disregard of the value of effortless action. According to the Taoists, a ruler should protect his people from experiencing material wants and should impose a minimum of government on them.

The Taoists also were often in conflict with the Buddhists. There were no physical battles over these differences, but many references in Chinese literature point to such animosities. This may surprise people who have visited both Taoist and Buddhist temples. They are much the same in floor plan and structure. The Buddhist architects used Taoist structures as their models and the Taoists copied the Buddhists. In order to determine to which of these two groups a particular temple belongs, one usually needs to find out the temple's name and the names of the various halls. Of course, the robes of the priests and the presence or absence of images of Buddha within the temple are also good clues.

An example of the conflict between Taoism and Buddhism is illustrated by the stone bridge erected in one of the courtyards of the White Cloud Temple in Beijing. This bridge was constructed during the Ming Dynasty (1368-1644) as protection against evil winds coming from a nearby Buddhist temple. The Buddhists, according to our Taoist guide, burned a particular kind of incense in their temple that was intended to harm the Taoists. I don't understand the fluid mechanics involved, if any, but our guide assured me that the bridge blocked the wind from progressing further. Perhaps the bridge's protection worked. In any case, the Taoist temple still stands and the Buddhist one is long gone.

MANY SECTS

As Taoism became a religion, it divided into many sects — altogether 86. The most influential and largest were the Wudoumi Tao (the Way of the Five Packs of Rice) and the Taiping Tao (the Way of Eternal Peace). Zhang Daoling (34-156) founded the Wudoumi Tao, which is also sometimes called Tianshi Tao (Heavenly Teacher Sect), because the followers of this sect considered Zhang Daoling their heavenly teacher. The Taiping Tao, founded by Zhang Jiao (?-184) and his brother, appeared a little later. At the beginning, the Taoist beliefs spread only among the common people. But after the Jin Dynasty (265-420), Taoism gained support among the upper classes.

By the Yuan Dynasty (1206-1368), Taoism had sorted itself into the two major sects that still exist today, the Northern and the Southern. The Southern Sect, also known as Zhengyi Tao (Way of Orthodox Unity), developed from the Tianshi Tao. Its members do not forsake home or family and can marry. They can drink alcohol and eat meat during non-fast periods. The Northern Sect, also known as Quanzhen Tao (Complete Perfection), was founded by Wang Chongyang (1113-1170). Members of this sect forsake home and family, do not marry, and are strict vegetarians.

Heading the list of commonly worshipped Taoist deities is a trinity (the Pure Trinity) that includes Yu Qing (also named Yuan Shi Tian Zun, the creator), Shang Qing (also named Ling Bao Tian Zun, next in importance only to Yu Qing), and Tai Qing (also named Dao De Tian Zun or Tai Shang Lao Jun, the supreme master).

Below this Pure Trinity are the Four Heavenly Emperors. The first of these is the Jade Emperor with the celestial way, or Tao, in hand. The second is the Emperor of the North Pole Star, a god who aids the Jade Emperor in managing the affairs of heaven and earth, the sun, moon, stars, and the four seasons. The next is the Celestial Emperor of the Gouchen Shanggong Star, who helps the Jade Emperor in taking charge of the North and South Poles and all geniuses in heaven and on earth, governs all constellations, and manages military affairs in human society. The last is the Empress of Earth, a goddess who determines birth, controls *yin* and *yang*, and is responsible for the beauty of all things.

Among the lesser gods are the God of Thunder, the God of Wind, the God of War, the God of Medicines, the God of Wealth, the God of Literature, and many more. There are gods that are worshipped as the guardians of individuals, the family, and village and town security, such as Door Gods, Kitchen Gods, and City Gods.

However, the most important contributions of Taoists are not in the area of defining gods. They are in the fields of culture, art, and science. Here their studies of health and the treatment of disease are the basis for Chinese traditional medicine and *kung fu* exercises.

In the early days all Taoists practiced various kinds of comparatively mild gymnastics that amounted to little more than extending and contracting the body. By later times these had evolved into many forms of strenuous and highly skilled exercises, generally called *wu shu*. These include the popular *taijiquan* exercises.

Qi gong, the Taoist way to keep in good health by deep breathing exercises also developed early. The aim at first was to try to return to the manner of breathing of an embryo in the womb. The Taoists tried to keep inspiration and respiration as quiet as possible and to hold the breath closed up as long as possible. Again the early exercises have evolved into forms that are now practiced by health seekers in many parts of the world, often persons with little or no interest in Taoism.

The Taoist health practices even included various sexual techniques aimed at nourishing life. Their basic aim was to conserve as much as possible of the seminal essence to promote the internal actions of *yin* and *yang*.

Tao Hongjin and Ge Hong were famous Taoist monks and medical experts. Ge Hong collected folk prescriptions and compiled the *Handbook of Medicine for Emergencies*. In this work is a report of smallpox, the earliest scientific mention of this subject, and a description of pulmonary tuberculosis (TB), a recognition of this disease that is some 1,000 years earlier than doctors recognized it in the West. Tao Hongjin developed an ancient theory of acute diseases. His annotated work *Commentaries on Materia Medica* is an important document of ancient Chinese herbal medicine.

The Taoists also contributed to chemistry and astronomy, as well as other sciences. Taoist monks engaging in alchemy produced a mass of ready-made traditional Chinese medicines while trying to get an elixir from cinnabar and mercury. The solution "golden liquid prescription," mentioned by the monk Ge Hong, was said to fuse gold. The discovery of gun powder was also the result of Taoist experiments in search of the elixir.

In art, Taoists produced striking statues and portraits of a characteristic style that reflect their ideas of creation. Many of China's greatest painters were Taoist monks. The preserved Taoist frescoes at the Yongle Temple in Shanxi Province and the huge mural paintings in the Daimiao Temple of Mount Taishan are masterpieces that incorporate the strong points from the best of Taoist paintings.

The use of music in Taoist ceremonies is thought to have a part in "moving the gods." Thus Taoist musicians strive for perfection in both performance and musical theory. There are various forms of solos, choruses, chanting, drum music, and instrumental ensembles of wind, plucking, string, and percussion instruments. Taoist music today not only preserves several ancient musical compositions, but also integrates some of the essentials of folk music.

When I visited the White Cloud Temple in Beijing, the priests were in the midst of a musical performance as we arrived. They were performing a chant for the dead. It was an awe-inspiring moment. I wanted to stay longer to listen, but our hosts were waiting for us. Among the musical chants one can hear in many Taoist temples are the *Jade Emperor's Canon*, the *Lasting Tranquillity Canon*, and the *Classic of the Tao and Its Virtue*.

Much of the excitement of Taoist writing comes from their use of paradox, contradiction, vivid poetic imagery, aphorism, and a spare but highly charged literary style. Among their published works is the *Collected Taoist Scriptures*, which includes all the important Taoist classics and documents. The *Collected Orthodox Taoist Scriptures* and the *Sequel of Collected Taoist Scriptures in the Wanli Reign* were compiled during the Ming Dynasty (1368-1644). The former consists of 5,305 volumes, and the latter of 180 volumes. They are important documents for research into the philosophy, history, literature and art, geography, medical science, physical culture, mathematics, biology, astronomy, geology, chemistry, and metallurgy of ancient China.

Taoist temples and monasteries are often located in picturesque mountains. Five well-known mountains, Mount Hengshan in Shanxi Province, Mount Hengshan in Hunan Province, Mount Taishan in Shandong Province, Mount Huashan in Shaanxi Province, and Mount Songshan in Henan Province are considered to be the five sacred mountains of Taoism. Other mountains of significance to Taoism include Maoshan, Qingcheng, Longhu, Zhongnan, Luofu, and Wudang.

In these mountains and elsewhere are 36 "Cave Heavens" and 72 "Blessed Realms," said to be the dwellings and resorts of Taoist deities. Monks in the past loved to live in quiet mountains and woods and often had their temples built in places said to have been visited by such deities.

Among the most famous Taoist temples and monasteries are the White Cloud Temple in Beijing; the Yongle Temple in Ruicheng, Shanxi Province; the Chongyang Temple in Huxian, Shaanxi Province; the Purple Sheep Temple in Chengdu, Sichuan Province; and the Jade Spring Temple on Huashan Mountain, Shaanxi Province. As a result of repairs and government protection of the sites, the ancient Taoist buildings stand today retaining much of their past splendor.

THE TAOIST ASSOCIATION

Taoism, for some time in decline, is now growing again in China, albeit more slowly than other religions. The number of Taoist sites is increasing. There are more than 3,000 temples, monasteries, and other Taoist places of worship that are preserved or have been restored since the Cultural Revolution. The number of priests and nuns is rising. And research work on Taoist philosophy is deepening. There are more schools, and more international exchanges going on, particularly with Taiwan and Hong Kong, but also with Japan and even the United States.

The affairs of the Taoists are coordinated by the Chinese Taoist Association. This national organization was initiated by Yue Chongdai, Chen Yingning, and others in April 1957. The first chairman was Chen Yingning, a well-known Taoist priest. Li Yuhang now serves as the association's chairman. The group was founded in Beijing and it has its headquarters there, at the White Cloud Temple.

There are 70 branches of the Chinese Taoist Association in the various provinces, autonomous regions, centrally administered municipalities, and counties of China. Each is directed by local Taoists. The association has no administrative powers. Its role is to help coordinate Taoist activities, help set up Taoist training academies, preserve Taoist writings and culture, and help implement state policy in regard to religion.

One of the first things the Chinese Taoist Association did after it was established was prepare for the teaching of advanced Taoist studies. Prior to this, there was no such training institute. Priests and nuns were taught by individual monks. It was quite hard to "enter the way," that is to become a Taoist disciple. Generally the teacher had to first observe the student for three years. Then the student had to observe the teacher for another three years. They were studying each other's behavior and integrity. Only after six years did the real teacher-student relationship begin.

The disciples were instructed apprentices in physical exercises; the use of large and small cymbals, bells, and drums; and in learning the scriptures by chanting. Many of these scriptures are in a form of ancient Chinese that is incomprehensible to persons outside the profession. The novices also learned how to operate a wooden fortune-telling device (much like a Ouija board used in the West) that had a compass in the center and various combinations of Chinese characters around the edges arranged according to the 60-year cycle of the Chinese calendar. Priests used the boards to decide auspicious days for burial and lucky orientations for graves.

Since 1982, advanced courses in Taoism have been taught for both priests and nuns at the White Cloud Temple. It is a two-year program. The students attend on recommendation of various local Taoist temples and with the approval of the provincial Taoist associations. They also must meet the qualifications of the White Cloud Temple in age (between 18 and 30), years of Taoism, cultural and educational level, and county quotas (only a certain number are accepted from any one county).

The course of education includes studies of Taoist classics, religious doctrine, and basic Taoism. In cases where students need to raise their educational level, special classes are taught in which they can do this. Approximately 50 trainees are enrolled at a time. Those who successfully complete this advanced-studies course become core members in running various temples, often the ones that originally sent them to school. Their education is paid for by the local associations. There are also scholarships for some that are provided by the national association.

There are now similar Taoist training schools in Shanghai and in Sichuan, Shaanxi, Zhejiang, and Gansu provinces. These are run by provincial and county Taoist associations. None of these schools accept any students from foreign countries, although this exclusion may change in the future.

A Chinese Taoist Institute was established in 1991. This provides a four-year course at the university level and awards a diploma approved by the State Education Commission. To enter, a student must have a high school education and meet the requirements of the institute administration. This institute is also located at the White Cloud Temple in Beijing.

Nowhere is there any Taoist education available for children. Part of the reason for this is that Taoist priests have no tradition of giving particular training to children, as do other religions. What religious instruction Taoist children receive usually comes from their parents. Another reason is the one provided by state law. This, as we have seen before, guarantees both the right for persons to believe or not to believe in religion. Members of the Chinese Taoist Association say that if they were to train children they would take away their freedom to choose. So religious training should not begin until after a person has passed age 18.

The association sponsors a quarterly publication, *Chinese Taoism*, which carries articles concerning Taoist research and the working experience of the association. A total of 13,000 copies are printed of each issue. The magazine is distributed both in China and abroad. Li Yuhang serves as its director and Li Yangzheng acts as its editor-in-chief.

In May 1990, the association established the Chinese Taoist Culture Institute, also located in Beijing, to do research on the historical records of Taoism. The Culture Institute maintains an Office of Research in Taoist History that helps compile and edit dictionaries, histories of Taoism, and various research papers. Among the scriptures and annotations that have come from the Taoist press are *A Taoist Dictionary*, *Elementary Knowledge of Taoism*, books on Taoist body cultivation and *qi gong*, and more than 300 articles and special works on Taoist research.

The association also has made contributions to compiling Taoist music, and it has published tapes, records, and music compositions. A Taoist philharmonic orchestra was established at Beijing's White Cloud Temple for the compiling, rehearsal, and performance of traditional Taoist music. The orchestra has played on various stages throughout China.

The Chinese Taoist Association promotes friendly exchanges with Taoists throughout the world. Several thousand such persons visit China every year to investigate Taoism as religion and philosophical thought. They come from Japan, Thailand, Hong Kong, Singapore, the United States, Canada, and France. Japanese scholars particularly are interested in studying Taoist rituals, culture, canons, organization, buildings, and mythology. The International Taoist Research Organization, sponsored by Taoists in the United States, has held several meetings that were attended by members of the Chinese Taoist Association. There have also been visits by Chinese Taoists to Canada and Europe. Usually six or seven priests travel together to such international meetings.

TEMPLE LIFE

Life in Taoist temples and monasteries is much the same today as it has been for centuries. Priests and nuns live in separate temples. There are famous ones for the nuns in Sichuan, Heilongjiang, and Zhejiang provinces. Wherever conditions permit, the temples maintain the Taoist tradition of growing grain, tea, and trees. They also provide medical clinics and inns for public use. There are monks who are not related to temples or monasteries and who live by themselves in the mountains as hermits. It is likely there are only a few of these, but those who live in this way maintain the same rigid diet and exercise regimen as the temple priests.

The daily routine for both priests and nuns is the same, with the exception of physical training. Here exercises for the nuns are different from those for the priests. They also get exactly the same religious training. Within each temple they eat together, work together, exercise together, and worship together. The exercise period at the White Cloud Temple in Beijing is one hour each day. The priests rise at 5:30 a.m. and go to bed at 9:30 p.m. There is also a time each day when the temple must be cleaned by the priests as they have many visitors.

Taoism has many fasting rules and many objects of taboo. Some of these rules are the same as those for Buddhism (no killing, stealing, loose morals, bragging, or addiction to alcohol). But others are rather complicated rules found in no other religion and related to the achievement of a closer unity with the Tao. Some of the Taoist canons have recently been abolished because they conflict with state laws. For example, Taoist trainees no longer can be beaten with bamboo poles or be made to kneel for long periods of time before images of the gods when they violate religious rules.

Most of the restoration of the White Cloud Temple in Beijing was paid for by the state after the Cultural Revolution ended. But now temple maintenance is financed through donations, tickets sold to visitors who wish to visit the temple, and by sales of Taoist artifacts. Such articles include small statues of the gods, books printed by the Chinese Taoist Association, tapes of temple music, and religious pictures and paintings.

There are more than 60 priests who live at the White Cloud Temple. Some are as old as 70 or 80 years, but the average age is 35. Thus many of them did not enter the priesthood until after the Communist government came to power.

During the Cultural Revolution this temple, and all others, was closed. Some of the priests returned to their villages and home towns. They worked in factories and on farms, continuing their religious practices secretly. Most, however, were able to continue to live in the temple, but without open religious observances.

The temple was occupied at that time by a unit of the army, which offered it some protection from the violence of the Red Guards. Yet conditions were crowded because the soldiers took over most of the living quarters. One priest saved their carved-jade, Tang-Dynasty (618-907) statue of Laozi by burying it in a section of the temple yard. In other temples where priests were able to remain on the temple grounds the priests tried, usually with little success, to protect the buildings from the periodic forays of Red Guard contingents.

All Taoists share a love for their country. There is an old Chinese saying "With the skin gone, what can the hair stick to?" Taoists say that they likewise cannot exist without their country as a basis for their religion. For this reason, whenever Taoists in China say prayers, they pray first for national stability and a peaceful life for the people. Taoism, with its attention to rendering a service in repayment for the kindness of the gods of heaven and earth, advises followers to do good works and make contributions to the country and its people.

There are two official Taoist representatives who attend the National Committee of the Chinese People's Political Consultative Conference (CPPCC) and many representatives who attend the city and provincial CPPCCs. There are also representatives in the People's Congresses at the provincial level who are known to be Taoists, but none in the National People's Congress.

INTERESTING TAOIST TEMPLES

Most Taoist temples and monasteries are located in places that are not easy to visit — on the sides and tops of mountains, and in counties remote from major cities. However, the effort to visit these temples is well worth it. There are usually only one or two Taoist places of worship in the largest cities, whereas there may be many Buddhist temples, Muslim mosques, and Christian churches.

In Shanghai, for example, there are only two Taoist sites

open, though this is the largest city in China and one of the largest cities in the world. One of these temples has the same name as the temple in Beijing, White Cloud Temple. It is only partly restored. The rest of it is rented as residential property. The other temple, called the Qingciyang Palace, is almost as complete as it was when built. Yet another Shanghai Taoist site, the Old City Guard Temple, is now being used by a commercial company and therefore not open for religious worship. The Shanghai Religious Affairs Bureau is working on the problem of getting this company to vacate the property so that it can be restored and returned to the Taoists.

In Quanzhou, a much smaller city, there are three Taoist religious sites open for visitors, but no Taoist priests to conduct the necessary rituals and prayers. One of these temples is named for the local goddess, Ma Zhu. It receives 2,000 to 3,000 visitors from Taiwan and Hong Kong each year. Another one has the name we've seen before, White Cloud Temple. There are many former Taoist facilities in this city that are now being used for factories and living quarters. They are all but impossible for a visitor to locate. Visitors will find it more rewarding to go north of the city and into the countryside where there is the oldest and largest statue of Laozi in all China, the Laojun Crag.

Chinese temples, whether Taoist or Buddhist, are never single buildings. They consist of a group of individual structures, usually one-storied, that follow a well-established pattern that is sometimes modified. The main buildings and their symmetrically corresponding secondary buildings form individual groups and courtyards that are connected to each other by walkaways. This characteristic style for temple buildings both in China and Japan developed early, probably before 200 B.C. The roofs of the buildings rest on a series of four-part brackets set on columns. They are graceful, overhanging roofs, sometimes in several tiers, with upturned eaves. The roofs are generally covered with glazed tiles, usually red, yellow, or blue in color.

The temple buildings are surrounded by an exterior wall

71

that is entered by an entry gate and then a spirit gate. Each building is dedicated to a particular god or complex of deities. For example, at the White Cloud Temple in Beijing there is one building that is dedicated to the Eight Immortals and includes statues of each. Another building contains 60 statues representing each of the 60 years of the Chinese calendar cycle.

If possible, one should time their visit to a Taoist temple to arrive on days set aside for special festivals. On such days there are usually grand ceremonies and Taoist scriptures are recited in front of special alters. Sometimes villages hold special country fairs during these same festival days.

The birthdays of each of the Pure Trinity gods are always Taoist festival days. The Winter Solstice is the birthday of Yuan Shi Tian Zun. The Summer Solstice is the birthday of Ling Bao Tian Zun. The 15th day of the second month of the lunar calendar is the birthday of Dao De Tian Zun. Other festival days include the Upper Yuan Festival (15th day of the first month of the lunar calendar), the Middle Yuan Festival (the 15th day of the seventh month of the lunar calendar), the Lower Yuan Festival (the 15th day of the tenth month of the lunar calendar), the birthday of the Queen Mother of the West (the 3rd day of the third month of the lunar calendar), and the birthday of the Celestial Master (the 15th day of the third month of the lunar calendar). There are many other festival days, some celebrated only at certain temples.

TAOIST MYTHS

Another thing that will make a temple tour particularly interesting is to consult a guide who can tell you the special stories about the particular temple or monastery. The priests or nuns in these temples all know such stories, but few of them can speak English and so you will probably need an able translator to get full delight from such tales.

This chapter began with one of these stories from a temple on Mount Huashan, the one about the emperor who lost the mountain in a chess game. Let us now return to Mount Huashan for some more examples. One of the Mount Huashan stories is the basis for a popular Chinese opera, *Cutting the Mountain and Rescuing the Mother*. This tale is about a scholar, Liu Yanchang, and a goddess he met one day on the road. The two fell in love and married. They had a son whom they named Chenxiang. But by marrying a mortal, the goddess violated the laws of heaven. She was punished by her elder brother, who crushed her under the weight of Mount Huashan. The son, Chenxiang, grew up and determined to rescue his mother. After many tries, he eventually was able to split the mountain in two with a magic axe. He thus rescued his mother. The place where this happened is on the West Peak of Mount Huashan, where temple priests will show you the mark of that axe blade. A huge axe lies nearby. On its 7 1/2-foot handle is an inscription telling about the rescue.

At one point along the road up Mount Huashan you can see a niche in the rock that is known as the Cave of the Green Haired Woman. The legend behind this name comes from the time of the China's first centralized government, the Qin Dynasty (221-207 B.C.). At that time there was a girl of 14 named Yujiang, who was chosen for burial in the first emperor's tomb at the time of his death. She learned of this dubious "honor" and escaped with six other maids from the palace at Xi'an. They crossed the forests and mountains on foot until they reached Mount Huashan. There they hid in this cave. They ate fruit and pine nuts and drank stream water. After many years, green hair grew all over Yujiang's body. People who saw her from a distance called her the green-haired woman. Later the cave was given its name in her honor and the peak was named the Peak of the Green-Haired Woman.

A more recent legend tells of Wang Changyue, a Taoist of the Qing Dynasty (1644-1911) who stood at a certain point on Mount Huashan to pay homage to the deities. Wang Changyue had abandoned his family to go to the mountain because he was so dissatisfied with the state of society. One day he said to his instructor in Taoism, "I have been a monk for more than three years, and I have not yet met a deity. What shall I do?"

His master replied, "As long as you are honest, you can certainly meet deities some day." The master then instructed him to recite the scriptures every day until a deity appeared.

For three more years Wang Changyue paid homage at this place. One day there was a thunder bolt and a golden beam of light appeared next to him. Out of this light stepped a deity. It had three heads and eight arms, and it was mounted on a strange animal with nine heads. The deity asked Wang Changyue what he wanted. But the monk was so frightened he just stood there, trembling. The deity, watching Wang's shaking feet and body, concluded that his desire must be to grow larger. So the deity granted this wish and disappeared.

Wang now found that his clothes and shoes were too small. He hurried back to tell his master of this event. The master then said, "When you met the deity, you neglected to answer his question. So all you got was a larger size. What a pity!"

Wang Changyue was overcome with remorse. He determined that he would again go to the place where he had been standing to continue to pay homage. Another three years passed and then one day the gold ray of light appeared again. It was so bright, he had to shut his eyes to keep from being blinded. But he heard a voice asking, "Monk, why do you pay homage to me?"

Wang was still too frightened to answer. Instead, he covered his mouth with his hand. The deity concluded that this was a sign that he wanted a beard. The deity disappeared and Wang suddenly found that he had a long beard that reached to his waist. Again Wang was overcome with regret and again he vowed to pay daily homage at this place.

Three more years went by and then a cloud appeared directly over his head. On the cloud sat a goddess with a face as bright as the full moon. She asked Wang why he was paying homage to her. This time he replied, saying that he desired to achieve the Taoist way. The goddess then told him that he must walk toward the northeast and there he would find the Taoist way waiting for him. Wang Changyue did this, reciting scriptures as he walked. Thus he became a true Taoist.

One last story from the temples of Mount Huashan is worth repeating. There is a place on the steep road leading up to the first peak that is named the Point of No Turning Back. This name does not come from timid travelers but from a tale about a priest who led two disciples up the mountain so he could show them how to cultivate themselves according to Taoist doctrines. The three of them spent their days cutting the path of the mountain and hollowing out caves in the rock face that solitary Taoist monks might someday occupy. Each time the disciples completed an assigned task they wanted to rest, but the priest insisted that they move on to a new one. Eventually the three had cut many steps and hollowed out 71 caves.

By then they were so tired and dissatisfied with this kind of life that they decided to kill the priest and return home. When they were working on the South Peak and the priest was hanging by a rope over the cliff face, they released the rope and let him drop to his death below. Then the two men packed up their things and started down the mountain.

But when they reached the Point of No Turning Back, they found the master standing there alive and well. The priest said to them, "Whatever you learn and whatever you do, always do it in honesty and steadfastness. If you are dishonest, all your previous efforts will be wasted."

The two disciples were deeply moved. They determined to change their ways. After this, they readily followed the master in his work on Mount Huashan. People later called this the Point of No Turning Back because this is where the disciples changed their point of view.

Before we move on to the chapter about Buddhism in China today, I will give a listing of noted Taoist religious sites. Visitors to China might wish to see these for themselves, particularly if they are on a Taoist pilgrimage.

VISITOR'S GUIDE TO TAOIST SITES

Among the more than 3,000 temples, monasteries, and other sacred places of the Taoists that are open to the public, a visitor will probably find these the most interesting.

1. White Cloud Temple (City of Beijing)

This was once the chief temple of the Quanzhen Taoist sect. It was first constructed during the Tang Dynasty, in 739, and was destroyed and repaired many times during the Ming and Qing dynasties. Since 1949 it has been renovated several times, and it is now the home of the Chinese Taoist Association. Among the 17 halls are the Hall of the Jade Emperor, Pavilion of the Three Parities with beautiful statues of these gods, Hall of the Eight Immortals that contains glazed statues of each, and the Yuanchen Hall that contains 60 statues, one for each year, of the gods of the Chinese zodiacal calendar. The Yuan Dynasty statue of Grand Master Qiu, flanked by his assistants, is in another hall worth visiting.

2. Temple of Supreme Purity (Liaoning Province)

The Temple of Supreme Purity in Shenyang has a number of beautiful halls with red pillars and intricately carved cross beams. There is a finely crafted statue of the Jade Emperor in the Jade Emperor's Tower. In other halls are a fine mural portrait of the God of the Soil and other excellent mural paintings. This temple is often used as a gathering place for Taoists from many other temples and monasteries at times of special celebration.

3. Temple of Infinity (Liaoning Province)

The Temple of Infinity is in the northeastern part of the

Qianshan Mountains, which are about 14 miles east of the city of Anshan. It was founded by Taoists in 1677. It has several well-preserved halls, including the Hall of Three Officials and the Hall of Guanyin. There are a number of other fine temples, monasteries, gates, and even pagodas on these mountains which make a climb up some of the peaks well worth the effort. The Qianshan, or Thousand Mountains, received their name because there are 990 peaks in this range of Northeast China.

4. Daimiao Temple and Temple of the Azure Cloud (Shandong Province)

The Daimiao Temple is at the foot of Mount Taishan and the Temple of the Azure Cloud is near its summit. There are numerous other temples, halls, pavilions, and stone inscriptions on the mountain to make the trip up this mountain (a journey of about five and a half miles) well worth the effort. The mountain can be reached by train or bus from the city of Jinan, and if one doesn't wish to climb, there is a cable car system that will take the visitor to the top. Its main peak is 1,545 meters high and thought to be a symbol of sublimity and dignity.

Daimiao Temple was erected as early as the Qin and Han dynasties. It was designated for the worship of the great ruler of the Eastern Mountains. Records from the year 1122 indicate that at that time the temple complex consisted of several hundred halls and pavilions. Today, only a few remain. The temple's focus is its main hall, built in 1009 and restored in 1956. It stands on a terrace surrounded by a white-stone balustrade. The double roof is composed of yellow-glazed tiles. A mural inside the hall depicts a grand procession of the god of the Eastern Mountains. The temple also boasts 157 stone stelae, the oldest engraved in 209 B.C. It is one of the oldest in China. A lion made of aloeswood, a jade scepter, and a porcelain gourd are called the temple's three treasures.

The Temple of the Azure Cloud was constructed between 1008 and 1016. Its roof is covered with bronze and iron tiles to make it invulnerable to storms. A Ming-dynasty bronze figure representing the Goddess of the Azure Cloud is located in its main hall. In the adjoining eastern and western halls, there are additional bronze statues depicting various gods. The view of the surrounding mountains and countryside from this temple or from the nearby Daiding peak is breathtaking.

5. Temple of Supreme Purity (Shandong Province)

The Temple of Supreme Purity, or Taiqing Temple, on Mount Laoshan, about fifteen miles east of the City of Qingdao, was founded by Zhang Lianfu in 140 B.C. The Hall of Three Emperors, Hall of Three Purities, and the Hall of the Three Officials are well preserved. Pu Songling wrote some of the stories in his famous book *Strange Tales from Liaozhai* at this temple. It is also a place from where one can get an excellent view of the ocean. There are several other Taoist temples of interest on Mount Laoshan if one has time to visit them.

6. Xuanmiao Temple (Jiangsu Province)

This temple, on Guanqianjie Street in the city of Suzhou, was built in 276 during the Western Jin Dynasty, and rebuilt in 1371 during the Ming Dynasty. It was renovated in 1956 and again in 1980. The temple originally consisted of 31 halls, but now only two remain. The temple contains tablet inscriptions and a portrait of Tai Shang Lao Jun (Supreme Master) by Wu Daozi, a famous painter of the Tang Dynasty. There is also an inscription by the Tang Emperor Xuanzong and a sample of the calligraphy of Yan Zhenqing, a famous calligrapher of the Tang Dynasty. One of the halls contains three gilded statues of Taoist immortals.

7. Yuanfu Wanning Temple (Jiangsu Province)

The Yuanfu Wanning Temple is on Maoshan Mountain, about 50 miles southeast of the city of Nanjing. It was built during the Tang Dynasty, and it is the place where Tao Hongjin (456-536), a noted Taoist of the Southern Dynasties, cultivated himself. The temple expanded during the rule of Emperor Zhezong (1086-1100) of the Song Dynasty. This temple along with the Jiuxiao Wanfu Temple on the same mountain are considered the most famous Taoist monasteries of the lower reaches of the Yangtze River.

8. Simplicity Embracing Monastery (Zhejiang Province)

The Simplicity Embracing Monastery is on Geling Hill in the city of Hangzhou. It includes the Red Plum Pavilion and several other buildings worth exploring. Also, on the same hill is the Gexian Nunnery with stone tablets and other artifacts to see.

9. Yongle Temple (Shanxi Province)

This temple located in Ruicheng County, in the southwestern corner of Shanxi Province, was originally situated on the banks of the Huanghe River in Yongle, a town bearing the same name as the temple. The government had to move the buildings to their present location when they constructed the Sanmenxia dike project during the 1950s. The temple is said to be the birthplace of Lu Dongbin, an important member of the Quanzhen Taoist sect. He is said to have been a philanthropist and to have possessed magic powers that enabled him to perform good deeds. He is generally depicted as an elderly figure with a sword in his hand or slung over his back.

The Yongle Temple was built in the mid-13th century and today consists of four halls. It is famous for its glorious murals, the creation of unknown painters who patterned their work after the great painter of the Tang Dynasty, Wu Daozi. The murals were done over a period of more than 110 years. The Pure Trinity Hall has 286 paintings of heavenly and earthly gods paying respects to the Pure Trinity. Chunyang Hall has 52 paintings that tell the story of Lu Dongbin from his birth to his deification. The realistic portrayal of the people and their environment have made this painting a rich source of information about life in the Yuan Dynasty. The Chongyang Hall has 42 paintings that tell the story of Wang

Chongyang, founder of the Quanzhen Taoist sect, and the lives of his disciples. There are also exquisite paintings in the Wu Ji Men (also called the Dragon and Tiger Hall), depicting the gods Yulei and Shentu, local deities, celestial warriors, and celestial scribes and officials.

10. Zhongyue Temple (Henan Province)

Zhongyue Temple on Mount Songshan, two and a half miles east of the village of Dengfeng and to the southeast of the city of Luoyang, was built during the Qin Dynasty and flourished during the Tang and Song dynasties. The complex is divided into eleven courtyards with numerous halls. Four iron men with angry faces are an interesting group of statues standing near one of the gates. They were cast in 1064. Although this temple is important to Taoism, the surrounding area is much better known for its Zen-Buddhist Shaolin Temple. This part of China, in fact, is often called a "treasure chest of cultural memorials" because of the many temples, pagodas, monasteries, and stone stelea that can be seen in the Songshan mountain range.

11. Temple of Eternal Spring (Hubei Province)

The Temple of Eternal Spring is in the city of Wuhan. Its Hall of Supreme Purity contains striking murals of Laozi traveling westward on a water buffalo and Laozi lecturing to a group of followers on the *Classic of the Tao and Its Virtues*. There are also other halls to see and a well-constructed stone bridge called the Meeting Immortals Bridge.

12. Wudang Mountain Temples (Hubei Province)

Wudang Mountain is located south of the town of Junxian and more than 200 miles north of the city of Yichang. It has been a sacred mountain for Taoists since the Tang and Song dynasties. Many temples and monasteries were there at that time, but by the end of the Yuan Dynasty most had been destroyed. In 1412 the Emperor Yongle gathered 300,000 workers to rebuild the temples. Within six years 46 temples and halls, 72 grottoes, 39 bridges and 12 pavilions were completed. Many are in good condition today.

Among the best preserved is the Temple of the Purple Cloud. Its roof, walls, ceilings, and sacred sculptures are highly impressive. The Temple of the Southern Rock hangs from the side of a steep slope just below the main peak. At one time it consisted of more than 640 rooms, but most are now gone. The Temple of Supreme Harmony, half way up the main peak, has bell and drum towers located to the sides of the main hall. A bronze bell made in 1416 still hangs in the bell tower. The travelers' aim in climbing this mountain, which takes about three hours, is the Golden Summit Hall, a bronze hall erected in 1416. It contains several bronze sculptures embellished with gold. From the courtyard outside this hall one can see a great distance across the mountain range.

13. Residence of the Heavenly Master (Jiangxi Province)

Near the base of Mount Longhu, southeast of the city of Nanchang and about 13 miles south of town of Yingtan is the birthplace of Zhang Daoling, the founder of the Wudoumi Taoist sect. The many halls of his home are preserved as a Taoist temple. At the end of 1990 a newly completed statue of the Heavenly Master was installed in one hall. Here one can also see his family tree, the jade seal he used when marking his writings, and a camphor tree he is said to have planted. If arrangements are made in advance, a visitor can take a trip down the nearby river to see scenic spots associated with the Heavenly Master and his followers. One can also climb Mount Longhu, which means Dragon and Tiger Mountain, to see places where many temples once stood.

14. Chongxu Temple (Guangdong Province)

The Chongxu Temple on Luofu Mountain, about 45 miles northeast of the city of Guangzhou, has several fine halls and statues of the Three Deities of Purity. There are also statues of the Simplicity Embracing Master and Goddess. This is the place where the Taoist monk Ge Hong compiled his famous handbook of medicine, and so you can see the pond where he washed medicinal herbs and the site of the stove he used for alchemical experiments.

15. Temple of the Eight Deities (Shaanxi Province)

This temple in the city of Xi'an has several fine buildings with bright red pillars and blue tile roofs. Among the most interesting halls are the Hall of Master Lu, the Hall of Master Qiu, the Hall of the Goddess Doumu, and the Hall Hidden in Clouds.

16. Chongyang Temple (Shaanxi Province)

This temple, located in Huxian County about 20 miles southwest of the city of Xi'an, was built over the grave of Wang Chongyang, the founder of the Quanzhen Taoist sect. It is regarded as one of the three major temples of Quanzhen Taoism. The stone tablets and inscriptions in the temple are of high artistic value.

17. Louguan Terrace on Mount Zhongnan (Shaanxi Province)

Located on Mount Zhongnan in Zhouzhi County, some 40 miles south of the city of Xi'an, the Louguan Terrace is the oldest of all Taoist temples. After continued repair and expansion through the centuries, it is now the preserve of more than 70 stelae and stone inscriptions written by celebrities from past dynasties. The temple includes a beautiful modern statue of Laozi holding a disk of the Eight trigrams, the reputed tomb of Laozi, and even an old cypress tree to which the master is supposed to have tied his ox. A Tang Dynasty carving of the ox stands not far away. The scriptures library is a rich source for research into Taoist history.

18. Jade Spring Monastery (Shaanxi Province)

The Jade Spring Monastery at the base of Mount Huashan, some seventy miles east of the city of Xi'an, was built more than nine hundred years ago during the rule of Emperor Renzong of the Song Dynasty. It was constructed in memory of the Taoist monk, Chen Tuan, who reportedly won ownership of the mountain in a chess game from the first emperor of the Northern Song Dynasty. The main hall contains a sleeping statue of Chen Tuan and many stone inscriptions. Travelers with the stamina to climb Mount Huashan will find several other Taoist temples and halls of note, one of which contains a colorful statue of the monk fully awake. The climb is quite difficult and will take a full day to reach the top. So the traveler should plan to sleep for the night at the inn provided by the Zhenyue Temple on the mountain's south peak.

19. Purple Sheep Temple (Sichuan Province)

The Purple Sheep Temple (Qingyang Gong) in the southwestern outskirts of the city of Chengdu is set in Wenhua Park. It is named for the two beautiful bronze sheep that stand inside the temple compound. Built during the Tang Dynasty, this temple has been renovated several times. The present halls date from the Qing Dynasty. Bagua Ting Hall attracts attention because of its yellow tile roof and eight stone columns, carved with dragon patterns. The main hall, Sanqing Hall, contains a gilded clay figure of the Taoist monk Sanqing. Every year on the 15th day of the second month of the lunar calendar there is a big flower celebration at this temple. Farmers from all over the surrounding counties come to Chengdu on this day to sell their flowers at the temple.

20. Qingcheng Mountain (Sichuan Province)

Qingcheng Mountain, long revered by Taoists, is well known for its fine scenery. It is located about 9 miles from the town of Guanxian which is, in turn, 37 miles from the city of Chengdu. A trip up the mountain and through the Taoist complexes takes two or three hours. The Jianfu Temple at the start of the foot of the mountain was constructed in 724 and reconstructed in 1888. Room and board are available here if the visitor wishes to stay for more than a day. The monks on this mountain cultivate tea gardens, and Qingcheng Shan tea can be savored here as well. It is an outstanding variety of tea that was only provided for emperors in the past.

The Tianshi Dong Temple is halfway up the mountain. Zhang Daoling, the founder of the Wudoumi Taoist sect, is said to have taught here. The temple halls were constructed in the Sui Dynasty and restored at the end of the Qing Dynasty. One can procure a fine vegetarian meal at the Tianshi Dong Temple. Further on is the Shangqing Gong Temple at the main peak of the mountain. It was constructed during the third century, but the present buildings date from the Qing period. The traveler can descend by another route and find many other points of Taoist interest.

Taoist Tourist Sites

BUDDHISTS:

Growing and Expanding

There are three distinct types of Buddhism in China. Each is of greater difference from the other two than Catholics are from Protestants. Yet the Chinese consider Catholicism and Protestantism separate religions, while they view all three kinds of Buddhism as one. The three types are Mahayana Buddhism, Hinayana Buddhism, and Lamaism. They are united only by a mutual desire for liberation from the pain of the material world and a claim to descent from India's Siddhartha Guatama (Buddha).

I am not talking of distinctions between Buddhist sects. Each of the three kinds of Buddhism has its own variety of different sects. No, the differences between these three kinds of Buddhism are more basic. Mahayana Buddhism, which the Chinese call Han Buddhism, puts emphasis on deeds that will effect the salvation of others. Hinayana, or Pali Buddhism, emphasizes individual salvation. And Lamaism, with its system of incarnating Living Buddhas, gives vast political powers to a small but select group of monks.

Considering the three types, as well as the multitude of different Buddhist sects in China, one can easily sympathize with Emperor Taizong of the Tang Dynasty (618-907) who despaired over which of the Buddhist sects really had the key to truth. For centuries advocates of one view after another had come to China from India, by way of the Silk Road. The first Mahayana Buddhists came as early as 2 B.C.

Emperor Taizong decided to dispatch an emissary to India to resolve the problem. He chose a Buddhist monk called Xuan Zang as his personal representative. Xuan Zang left for India in 629, and returned sixteen years later. He brought back huge box loads of scriptures and some Indian assistants skilled in reading Sanskrit texts. Within 19 years Xuan Zang translated into Chinese 75 Buddhist works in 1,315 fascicles, or sections. He also wrote, with the help of his disciple Bai Ji, *Records of Western Travels*. In this, Xuan Zang described the geographical features, customs, and religious myths of the 111 states he visited during his journey.

Far better known, however, are the myths and popular folk tales that grew up around Xuan Zang's journey. These imaginary stories were recited over and over again for centuries by professional story tellers. Some four hundred years ago they were gathered by Wu Cheng'en in his 100-chapter *Journey to the West*. The book has become one of the greatest classics of Chinese literature. Its episodes are the basis for many Chinese operas, and parts of it have been made into a full-length Chinese motion-picture cartoon.

The pantheon of gods depicted in the *Journey to the West* come out of a Taoist heaven, not a Buddhist one. But the tale is clearly Buddhist in intent because its pages are sprinkled with hostile remarks against Taoist priests, always depicted as dishonest and devious in their nature. The book illustrates the conflict that has long existed between Buddhism and Taoism in China. It also shows how Buddhism has become popular in China through its willingness to incorporate elements of Confucian and Taoist thought and mythology.

The actual journey of Xuan Zang to India and back did nothing to clear the confusion over which of the many Buddhist sects has the key to truth. However, it did advance China's knowledge of the world. And it led to the translation of many Sanskrit texts into Chinese, establishing the first Buddhist library in China, and an increase of popular interest in Buddhist teachings.

Buddhism succeeded in China in spite of the fact that some of its teachings contradict elements in the indigenous culture of the people. The Buddhist teaching that all is suffering and illusion is quite different from the traditional Chinese view that life is good and is something to be enjoyed. Also the Buddhist insistence on celibacy for monks and nuns is not in keeping with the Chinese emphasis on family and on having children to care for parents in old age.

The religion grew in China in part because here it began to put a stress on filial piety, which fit into Chinese traditions. The Buddhists also began to chant prayers for the well-being of the departed, which met the common people's desires. Buddhism brought solace to those in sorrow, offered divine aid through ever-compassionate Buddhas, and brought the promise of reward for a good life or punishment for a bad one through reincarnation. Such promises were not provided by Confucian ethics or Taoist teachings.

Today there are more than 9,000 Buddhist temples (Han, Lama, and Pali) throughout the country. The oldest one is the Han Buddhist Baima (White Horse) Temple in Luoyang, Henan Province. Two Indian monks, Kasyapa-matanga and Gobharana, helped to build this temple in 67 A.D., during the reign of Emperor Mingdi of the Eastern Han Dynasty.

The number of Buddhists today in China is probably more than 72 million, though Zhou Shaoliang of the Buddhist Association in Beijing told me he estimated the Buddhist population at more than 100 million. Official figures put the number of Lamaists at 17.68 million and the number of Pali Buddhists at 1.5 million. No such statistics are available for Han Buddhists, but an educated guess puts their number at about 54.72 million.

The number of Buddhist monks and nuns comes to about 200,000. The breakdown here is 82,000 Han monks and nuns, 110,000 Lamaist, and 8,000 Pali. In the case of the Han and Lamaist religious professionals, this number is considerably less than it was before 1949 — one-sixth of the 1949 figure for the Han Buddhists. It also should be pointed out that the figure for the Han Buddhists represents a much larger percentage of nuns than of monks. There are an estimated 50,000 nuns to just 32,000 monks among the Han Buddhists.

I asked Zhou Shaoliang why so many more women than men committed themselves to full-time religious work. He said he believed this is because women suffer more, and the aim of Buddhism is to relieve suffering.

I am not surprised at the high figure that this leader of the Buddhist Association gives to the number of Buddhists in China. Everywhere I visited Buddhist temples and monasteries I saw people worshipping. On special temple days and religious holidays, there were large crowds of people burning incense, lighting candles, and offering prayers. Sometimes there were small groups standing in doorways to temple halls to watch the monks, both young and old, as they chanted Mantras to the accompaniment of drums and other musical instruments. Clearly Buddhism in China is in the midst of a period of growth.

Many temple visitors, of course, are tourists and sightseers. This is why most of the temples charge a small admission fee to those who enter. But a significant number are worshipers. I was told that people's interest in Buddhism is often stimulated by their visits as sightseers to temples and sacred Buddhist mountains. Such visitors begin to ask questions of the monks, and then stay to listen to lectures given by the head abbot.

Except for monks and nuns, Buddhist worship in China is a personal and solitary activity. The believer can enter the temple or monastery on any day, after the gate opens, to bow, offer prayers, and burn incense before the various images of Buddha that are found there. Worshipers often bring fruit and vegetables, money, or other gifts to lay as an offering before Buddha. Sometimes they will stop to shake and toss joss sticks (bamboo slats with individual fortunes written on them) in front of the image in the hope of getting an answer to their prayers.

On special temple days, the worship area in front of an image may become so crowded with worshipers that an individual will have difficulty in reaching it, yet each worshiper will still offer only individual and personal prayers. Every temple has a schedule of such special days, but most relate to events specific to that temple (the date of its founding, the date of some miracle that took place there, the date that some abbot achieved enlightenment) and are not universal throughout Chinese Buddhism. An exception is Buddha's Birthday, (the eighth day of the fourth lunar month), which is celebrated everywhere.

The worship by the monks and nuns is quite different. This is a collective activity that takes place at set times, both day and night. The monks chant set prayers together at worship, just as they eat together and study together. Each monk is assigned a specific task, such as cleaning and caring for a particular part of the temple, during times other than the communal activities. A Buddhist motto has it, "Once in their robes, Buddhists are all fully occupied."

Today the Buddhist temples in China appear to be running so efficiently it is easy to forget that just fifteen years ago, during the Cultural Revolution, all such temples were closed and the nuns and monks were laboring in fields and factories throughout China. Now the monks and nuns have returned and the temples are back in working order. It should be noted, however, that there are fewer temples today than there were before 1949. Some that were in disuse at that time have been closed and torn down, but there are still so many that Chinese Buddhists have seen no need to build any new ones.

To give some examples of Han Buddhist activity, the Jade Buddha Temple in Shanghai has more than 160 monks taking care of temple activities. The Longhua Temple, also in Shanghai, has more than 100 monks. In the various lama temples of Tibet, Inner Mongolia, and Qinghai Province the number of monks is often higher than 1,000. The Yonghe Lamasery in Beijing has more than 90 monks. The Shaolin Temple in a rural part of Henan Province has 50 monks, and the temple run by nuns outside Quanzhou has 20 nuns. Buddhist monks and nuns never live in the same temples.

Wherever there are Buddhist monks or nuns there are also lay Buddhists who participate in worship and take care of temple repairs and other services that keep the institutions functioning smoothly. Some of these lay Buddhists eventually decide to become monks or nuns. Many have done so since the Cultural Revolution. At the time I visited the Fayuan

Temple in Beijing, I was told there was a consecration ceremony in progress in Jiangsu Province for 1,300 monks and nuns. This ceremony is a long one, taking about 25 days to complete. Of the 700 aspiring monks, 400 were below the age of 40, and 100 were between the ages of 40 and 60.

HAN BUDDHISM

Han Buddhism is so named because most of its proponents are from the majority Han ethnic group in China. It reached its peak of popularity during the Sui (581-618) and Tang (618-907) dynasties. But as early as 425 A.D., there were 1,367 Buddhist temples in the northern capital of Luoyang alone, as shown by archaeological studies. At that time this city only had a population of about half a million.

Han Buddhists emphasize the existence of many Buddhas. They focus attention on Buddhas in heaven and on people who will become Buddhas in the future. They believe that these present and future Buddhas can save people through compassion and grace. Although Han Buddhists accept the basic Buddhist *Tripitaka* (three classes into which the sacred writings of Buddhism are divided), they believe that their own scriptures reveal an even higher level of truth.

Han Buddhism formed many sects and eventually spread to Japan, Korea, Vietnam, and other countries in Asia. Today there are eight main sects of Han Buddhism. These are the Sanlun (Three Treatises) Sect, the Faxiang (Dharma Characteristic) Sect (also known as the Yoga Sect), the Tiantai Sect, the Huayan (Flowery Splendor) Sect, the Jingtu (Pure Land) Sect, the Chan (Zen) Sect, the Ritsugaku Sect, and the Esoteric Sect.

The Pure Land Sect's chief tenet is salvation by faith alone. The sect demands only that followers worship and pray to Buddha. All those who have faith in Buddha and keep praying to Buddha will be reborn after death in the Pure Land of the West Paradise. Worshipers need neither full understanding of Buddhist scriptures nor the practice of long meditations.

The Chan Sect, founded in 520, promises salvation through one's own perceptions following long meditation exercises. This sect has become particularly influential in Japan, where it is known as Zen Buddhism. Many in this sect believe that enlightenment comes through a sudden flash of insight. Others say it comes gradually through a long process of self discipline, meditation, and instruction.

The doctrines of the various Han sects played an important part in the development of philosophical ideas in China. This cannot be said of the other two forms of Chinese Buddhism (Lama and Pali), since the influence of these was experienced only among certain ethnic minorities within China. Han Buddhist influence is seen in the thousands of Chinese classics. Many of these are of high literary value. The *Vimalakirti, Saddharma-pundarika-sutra* (Lotus Sutra), and *Surangama-samadhi-sutra* have always been special favorites of scholars. Buddhism brought to Chinese literature new conceptions, literary styles, and techniques of wording and phrasing. The first Chinese wood-block printing was a series of pictures based on the *Tripitaka* in Chinese.

Buddhist painting and sculpture have left a rich source of material for the study of Chinese art and history. Whether it be the murals of the Dunhuang caves or the stone carvings in the Longmen, Yungang, and Dazu grottoes, the works highlight a brilliant chapter in China's cultural history. China's pagoda architecture and statue art, at least before the twentieth century, are mostly the work of Han Buddhist designers. The pagodas can be divided into two types, one Indian with Chinese characteristics and the other purely Chinese.

China's music, astronomy, medicine, and gymnastics also reveal Han Buddhist influences. As early as the 2nd century, Buddhist songs were being sung by the Chinese. Yi Xing (673-727), a monk of the Tang Dynasty, was the first to compute the length of the meridian. He compiled a number of books on astronomy and mathematics. In medicine, there were more than ten prescription texts from India that Buddhists translated into Chinese and that were used in

China during the Tang Dynasty. Finally, in gymnastics, the monks of the Shaolin Temple developed various exercise methods imported from India into a special form of *wu shu* through the incorporation of Chinese martial arts techniques.

Four mountains in China are particularly sacred to Han Buddhists. These are Wutai in Shanxi Province, Putuo in Zhejiang Province, Emei in Sichuan Province, and Jiuhua in Anhui Province. A total of 140 monasteries and temples have been rebuilt on and around these mountains. Legend has it that the great Buddhas, Manjusri (Bodhisattva of Wisdom), Samantabhadra (Bodhisattva of Universal Benevolence), Avolokitesvara (Goddess of Mercy) and Ksitigarbha (Guardian of the Earth) respectively visited these four mountains.

The famous temples and monasteries of Han Buddhism include the Fayuan Temple in Beijing; the Daxingshan Temple in Xi'an; the Shaolin Temple in Dengfeng, Henan Province; the Lingyin Temple in Hangzhou; the Hanshan Temple in Suzhou; the Kaiyuan Temple in Quanzhou, the Yufo (Jade Buddha) and Longhua temples in Shanghai; the Daming Temple in Yangzhou; and the Guoqing Temple in Tiantai, Zhejiang Province.

WELFARE SERVICES

Today Han Buddhists are widely recognized for their contributions to social welfare. As one of the monks at the Fayuan Temple told me, the aim of Buddhists is to save people from suffering. In this, they try to inspire the intellect and to purify life.

One of the public service areas for which they are known is afforestation. The monks in the temples of Ningde Prefecture in Fujian Province, 16 temples in all, have planted more than 310 hectares of pine, fir, bamboo, palm, and tea-oil trees. Master Ling Zhao on Wutai Mountain planted more than 5,000 trees while he was living in the Lingfang Temple. After he moved to the Nanshan Temple on the same mountain, he directed 40 monks in the planting of

45,000 trees over a ten-year period.

Because many temples and monasteries are built on high mountains, they are difficult to reach. The Buddhists, therefore, build bridges, repair roads, and provide parking places in front of their temples to accommodate believers and visitors. Such roads and bridges are useful to the public at large as well as to temple goers. A lay Buddhist named Wang Tianhong in Linhai County, Zhejiang Province, has, since the beginning of the 1960s, spent more than 100 days each year voluntarily paving roads. By 1990, he had constructed 33 roads totaling more than 62 miles, and reportedly worn out 138 spades in the process.

Buddhist temples have set up hospitals and clinics that use traditional Chinese medical techniques. A hospital they operate on Wutai Mountain has 150 beds. They claim that about 3,000 patients with leg, hip, and other injuries have been cured by Master Zang Ming at this hospital. The Dichun Central Hospital in Taiyuan City, Shanxi Province, was established in 1958 by a monk named Guang Qing of the Baiyun Temple there. It now has more than 20 medical workers, most of whom are Buddhists. The Buddhist Tianjia Convent in Anhui Province runs a special plaster clinic for persons with severe pains, inflammation, and swelling. The health-producing plasters are made according to secret recipes passed down by nuns from generation to generation for hundreds of years.

At the Cao'an Temple run by nuns near Quanzhou, there is an orphanage for girls. Many local peasants abandon girl babies at the temple gate, particularly if these babies are deformed in any way. I saw one child there, about eight years old, who had a genetic anomaly — hair growing all over her back. The nuns cared for this child just as they did for the others. They had taken her to various hospitals in the hope that the condition could be cured, but so far with no success. The nuns also took care of a stray dog with only three legs. It apparently lost one when it tangled with some agricultural machinery.

In Shanghai, I was told of the many public welfare

programs to which the Buddhist temples contribute. The temples of this city gave over one million yuan to flood relief in 1991. In earlier years they donated large sums to earthquake victims in Yunnan Province and forest-fire victims in Heilongjiang Province. They have a special fund for welfare of the handicapped to which the temples make regular donations about four times a year, and they donate to the foundation to save giant pandas.

Finally, in the area of Han Buddhist services to the needy is the openness of Buddhist monasteries and temples to free hospitality for fellow believers. One Buddhist monk I know of has been wandering the mountains and rivers of China for more than thirty years. Being a monk, he says, he "can wander the whole country with empty pockets." All temples provide food and temporary shelter to such wandering monks. "If you are short of cash or traveling money, the abbot will probably give you some. However, if you want to stay for a long time in a well-known temple, then you will have to apply for a position." When this monk travels, he carries documents with him that are acknowledged by temples nationwide.

LAMAISM

Mahayana (Han) Buddhism didn't reach Tibet until the 7th century A.D., then entering from the central plains of China and from Nepal rather than from India. It immediately came into conflict with Bon, the indigenous religion of that area (a mixture of shamanism and sorcery), whose followers began to blame Buddhism for all their calamities. The followers of Bon said that each pestilence that fell on them was the result of Buddhism having annoyed the divinities and spirits of the earth, mountains, rivers, and heavens.

In the early 9th century, two Bon believers killed Tsanpo, a local leader who had been converted to Buddhism. An advocate of Bon replaced Tsanpo and soon closed all the Buddhist monasteries in the area, destroyed or buried Buddhist figures and scriptures, and forced the nuns and monks to either return to a secular life or face death. But within a few years, this Bon leader was killed by one of the deposed Buddhist monks and the Bon regime collapsed. Much of Tibet was plunged into social chaos.

Only after ages of struggle between Bon and Buddhism did the gap between the two religions begin to narrow. Tibetan Buddhism slowly adopted some of the Bon rites, while Bon eventually took on Buddhist teachings and disappeared. From time to time, a few Buddhists from India were invited to bring their teachings into Tibet, but Lamaism mainly gained its Buddhist knowledge from Chinese Han Buddhist sources.

Of the various sects that eventually developed within Lamaist Buddhism, the main ones are the Nyingma, Sakya, Kagyu, Bon, and Gelug. The Nyingma Sect was founded by Padmasambhava, an Indian master of Esoteric Buddhism who was invited to Tibet to preach Buddhism during the later half of the 8th century. This sect is also called the "Red Sect" because the monks of this school wear red hats. Its principal monasteries are the Dorjida and Minduling.

The Sakya Sect is also known as the "Striped Sect" because of the three stripes of red, white, and black that are painted on the walls of all its monasteries. These stripes represent Manjusri (Lord of Wisdom), Avolokitesvara (Goddess of Mercy) and Vajrapani (a mighty god of two heads and many arms). The principal monastery of this sect is the Sakya Monastery.

The Kagyu Sect is also called the "White Sect" because its monks wore white robes in the past. The Digun and Papang monasteries are the main monasteries of this sect. The Bon Sect is also known as the "Black Sect." It grew directly as an overlay of Buddhism on top of the Bon traditions.

By far the most powerful of the Lamaist sects is the Gelug, or "Yellow" Sect, called this because the monks wear yellow hats. It was founded in 1392 by Tsongkapa, an advocate of religious reform, and it grew rapidly into the sect with the largest following. Part of the reason for this is the political support the Yellow Sect received from the Qing Dynasty (1644-1911) government, which appointed their leader, the Fifth Dalai Lama, to "unify the tribes" in Tibet. Ganden, Sera, Drepung, Tashilhunpo, Ta'er, and Labrang are the principal monasteries of this sect.

Buddhism became the core, the very reason for life in Tibet. A religious caste of lamas (Buddhist monks) arose. This caste superseded all secular authority. Fully one quarter of the male population was recruited for the monasteries, and Tibet remained an authoritarian theocracy until the Communist revolution of 1949.

In taking on some of the traditions of Bon, Lamaism created its own system of leadership, that of rule by persons designated as Living Buddhas. Such persons are believed to be the reincarnations of deceased Living Buddhas. Thus, in Lamaism special persons are literally born into Buddahood, whereas in Han Buddhism followers move toward Nirvana only through good works and in Pali Buddhism they can attain the same condition through devotion.

This system for designating Living Buddhas was formulated by the Kagyu Sect more than one hundred years before the Yellow Sect came into existence. It relies on a committee of monks who search for a soul boy (one into whom the soul of a previous Living Buddha has settled). The monks start this search one year after the death of the previous Living Buddha. They travel in different directions from their temple to find all male children born at the time the former Living Buddha died.

When such soul boys are found (there may be several), each is presented with a group of utensils, some of which were possessions of the previous Living Buddha. If the child takes an interest in one of the utensils owned by the previous Living Buddha, the boy is assumed to be the possible reincarnation. A second test is then administered to make sure. This involves the ritual of asking advice from a protecting spirit. If two or more potential soul boys pass these two tests, lots are drawn from a gold urn to determine the correct identity.

The process of selection and control remains in the hands of a select group of monks — the search committee. One of their number acts as regent until the boy reaches an age when he can be elevated in a grand ceremony to the position of Living Buddha, usually sometime between the ages of 12 and 18. The members of the search committee then remain as the Living Buddha's assistants until he is old enough and wise enough to replace them. Should the new Living Buddha die young, the same group of monks becomes the committee to select the next Living Buddha.

The Living Buddha known as the Dalai Lama is so famous in the West that few people realize there are actually more than 1,000 Living Buddhas in Tibet and other Lamaist communities of China. However, the line of the Dalai Lama (the present one is the 14th) is considered the most powerful, both spiritually and politically. It became so through the action of China's first Qing Dynasty emperor, who, as noted above, used the Fifth Dalai Lama to pacify rebellious tribes in Tibet. The second Qing emperor gave similar powers to a different lama of the Yellow Sect, the Bainqen Lama (also called the Panchen Lama), whose line stems from the Tashilhunpo Monastery in Tibet.

The relations between the Dalai Lama and the Bainqen Lama and to the Chinese government are far too complex and changing to be developed in detail here. Suffice it to say that Emperor Qianlong (1736-95) favored the Bainqen Lama and built a palace in Jehol for him, next to the emperor's own summer palace. The next emperor favored the Dalai Lama and some of the subsequent ones favored the Bainqen Lama. Throughout the present century the Dalai Lama's line has been the dominant one.

It is tradition that the government of China is always asked to ratify the selection of these two Living Buddhas, although this has been more of a formality than a legally binding action. The Nationalist government ratified the elevation of the Dalai Lama in 1938 and ratified the elevation of the recently deceased Bainqen Lama in 1949.

It may come as a surprise that more Tibetans in China

live outside Tibet than inside this autonomous region. Many live in Yunnan, Sichuan, and Qinghai provinces. And there are many followers of Lamaism in China who are not Tibetans at all. Others who follow Lamaist Buddhism include the peoples of the Mongolian, Manchu, Yugur, Luoba, Menba, and Tu ethnic minorities, and part of the Qiang and Pumi people.

The historical relation of Tibet with China is usually taken as beginning in 641 A.D., when Tibet's first notable king, Srongtsan Gampo, married the princess Wen Cheng of the Tang Dynasty. Tibetan kings thereafter paid tribute to the Tang emperors. The princess is still honored in Tibet through songs, fairy tales, and operas that say she "brought Buddhism to Tibet with her dowry." She also brought silk-worms, water-wheels, and other superior techniques of the Tang Dynasty. The famous statue of Buddha that the princess carried with her, said to have been self-created and therefore most holy, stands in a shrine of the Jokhang Monastery in Lhasa.

A century later another king of Tibet married another Tang princess, and in 821 A.D. the Tang emperor Muzong built a monument in Lhasa "to the unity of uncle and nephew" (China and Tibet). Then, in 1271, Kublai Khan made the relationship more secure by the "political unification" of Tibet and China under the Mongol Empire, or Yuan Dynasty. In later years, China more than once broke into warring factions. When this happened, Tibet broke off as one of them. Whenever China was again united under a strong central government, Tibet became again part of China. The Tibetans, however, never allowed the Chinese to station an army in Tibet or to act as the region's police force. This power the monks held for themselves until after the Communist revolution in 1949.

In late 1950, the Chinese Communist army entered Tibet to secure its control over the region. There were scattered revolts against the Chinese after 1956 and an armed uprising of Tibetan monks in 1959, led by the Dalai Lama. This failed, and he fled with some of his supporters to India. There he joined the large community of Tibetans who had migrated to India over the centuries, many to escape the tyrannical excesses of the Tibetan theocracy. From this refuge, the Dalai Lama has issued many proclamations and position papers about the suppression of religion in Tibet.

Some of his allegations about the destruction of religious artifacts and confiscation of temple lands are true. Because the 1959 rebellion was engineered by the monks, the Chinese army raided their temples and confiscated temple land that was used for agriculture and other "non-religious" purposes. But many of the Dalai Lama's examples of the abrogation of religious freedom are related to the period of the Cultural Revolution when all religious activity in China was suppressed.

One needs to remember that the goal of this "revolution" was the eradication of religion completely and forever. Temples, monasteries, and churches of all religions, not just Tibetan Lamaism, were closed at that time, and converted to other uses. Some of these structures suffered savage attacks and depredations. In some cases, the devastation wrecked by marauding Red Guards on the buildings and religious artifacts was total. According to eyewitness accounts, those of Tibetan Buddhism suffered the most damage of all religious structures in China. This is why the Chinese government has allocated more money to the restoration and rebuilding of Tibetan temples than to the restoration of worship sites for any other Chinese religion.

The Dalai Lama's plea for religious freedom in Tibet needs to be balanced against the issue of social justice, and here Tibetan society before 1959 was woefully lacking. At that time, and for centuries before, the population consisted of two basic classes: nobles and serfs. In Tibet's largest city, Lhasa, it is estimated that some two percent of the population were nobles, an additional three percent were their immediate agents (overseers, stewards, and members of private armies), and ninety percent were serfs, tied to the land. The remaining five percent were slaves, persons treated as chattels. All small merchants and handicraftsmen were serfs, who worked for their lords or paid taxes to these lords for the privilege of engaging in trade.

Serfs had to get their lord's permission to marry. Their marriage might be broken by arbitrary transfer of one partner to another estate. A poll tax was imposed on all the serfs, not only men and women, but also the children, including infants. The serfs, of course, ran away with some frequency. If caught, anything might happen to them, including torture, maiming, or death. The law only protected nobles. So many serfs ran away to India, in fact, that the population of Tibet was seriously depleted by 1959. Historical records put the population at 10 million in 634, 8 million in 1737, and 1.19 million in 1959.

Even in monasteries this division of labor between nobles and serfs continued. Sons of the upper class who became monks often had houses of their own, which their families paid for, inside the monastery compounds. Sons of serfs who became monks had to work like slaves for these upper-class lamas. The lower-class ones were reportedly sometimes flogged and tortured like serfs. Many of the monasteries had jails, as did the manor houses of the nobles. In 1947, for example, a Living Buddha known as the Fifth Reting Living Buddha died in the jail cells of the Dalai Lama's Potala Palace in Lhasa because he refused to support edicts issued by the ruling clique.

It was not until reforms were instituted by the Chinese, in 1959, that most of the serfs for the first time won any kind of personal freedom. This is also when the first modern schools and hospitals were established in this region, and when the first major highways, hydropower plants, and industrial projects were constructed. Life expectancy has increased from 36 years of age in 1959 to 64 years of age in 1989.

The Tibetan ruling classes of the past maintained their positions by resisting changes, such as the introduction of modern medicine. Scientific experiments were opposed, and anyone proposing alternative theories of the universe to those of Lamaism was burned as a sorcerer. No roads were allowed, since they would have facilitated the entry of persons with modern ideas.

The monks of Tibet no longer own land, nor is their power as great as it once was. However, religion is still strong in the hearts of the Tibetans. Every visitor to Lhasa will testify to that. There are today 1,400 temples, monasteries, and other religious sites in Tibet alone, which has a population of only 2.196 million.

Over the centuries the Lamaists developed great libraries of Sanskrit and Tibetan manuscripts, the most popular of which is the *Tripitaka Sutra*. It consists of two parts, the Kagyur (the translated scriptures) and the Dangyur (the translated elucidating treatises). The Kagyur has 1,008 entries while the Dangyur contains 3,461 entries. The mandalas that the Lamaists designed are an inspiration to Buddhists and others all over the world. Tibetan art and architecture are almost entirely religious in character. The insights and religious development of Tibetan Buddhism grew despite the social and economic backwardness of this part of China, just as some of the deepest insights in Christianity emerged during the most socially oppressive years of the Middle Ages.

The Tibetans, though not the first to make use of endlessly repeated religious phrases as an aid to worship, have discovered deep religious meanings in such repetition. Their protective formula, *Om mani patime hum* ("Om," the jewel in the lotus), is repeated constantly. It is inscribed on rocks and walls, tallied on prayer wheels, and displayed on banners and. streamers. Their worship also includes reciting prayers and intoning hymns, often to the sound of horns and drums. In some of these the primitive, shamanistic origins of this form of Buddhism can be heard. "Unseen demons inhabit every tree, rock, stream ... not a gesture, not a word, but can draw malevolence ... that only the prayers of priests can exorcise."

The Lamaist monastic orders include abbots, monks, and nuns; novices (candidates); and neophytes (children on probation). The number of Lamaist nuns is small and their standing within this form of Buddhism is inferior. The few temples of Lamaist nuns are all in Tibet. The ordinary monks are called "Dapa," while the well-learned monks with higher social positions are called "Lama," which means "master."

The rules that govern the lama temples are different from those of Han and Pali Buddhism. For example, although Han monks and nuns must be strict vegetarians, Lamaist monks can eat fish and some meat.

A MONGOLIAN LAMA TEMPLE

The lama temple in Beijing, the Yonghe (Everlasting Harmony) Lamasery, is a Mongolian institution and not a Tibetan one. My interview there with Jiamyang Tubudan, the Deputy Director, and Zhang Yu Long, his assistant, had to be translated from Mongolian into Chinese before it could be understood. The temple's more than 90 monks are almost all Mongolian, though some are Tibetans. Tea was served us by their youngest novice, Hu He, a 15-year-old Mongolian youth.

According to the Deputy Director, they estimate of the more than a million visitors each year, about 13,000 of them are Buddhist worshipers. The temple upkeep is financed mainly by the gate entry fees they charge. They also receive donations from the faithful and rent from homes and apartments they own in the surrounding neighborhood.

During the Cultural Revolution this temple was spared from damage because of the personal intervention of Premier Zhou Enlai. Some monks were permitted to remain there to care for the property, but the temple was closed to all worshipers and visitors. In one of the courtyards I noticed a cement urn of modern design. Thinking this might be a significant temple object, I asked about its history. They explained that the urn is actually a vent to an underground shelter, built here during the Cultural Revolution when China expected imminent attack by the Soviet Union. Such shelters were constructed all over Beijing and other major cities of China. This one is no longer used, not even for storage.

The temple is a training center for Lamaism, and 60 of

its more than 90 monks are considered students. They can enroll in the school at age 14, if they have completed junior high school. The students at this lamasery come from Inner Mongolia, Liaoning Province, and Qinghai Province. They work at temple duties and take courses for a fifteen-year period before they can become monks. Their vacation period is the same as that for students in the public high schools and colleges.

I asked how they can enroll students at age 14 when Chinese law forbids religious instruction for minors. They explained that the law does not apply to ethnic minorities, some of whom have a long history of assigning children to life in a religious vocation. Before 1949, boys as young as five were sometimes sent by their parents to such lamaseries to become monks.

The courses here are taught in Mongolian, though the students also learn Chinese and Tibetan. When they complete their studies, most of them remain at this temple, though some will go back to their home temples. Occasionally there are students who realize they are unsuited to a religious life after they have been at the school for a few months. These students are free to leave. Others can return home for a time if their parents need care, and then return to the lamasery studies later.

I asked each of our hosts about their own backgrounds. The Director, a man of 67, became a novice at age seven when his parents sent him to the largest monastery in Qinghai Province. After he became a monk, he was assigned to this lamasery and has been here ever since. His assistant was born in a Tibetan region of Liaoning Province. Because his family is Mongolian, he was raised in the Buddhist faith. He decided to become a lama at age 22 when he heard this lamasery in Beijing was recruiting novices. He has been here ever since (except for the time during the Cultural Revolution when he worked in a factory).

Because these lamas represent the same type of Buddhism as the Dalai Lama, I asked their opinion of his campaign for Tibetan independence. Both became somewhat excited as they answered rapidly in Mongolian, which was difficult for the Chinese translator to follow. The Deputy Director said, "The Buddhist religion has nothing to do with political independence. It just isn't right, according to Buddhist doctrines, to promote this cause. Buddhism should unite and not divide." He further said that independence for Tibet is not in the interests of Mongolian lamas, who travel frequently to that region for meetings with other monastery leaders. I got the impression from this comment that they believed such independence would mean that Lamaism would become the national religion of a Tibet separate from China. The many other lamaseries in China and elsewhere in the world (there is one in the United States) might then be cut off from the source of their religion.

Though there are lamaseries in many parts of China, the best known are in Tibet, particularly in the city of Lhasa. The best known outside of Tibet are the Kumbum Lamasery of Qinghai, the Labrang Lamasery of Gansu, the Wudang Lamasery of Inner Mongolia, and the Yonghe Lamasery of Beijing.

PALI BUDDHISM

Hinayana Buddhism was introduced from Burma, about the 9th century A.D., into regions inhabited by the Dai, Bulang, Achang, and De'ang ethnic minorities in Yunnan Province. Today its followers are mainly people from these ethnic minorities, as well as part of the Bai, Jing (Ginzu), and Lahu people. In China it is called Pali Buddhism because Pali is the language of ancient India that is spoken in the temples.

Pali Buddhists emphasize the importance of Buddha as a historical figure, the virtues of monastic life, and the authority of the *Tripitaka*. For them the ideal Buddhist is what we might call a saint and they call an *arhat*. There are several sects of Pali Buddhism just as there are many sects of Han and Lama Buddhism, but the Pali sects differ only in rituals rather than doctrine.

Monks are recruited at a young age. The abbot at the Jade Temple in Shanghai told me that when he last visited Yunnan Province, he saw many young Buddhist monks. They were teen-agers and younger, all wearing the distinctive yellow robes that showed they were monks. He said that even in public middle schools and high schools he saw monks among the students.

The Demenglong Fota Pagoda in Xishuangbanna and the monastery at Ruili, both in Yunnan Province, are fine examples of Pali Buddhist temples.

BUDDHIST ASSOCIATION

The Chinese Buddhist Association was established in 1953, in Beijing, by a group of distinguished Buddhist leaders. These included Chen Mingshu, Ye Gongchuo, Yuan Ying, Neng Hai, Xu Yun, Lu Zheng, Zhao Puchu, Xirao Jiacuo, and Zhou Shujia. The association unites Buddhists of all types and sects. Zhao Puchu serves as its chairman. There are also provincial and regional Buddhist associations, each of which has representatives in this national Chinese Buddhist Association. One of the representatives from Sichuan Province is a leading nun, Long Lian, who is also in charge of the Sichuan Buddhist Association and the Sichuan Nizhong Buddhist Institute for Nuns, the first training center of its kind in the world.

The association sponsors the journals *Modern Buddhism* and *Dharmaghosa* (*Voice of the Dharma*). These carry academic papers on Buddhism and translations of famous works written by foreign scholars. A total of 15,000 copies of each issue of *Fa Yin* are printed and distributed in China and in 20 countries abroad. The editor-in-chief is Buddhist Master Jing Hui. The association has established a library of 160,000 Buddhist books and a museum of replicas of Buddha from almost every dynasty. It is located at the Fayuan Temple in Beijing.

In 1956 the association founded the Chinese Institute of Buddhist Studies to train Buddhist professionals. This offers four-year and two-year programs. There are about 70 students now taking the four-year course. They are admitted on the recommendation of provincial associations and local temples. The students must be high school graduates, must have at least two years' experience as monks, and must pass an entrance examination. A committee of the Buddhist Association is in charge of teaching and administrative affairs, and the students have their own students union. The Buddhist Association covers all student expenses. Students receive a university diploma on graduation.

About 70 percent of the course work is on Buddhist scriptures and the history of Buddhism; 10 percent is on literature both ancient and modern; 10 percent is on language, either English or Japanese; and 10 percent is on current affairs, such as religious policies in China and the world. Most students return to the temples that sent them after graduation. Some go on to graduate schools in the public universities. Students from Japan and Sri Lanka have come to China to study at this institute.

Two branches of the Chinese Institute of Buddhist Studies have also been opened on Lingyan Mountain in Suzhou and on Qixia Mountain in Nanjing. In 1987, another branch for training senior researchers in Lamaism was founded in Beijing, and special training schools for Lamaism are operating in Tibet, Sichuan, Gansu, and Qinghai provinces. There is one school for Pali Buddhists. Pali Buddhists have also gone to Sri Lanka for advanced studies. All of these are under the sponsorship of the Chinese Buddhist Association.

Local Buddhist colleges and training classes are operating at various places, such as the Shanghai Buddhist Institute, the Sichuan College for Buddhist Nuns, the Fujian Buddhist Institute, and the South Fujian Buddhist Institute. There are furthermore many training courses for monks in various temples and monasteries. Nuns attend schools in Shanghai, Sichuan, Xiamen, and some other places. Again, the Buddhist Association acts as the sponsor of all these institutions.

Beyond this, they maintain lay Buddhist training schools, some of which hold classes on weekends and holidays so that workers can attend in their off hours. These schools teach foreign languages, particularly English and Japanese, and history, as well as the tenets of Buddhism.

The Chinese Buddhist Association has helped in the renovation and reopening of temples and monasteries closed during the Cultural Revolution, has printed hundreds of scriptures and classics, and catalogued more than 125,000 pieces of scripture kept in the Buddhist Scripture Engraving Center in Nanjing. For the Lamaist temples, the association has made a number of porcelain statues of Buddha, painted with gold, and produced more than 700,000 portraits and pictures of Buddha. They have printed pictures for the Pali Buddhists and established libraries and museums for research into Buddhist history and cultural relics.

Since the founding of the Chinese Buddhist Association, contacts with Buddhist organizations in more than 20 countries have been established and friendly visits have been exchanged. In 1962, the Chinese and Japanese governments jointly organized commemorative activities marking the 1,200th anniversary of the death of Jian Zhen, a monk of the Tang Dynasty. In 1964, on the 1,300th anniversary of the death of Xuan Zang, the Chinese Buddhist Association hosted delegations from Japan, Sri Lanka, Kampuchea, Vietnam, and six other countries. The Chinese Buddhist Association has sent delegations to Kampuchea, India, and Nepal for the commemoration of the 2,500th anniversary of the Nirvana of Sakyamuni Buddha. And in 1984, 1986, and 1989, the Chinese Buddhist Association sent delegations to the world Buddhist conferences in Sri Lanka, Nepal, and the United States.

WORLDLY BUDDHISM

The leaders of the Chinese Buddhist Association have pioneered a new concept in Buddhist understanding, "worldly Buddhism." As Zhen Chan, the abbot of Shanghai's Jade

Buddha Temple puts it, "Buddhists engage in worldly affairs with an unearthly spirit, and have the welfare of all sentient beings at heart." Worldly Buddhism goes against the traditional tendency to emphasize the next life and stresses Buddhist contributions to human society today. It regards the world as its base of operation and engages in charitable undertakings as a means to carry out Buddha's behests and fulfill the Buddhist vows in lifelong practice.

Zhao Puchu, Chairman of the Chinese Buddhist Association, says that worldly Buddhism means that through the five precepts, ten goodnesses, four compassions, and six methods to Nirvana, Buddhists are encouraged to build the Pure Land consciously in this world and thus make a contribution to the building of socialism. The five precepts are admonitions against killing, theft, evil rumors, wild speeches, and drinking alcohol. The ten goodnesses are basic Buddhist ethical creeds too long to detail here. The four compassions are conditions for unity among people, such as alms giving, harmonious speeches, and service to others. The six methods to Nirvana include donations to Buddhist temples, observance of monastic discipline, tolerance, and unremitting efforts to behave well in one's vocation.

According to Zhao Puchu, all Buddhists "regard it as their duty to realize the ideal of a 'pure land' in this world and to do their bit for modern socialist construction, a lofty cause to honor the country and benefit the people." In his book *Questions and Answers on Common Knowledge About Buddhism*, he elaborates on the concept of worldly Buddhism in this way:

"If everybody acts by the Five Precepts and Ten Goodnesses, people will live happily and in a peaceful world, society will be stable and united, and the country will be prosperous. Then a peaceful world, a world of high civilization will appear. This is the aim of worldly Buddhism.

"According to Mahayana, all living creatures can become a Buddha. But to become a Buddha, one has first to be a good person, a pure and honest person. Only on the basis of being a good person can one learn from the Buddha

110

and become a Buddha. Only by benefiting others can one benefit oneself. This is Buddha's dialectical aim of salvation of all living creatures first before attaining self-salvation. This is also the theoretical basis of worldly Buddhism.

"If everybody acts according to Buddha's instruction not to say whether one will someday become a Buddha or not, their actions, at least at present, may be conducive to building the country and society. They will be helping to build up a noble morality and a spiritual civilization of helping others, that is, by making the world a pure land. This is where the doctrine of worldly Buddhism lies."

The Chinese Buddhist Association presented me with a small medallion that has on it what they told me were the instructions of Buddha himself. It reads, "Give thanks to country; give thanks to parents; give thanks to teachers; and give thanks to all living things." The Buddhists in Shanghai told me that they have a saying that translates, "Make the Buddhist kingdom prosperous; make the people's living happy." They also said that if Buddhism is to prosper in China, they will need stability and prosperity. For this reason, they believe their fate is closely connected to the fate of the country as a whole.

The Jade Buddha Temple in Shanghai holds two services each day at which they pray for stability of China and for world peace, one in the morning and one in the evening. They say they can only help to develop China in a peaceful environment.

This connection between love of religion and patriotism is symbolized by the fact that many persons serving at various levels in the government decision-making process are identified as Buddhists. Zhao Puchu is vice-chairman of the National Committee of the Chinese People's Political Consultative Conference, one of the highest bodies of government. Hundreds of Buddhists serve on provincial and city consultative organizations. Before 1949, they were denied such political posts. As a member of the Shanghai Buddhist Association told me, "The government now listens to what we say."

Many lay Buddhists, in all walks of life, have been honored by the government as model workers. The awards not only mention their work but also that they are Buddhists.

What does the future look like for Chinese Buddhism? The answer comes again from Zhao Puchu. In comparing the past with the present, he recently said that he "is pleased with the present state of Chinese Buddhism and Buddhists. Chinese Buddhism will definitely prosper with the advances in China's economic construction, and Buddhism will do its share in honoring the country and benefiting the people by safeguarding world peace, progress, and happiness." Looking forward, Zhao Puchu says that he believes there is a bright future ahead for Chinese Buddhism.

Following a description of some to the most interesting places of Chinese Buddhism, we will turn to Islam in China. Unlike the Buddhists, the Chinese Muslims are almost all one sect, though they represent many different ethnic groups.

VISITOR'S GUIDE TO BUDDHIST SITES

There are Buddhist temples everywhere in China, but the temples and lamaseries we have listed below are the most significant ones. We include, at the end, a listing by sect for those visitors seeking such specific types.

HAN BUDDHISM

1. Fayuan Temple (City of Beijing)

Located on Xuanwumenwai Street, this temple was built in 645, during the Tang Dynasty, and restored several times. It has six courtyards. The first of these contains the bell and drum towers. In the second courtyard is the main hall of the temple, containing statues of three generations of Buddhas — past, present, and future — as well as 18 arhat figures. The temple has many historical relics and a museum of Buddhas from almost every dynasty, but the museum is not open to the public. By request one can obtain special permission to see it. One of the most valuable objects is a ceramic statue of Buddha from the Eastern Han Dynasty (25-220). The temple is the site of the Chinese Institute of Buddhist Studies.

2. Yufo (Jade Buddha) Temple (City of Shanghai)

Located on Anyuan Street, this temple is noted for its two valuable jade Buddha statues, one a large sitting Buddha carved from a single piece of solid white jade and the other a reclining Buddha also made from a single piece of white jade. The monks here take pride in the fact that it is in the center of the city, "a quiet land surrounded by a noisy place." The temple was built more than 100 years ago in the style of the Song Dynasty. It contains three main halls and two courtyards. The first is the Heavenly King Hall; the second, the Grand Hall; and the third, the Abbot's Hall of Wisdom. Above this third hall is a chamber for the sitting Jade Buddha, on either side of which is kept a collection of 7,240 volumes of wood-block printed Buddhist scriptures.

The surrounding halls include a Meditation Hall, Reclining Jade Buddha Hall, Bronze Buddha Hall, Bronze Mercy Buddha Hall, and Charitable Hall. There is also a guest house and a fine vegetarian restaurant. Reservations are advised. Among the many statues, the oldest of which dates from the 5th century, are the four celestial kings, three large gilded Buddha statues (past, present, and future), and 18 gilded arhat statues. This temple was protected by Premier Zhou Enlai during the Cultural Revolution, while all the other Buddhist temples in Shanghai were badly damaged or destroyed. The abbot, Zhen Chan, is a noted author of four books on Buddhism. The temple belongs to the Chan Sect.

3. Longhua Temple (City of Shanghai)

The Longhua Temple, the largest Buddhist temple in Shanghai, is said to have been built in 242, during the period of the Three Kingdoms. It was damaged many times and rebuilt in 1875. The seven-story, octagonal-wooden pagoda in front of the temple was built in 247 and rebuilt in 977 during the Song Dynasty. It is the only pagoda in Shanghai. The pagoda is not open to visitors and has been separated from the temple for more than fifty years. There are plans to connect it again and reopen it, but such a process will cause the displacement of about 20,000 persons who live in the surrounding area and so it may be many years before this can be done. The temple has five courtyards surrounded by halls and rooms and includes a bell tower and a drum tower. In one of the halls is the largest 1,000-hand statue of the Goddess of Mercy in China. It is a gilded statue surrounded by other Buddhas and heavenly figures.

The temple underwent renovations in 1957 and 1979. Some of its Buddhist statues were destroyed during the

Cultural Revolution, but these have now been restored. A bronze bell from 1382 is one of the features of interest. The temple has a three-star guest house with more than 100 rooms and an excellent vegetarian restaurant. Some people say this is the best vegetarian restaurant in China, and the best of all Buddhist ones in the world. Reservations are advised for those who wish to eat here. A Longhua Temple Fair, held around the third day of the third lunar month, has developed from a religious ceremony into a popular commodity fair. The temple belongs to the Lotus Sect.

4. Hanshan Temple (Jiangsu Province)
Situated about two miles west of the city of Suzhou, in the village of Fengqiao Town, this temple was founded in 503. It was later named for a famous Buddhist monk, Hanshan, who lived here for a time during the 7th century. The present buildings date from the Qing Dynasty. The temple bell, no longer in existence by the Ming Dynasty, was lauded in a poem by Zhang Ji (8th century). One can now see a bronze bell, patterned after a model from the Tang Dynasty, that was presented to this temple by Japanese Buddhists.

5. Lingyan Temple (Jiangsu Province)
This temple, also known as Congbao Temple, stands on the summit of Lingyan (Elephant) Hill near the small town of Mudu and about six miles southwest of the city of Suzhou. Its pagoda dates from 1147, but the buildings were all rebuilt between 1919 and 1932. The hill itself has been praised for its beauty by poets and writers from many periods of China's history, including Li Bai, Bai Juyi, Li Shangyin, and Tang Yin. The temple, though rebuilt, is still considered one of the earliest structures of the Pure Land Sect.

6. Qixia Temple (Jiangsu Province)
This temple, about 14 miles east of the city of Nanjing, was erected about 483. It burned in 1855 and was then rebuilt. Only the main gate, three halls, and the Tower of

Holy Books remain. There are also stone pagodas from the time of the Five Dynasties and stone stelea from the Tang Dynasty. One pagoda is said to date to 601, but the Buddhas chiseled into its seven walls are from the 10th century. The temple belongs to the Sanlun Sect.

East of this temple is the Thousand Buddhas Rock, which is also worth visiting. Tradition has it that two Buddhas were chiseled into this rock around the year 500. Later, more and more figures were added until there are now some 299 niches containing 515 Buddhist sculptures. The Wuliang Hall hall that stands next to this rock was erected in 484. Its outer walls and arched gate are of stone.

7. Daming Temple (Jiangsu Province)

This temple, built between 457 and 464, is 3 miles northwest of the city of Yangzhou. It was rebuilt between 1860 and 1870 and is also known as the Fajing Temple. Monk Jian Zhen, an abbot of this temple, crossed the sea to Japan with some of his students during the Tang Dynasty and established Buddhism there. In 1973 a new hall of this temple was dedicated to the memory of the monk. There are three big Buddha statues in the main hall as well as 18 arhats and one Guanyin statue. In 1963, on the 1,200th anniversary of Jian Zhen's death, Chinese and Japanese Buddhists held a joint festival here in his memory. The temple belongs to the Ritsugaku Sect.

8. Longchang Temple (Jiangsu Province)

This temple is on Baohua Mountain north of Jurong County and about 50 miles east of the city of Nanjing. It is a significant temple because it is one of the earliest built of the Ritsugaku Sect.

9. Lingyin Temple (Zhejiang Province)

This temple, also known as Yunlinchan Temple, is located in the city of Hangzhou, northwest of West Lake and at the foot of Lingyin (Hidden Saints) Mountain. It was built in 326 and has been repaired and expanded many times since then. According to legend, an Indian Buddhist monk came here in 326 and saw a mountain peak, now called Feilai Feng, that so resembled one in India that he concluded the peak must have miraculously flown here. He therefore erected the temple at this site. The peak contains many ancient trees, caves, and the strangely shaped rocks. More than 380 Buddhist sculptures have been placed on this peak, including one of the Maitreya Buddha, dating to the Song Dynasty, that can be seen from some distance away. He sits in one of the large niches, laughing and playing with a string of pearls.

The temple itself at one time had nine towers, 18 pavilions, and 270 halls. More than 3,000 monks were living there. The present complex dates from reconstruction after the Taiping Revolution in 1856. A laughing Maitreya Buddha is in the center of the Hall of the Celestial Kings. Along the walls of this hall are the four celestial kings and a Song Dynasty, sandalwood statue of the youthful warrior Weituo. The Grand Buddha Hall contains a gilded statue of a seated Sakyamuni Buddha made of camphor wood. Behind a partition in the same hall is a statue of the bodhisattva Guanyin. There are also two octagonal stone pagodas with nine tiers in front of this hall. They date from the 10th century. Visitors should take time to walk through the area surrounding the temple. The paths lead through forests and past steep gaps and mountain springs.

10. Jiaxiang Temple (Zhejiang Province)

This temple in the city of Shaoxing is significant because it is one of the earliest temples of the Sanlun, or Three Treatises, Sect.

11. Yanqing Temple (Zhejiang Province)

This temple in the city of Ningbo is one of the earliest temples of the Tiantai Sect, and is important for that reason alone. It has a Vairocana Buddha as one of its few sculptures.

12. Guoqing Temple (Zhejiang Province)

This temple in Tiantai County, about 100 miles south of the city of Ningbo, is the primary temple of the Tiantai Sect (a rationalist school of thought based on interpretations of the Lotus Sutra). It is far from normal tourist areas, but can be reached by bus from Ningbo, Shaoxing, or Hangzhou. The temple was completed in 598 during the Sui Dynasty and renovated in 1973. It has 13 halls and more than 600 chambers. Outside the temple is a stupa devoted to the Buddhist monk, Yi Xing, who was an astronomer during the Tang Dynasty. Inside are several exquisitely carved statues of Buddha.

13. Putuo Mountain (Zhejiang Province)

This is one of the four sacred mountains of Buddhism. It stands on a small island off the coast of Zhejiang Province and can be reached by a boat trip from the city of Ningbo, a journey that takes about five hours. The mountain is dedicated to the bodhisattva Guanyin, the personification of compassion, goodness, wisdom, and love. Guanyin has the ability to appear in different forms, both male and female. The bodhisattva is often portrayed as figure with a thousand arms so as to emphasize his unending goodness and willingness to help. He is said to have meditated and given sermons here for many years. At one time there were more than 300 temples and monasteries on this mountain and 3,000 monks. Visitors can stay in one of the guest houses of the village, about a 20-minute walk from the harbor.

The three most sacred temples on Putuo Mountain are Puji Temple, the oldest and largest, Fayu Temple, and Huiji Temple. Puji Temple was founded in 1080 and has been expanded through the years. The main hall has a gigantic Guanyin statue. There are many other temples, convents, and Buddhist pagodas on the mountain that are worth visiting. Also of interest are the two large rocks above the Guanyin Gudong Convent on the west side of the mountain that are naturally shaped like turtles. One seems to be stretching out its head. A beach on the eastern shore of this island provides a good place for swimming.

14. Kaiyuan Temple (Fujian Province)

This temple, also called the Mulberry and Lotus Temple, is in the city of Quanzhou. It was built in 682, during the Tang Dynasty. At its prime, it had 120 attached buildings that housed 1,000 monks. Today it includes a Grand Buddha Hall, Ganlujie Alter, Buddhist Scripture Library, and East and West Towers. According to legend, the site of the temple was once a mulberry field. Its owner dreamed one day that a Buddhist monk asked him to give up the field for the construction of a temple. The owner answered that he would do so only if the mulberry trees blossomed with white lotus flowers. Three days later the trees did indeed produce lotus blossoms.

Almost one hundred stone pillars were used in the construction of the Grand Buddha Hall. On the crossbeam in the hall are 24 music birds with human faces that are said to have landed there to listen to the recitation of Buddhist sutras. Their heads help to prop up the beams of the roof. They symbolize the 24 divisions of the solar year of the Chinese calendar. A statue of Guanyin and eighteen arhats are enshrined on the north side of this hall. The Ganlujie Alter is an octagonal structure where Buddhists are confirmed as monks and nuns. It is the biggest and best preserved alter of this type in China. It is divided into five levels. The statue of the supreme Buddha Losana sits on top, perched on a lotus-flower platform consisting of 1,000 petals. On each of the petals another Buddha is carved.

There are some 37,000 volumes of Buddhist scriptures and other relics in the Scripture Library. There are also two stone pillars that hold up one of the roofs that come from a Brahman temple that previously stood on this site. The pillars have Brahman inscriptions on them. A pair of towers are a special feature of this temple. The eastern one dates from the end of the Tang Dynasty and the western one from the Five Dynasties era (907-960). Both were formerly made of wood, but between 1228 and 1250 they were rebuilt in stone.

119

15. Nanhua Temple (Guangdong Province)

This temple is near Shaoguan, about 100 miles north of the city of Guangzhou. Shaoguan is on the railway line between Guangzhou and Beijing. The temple was built in 504 and is still in good condition today. It has three gilded Buddhas, seated on lotus blossoms, in the Grand Buddha Hall. These represent the past, present, and future. Along the walls are 500 arhat figures in five rows, one above the other. A huge water vessel from 1338 stands behind the hall. The Depository of Buddhist Texts contains valuable sutras and original decrees from the Tang, Yuan, and Ming dynasties. A brick pagoda from the 8th century stands behind this depository. The Liuzu Hall is dedicated to the monk Hui Hui Neng. The temple belongs to the Chan Sect.

16. Yungang Rock Temples (Shanxi Province)

These rock temples are located about seven miles west of the city of Datong, in a valley on the south side of the Wuzhou Mountain. Most of them were constructed about 1,500 years ago during the Northern Wei Dynasty. In 460 the emperor commissioned the famous monk Tan Yao to carve five large Buddhist statues into the sandstone of the mountain. This was followed by other carvings in caves hollowed out of stone. Approximately 100,000 statues were produced here. In the 53 caves that are preserved today, there are 51,000 sculptures. Although they are of Chinese design, they show elements of Indian, Persian, and even Greek influence. Many of the statues have been damaged by weather and humans. At least 1,400 of them were stolen, and many of these are on display in museums throughout the world. Attempts are now being made to restore and preserve the damaged statues and the caves that house them. There are three groups of caves. A wooden monastery building protects the cave with the largest Buddha.

17. Wutai Mountain (Shanxi Province)

This is another one of the four sacred mountains of Buddhism. It is in the eastern part of the province on the border of Hebei Province. It can be reached by bus from the city of Taiyuan, a drive through mountainous country that takes about nine hours. The mountain consists of five platform-shaped peaks, standing in a ring that separates the mountain into Outer and Inner Wutai. On the tops of the peaks of Inner Wutai are 39 well-preserved temples, including the fine Temple of Revelation, and Dagoba Temple. The Outer Wutai has eight monasteries, including Buddha's Light Temple and Nanchan Temple. Tradition has it that this is the place where Manjusri, Bodhisattva of Wisdom, displayed his power and lectured.

The first monastery on Wutai Mountain was built during the Eastern Han Dynasty, and historical records show that more than 200 such temples and monasteries were standing here by the year 557. Among the structures today are the Bishan Temple, built during the Northern Wei Dynasty, that contains a Buddha carved in white jade; the Nanashan Convent, built during the Yuan Dynasty; and the Longquan Temple, built during the Song Dynasty, that has a white-marble ornamental gate. Several of the temples provide sleeping and eating accommodations for visitors. There is a big Buddhist festival held on Wutai Mountain in the sixth month of every year of the lunar calendar. It attracts many foreign and Chinese Buddhists.

18. Xuanzhong Temple (Shanxi Province)

This temple, also called the Stone Wall Temple, is on Shibi Mountain about two miles southwest of Jiaocheng County seat and about 30 miles southwest of the city of Taiyuan. The area is impressive for its mountains, but quite difficult to reach. The temple was set up in 472, during the Northern Wei Dynasty. It is the primary temple of the Jingtu, or Pure Land, Sect. All its halls, pagodas, and monk's chambers have been renovated since 1954. The most precious relics in the temple are scores of ancient stone tablets and about 1,000 large and small Buddhist statues.

19. Baima Temple (Henan Province)

This temple, the name of which means White Horse, was the first ever built by Buddhists in China, is located about five miles east of the city of Luoyang. It was erected in the year 67, during the Eastern Han Dynasty. Legend has it that two Indian monks who brought Buddhist teachings to China came there riding on white horses. The temple was established where the horses came to a halt. The temple complex has been renovated and restored many times. Its present buildings date from the Ming Dynasty. They include the Tianwang, Dafo, Daxiong, and Pilu Ge halls. There are also two tombs inside the temple gates that contain the remains of the two Indian monks. A pagoda, built in 1175, stands in the temple's eastern section.

20. Longmen Caves (Henan Province)

About five miles south of Luoyang is Longmen Mountain into which caves and grottoes were carved as early as the Wei Dynasty. More were added during the Tang Dynasty so that today there are 1,352 caves, 750 niches, 39 pagodas, 97,000 sculptures, and 3,680 inscriptions on this slope and on the slope of the mountain that stands opposite it on the other side of the Yihe River. As at the Datong Caves in Shanxi Province, many of the statues have been removed by unscrupulous persons. Some of them are found in the museums of Europe and North America. The most impressive caves include Qianxi Temple, which has a sculpture of Amitabha with a disciple at each side; Binyang Cave, with 12 statues of Buddha and musicians and dancers depicted on the roof above; and Wanfo Cave, with more than 15,000 figures of Buddha carved into the cave walls.

21. Shaolin Temple (Henan Province)

The Chan-Buddhist Shaolin Temple is located in the Songshan Mountain area, about 35 miles southeast of the city of Luoyang and 40 miles southwest of the city of Zhengzhou. It was built in 496 during the Northern Wei Dynasty and now serves as the primary temple of the Chan

Sect. The temple is well known around the world because this is where one of the most famous styles of martial arts developed. It is said that an Indian monk, Bodhidharma, came to China to spread Buddhism and introduced an Indian form of exercise. The Chinese monks that he gathered here as followers then combined this with Chinese techniques to produce this unique form of *wu shu*. The militia monks of Shaolin gradually gained fame during the early Tang Dynasty by helping Li Shimin, the first emperor of that dynasty, to suppress a local feudal ruler who wanted to set up a separate government by force. At one time 1,000 monks lived at this temple.

The temple has a mountain gate, guest rooms, Dharma Pavilion, Baiyi Hall, Ksitigarbha Hall, and a hall housing 1,000 statues of Buddha and murals depicting 500 arhats. There are also many stelae handed down since the Tang Dynasty. Two rows of depressions can be seen in the brick floor of the temple caused by monks practicing their fighting styles. There is also a mural depicting 30 monks practicing this form of *wu shu*. The temple has been renovated many times. Beside the temple stand 220 stupas, first built in 791. In addition, convents and pagodas are scattered over the mountain.

22. Jiuhua Mountain (Anhui Province)

This mountain, another of the four sacred Buddhist ones, is in the southern part of the province, about 40 miles west of the city of Anqing. A bus from this city will take the visitor to the foot of a series of peaks that compose this mountain. Here there are hotels, restaurants and several famous temples along the road that takes the visitor to the other Buddhist sites. Legend has it that Ksitigarbha, the Guardian of the Earth, demonstrated his power on Jiuhua Mountain. During the Tang Dynasty, Prince Kim Gio Gak of the Kingdom of Silla on the Korean Peninsula came to this mountain to become a monk. A long time after his death, his corpse was found intact and so people regarded him as the reincarnation of Ksitigarbha. There is now a golden stupa on the mountain that contains his remains. There are also more than 80 large and small temples.

During its golden age, the mountain had more than 200 temples and more than 5,000 monks. Today the largest is Zhiyuan Temple, built during the Ming Dynasty. It contains three large gilded Buddhas in its main hall. Baisui Gong, the Hundred-Year-Old-Palace, contains the gilded mummy of Hai Yu, a noted monk who lived during the Ming Dynasty. He died at the age of 120. There are many other interesting things to see in this area, including its waterfalls, stone caves, creeks, trees, and general scenic charm. The name of the mountain means Nine Blossoms and comes from a poem by the Tang Dynasty poet Li Bai.

23. Yuquan Temple (Hubei Province)

This temple at Dangyang, a town about 25 miles east of the city of Yichang, is one of the earliest temples of the Tiantai Sect.

24. Zhenjue Temple (Hubei Province)

This temple in the northeastern part of Huangmei County, about 35 miles north of the city of Jiujiang, is one of the earliest temples of the Chan (Zen) Sect.

25. Dongling Temple (Jiangxi Province)

This temple stands at the northwest foot of Lushan Mountain, which in turn is a little south of the city of Jiujiang on Poyang Lake. It was built in 384 by Hui Yuan, a famous Buddhist monk. It is believed that the Pure Land Sect was started here. During the Tang Dynasty, many Buddhist monks came here from foreign countries to study the teachings of this sect. The temple has several halls. The main one, Shenyun Baodian, contains numerous statues, including ones of Sakyamuni, Manjusri, Samantabhadra, and Kasyapa. The mountain contains a number of other temples and pagodas that should be of interest to any visitor.

26. Daxingshan Temple (Shaanxi Province)

This temple in the city of Xi'an, originally built during

the Jin Dynasty, competes with the Qinglong Temple (also in Xi'an) as the primary temple of the Esoteric Sect. The three great Indian Buddhist monks of the Tang Dynasty — Subhakarasimha (637-735), Vajrabodhi (669-741), and Amoghabajra (705-774) — taught here. These monks reportedly translated 500 Buddhist classics into Chinese at this temple. It is also a temple where Japanese Buddhists came to study during the Tang Dynasty. All the present buildings date from the Ming and Qing dynasties. They were restored in 1956.

27. Qinglong Temple (Shaanxi Province)

This temple is one of two temples in the city of Xi'an that are each considered to be the primary temple of the Esoteric Sect. The other is the Daxingshan Temple. During the Tang Dynasty, Master Hui Guo of the Esoteric Sect was the abbot here. His disciple, the Japanese monk Kukai, later established the Esoteric Sect of Japanese Buddhism. There were also disciples here from the Kingdom of Heling (today's Java Island in Indonesia) and the Kingdom of Silla (today's Korea). The temple fell into ruin in 1086 during the Northern Song Dynasty. In 1982 a monument to Kukai was erected at the ruins. Memorial halls to Hui Guo and Kukai were also built in recent years.

28. Cien Temple (Shaanxi Province)

This temple is in Yanta Village, in the southern outskirts of the city of Xi'an. It is the primary temple of the Faxiang (Dharma Characteristic) Sect, also known as the Yoga Sect. The temple was built in 589, during the Sui Dynasty. At one time it had 10 courtyards, 1,897 rooms, and 300 monks. It was destroyed toward the end of the Tang Dynasty. The present buildings date from the Qing Dynasty. There are three Buddhas and 18 arhat statues in the main hall.

The temple's Dayan (Wild Goose) Pagoda was built in 652 to protect the 615 volumes of Buddhist sutras that Xuan Zang brought back from India during his journey to India. The pagoda was named by Xuan Zang after an old Indian legend telling of a monastery where the monks were allowed to eat veal, venison, and wild goose. One day a flock of wild geese flew over the monastery and admonished the monks to give up eating meat. As a warning, one of the geese sacrificed itself by falling to the earth at the monks' feet. They buried it there and then built a pagoda in honor of the goose. From then on, the monks never ate meat. The Dayan Pagoda is square and originally had five stories. It was torn down in 705 and rebuilt on a grander and higher scale — 10 stories. Today only seven of these remain. Over the years a layer of brick was added to the walls to stabilize the building. Otherwise, it has remained well-preserved for more than 1,200 years. It is possible to climb to the top floor and view the city.

29. Jingye Temple (Shaanxi Province)

This temple on Zhongnan Mountain, about 20 miles south of the city of Xi'an, is one of the earliest of the temples of the Ritsugaku Sect. The mountain itself is also worth visiting since it is a favorite cultural, recreational, and scenic area.

30. Xingjiao Temple (Shaanxi Province)

This temple, 24 miles south of the city of Xi'an, was built in 669. It is one of the earliest temples of the Faxiang (Dharma Characteristic) Sect in China. The three-story pagoda was erected to hold the remains of the monk Xuan Zang. The temple gradually went into decline and deteriorated. In 1922 new buildings were constructed at this site, and a Buddhist library was put up in 1939. The temple is noted for its jade statue of Buddha that came from Burma.

31. Caotang Temple (Shaanxi Province)

This temple in Huxian County, 36 miles southwest of the city of Xi'an, is the primary temple of the Sanlun Sect. It was originally the site of a Chinese palace, built in the 5th century, but after the Indian monk Kumarajiva (344-413) came to teach in this area it became a temple. The octagonal stone pagoda, which is part of the site, was constructed in the Tang Dynasty. Renovations were initiated twice, in 1952 and 1956. In 1981, the large temple hall and monks' chambers were rebuilt.

32. Famen Temple (Shaanxi Province)

In the north part of Fufeng County, about 70 miles west of the city of Xi'an, is the Famen Temple, built during the Eastern Han Dynasty. It became famous because it is said to have a relic of Sakyamuni, the founder of Buddhism — his finger bones. The temple has attracted many Buddhist pilgrims over the years. One finger bone is still preserved in a seven-layered casket made of gold and precious jewels. During the Tang Dynasty, a four-level wooden stupa was constructed above an underground tomb in which this casket was placed. The stupa collapsed during the Ming Dynasty and was replaced by a 13-level brick stupa. This, too, fell into disrepair.

In recent years archaeological excavations were conducted in the area, prior to rebuilding the brick stupa. These uncovered many special porcelain items, glass vessels, and 7,000 silk fabrics from the Tang Dynasty, as well as copper, gold, and silver objects, stone carvings, coins of various types, and some buried sutras written in the Northern Song and Yuan dynasties. An exhibition hall has been constructed to display these items to the public. On November 9, 1989, a special ceremony was held to commemorate the construction of the new stupa. It was attended by some 50,000 persons, including Buddhists from Japan, Singapore, Hong Kong, and Australia.

33. Emei Mountain (Sichuan Province)

This mountain is one of the four sacred mountains of Chinese Buddhism. It is located about 100 miles southwest of the city of Chengdu. There is a train that takes the visitor from that city to a point near the base of the mountain. One can also drive by car part way up to the top. According to legend, Buddha Samantabhadra often displayed his power on this mountain. At one time there were about 200 big and small temples here, but today only 20 remain. Four are still well preserved. Fuhu Temple is at the foot of the mountain. It was founded during the Tang Dynasty, and rebuilt in 1651. It has a guest house and a restaurant. Not far away is Baoguo Temple, built in the 16th century. It has four halls, the Maitreya Hall, the Grand Buddha Hall, the Seven-Buddha Hall and the Depository of Buddhist Texts, as well as decorative pavilions and towers. Its colorful ceramic statue of Buddha dates from 1415. There is also a bronze pagoda, the walls of which are decorated with 4,700 Buddhist figures, and a model of Emei Mountain.

The Guangxiang Temple dates from 1612, during the Ming Dynasty, though the halls that are open to the public were built during the Qing Dynasty. Further up the mountain is the Elephant's Bathing Pool where the Buddha Samantabhadra's flying elephant is said to have taken a bath. Near this is the Wannian Temple that has three Buddhist sculptures: Guanyin, Ksitigarbha, and Sashi Zhi. The highest point of the mountain is the Golden Peak, about a two-hour walk from the Elephant's Bathing Pool. The special feature of this peak is "Buddha's Glory," a circular rainbow that can sometimes be seen when looking over the cliff below. Many Buddhist pilgrims have seen their own shadows in this rainbow and assumed this meant they had achieved illumination. They then jumped into the rainbow ring and fell to their deaths below. There is now a fence to prevent persons from getting too close to the edge of the cliff. The rainbow can be seen several times a month and almost daily in October and November.

34. Dazu Grottoes (Sichuan Province)

These Buddhist cave temples are about 110 miles northwest of the city of Chongqing, about three hours distance by car. They date from the end of the Tang Dynasty and beginning of the Song Dynasty. There are 50,000 stone sculptures altogether in about 40 different caves spread over several mountains. The best ones are found on Beishan Mountain and on Baoding Mountain. Many of the sculptures have been restored in recent years.

35. Dunhuang Caves (Gansu Province)

These caves, also known as the Mogao Grottoes, were begun in 366 by Buddhist monks. The caves are located about 15 miles southwest of Dunhuang, which is in the western part of the province. To get there one travels by train toward the city of Urumqi, in Xinjiang Uygur Autonomous Region, gets off at the town of Liuyuan, in Gansu Province, and then takes a bus or car south to the town of Dunhuang. The traveler can stay at the Dunhuang Hotel as many days as necessary to study the art in the grottoes. A Tang Dynasty inscription says that the site for these caves was determined by a Buddhist monk who was traveling west. The monk arrived here at sunset and saw that the surrounding mountains were sparkling as if lit by a thousand Buddhas. He took this to be a holy sign and built the first grotto in a sandstone wall opposite the mountain. Buddhist monks and lamas continued to build caves there until the 11th century, when the site was abandoned and forgotten. It was rediscovered by a wandering Taoist monk named Wang Yanlu, in 1899.

Wang Yanlu discovered an old monastery library in one of the caves that contained the oldest extant printed book (dated to 868). He also found bronze figures, silk paintings, and embroidery that probably belonged to monks living in the cave temples during the 11th century. He told the authorities about his find, but the Chinese government at that time didn't see much value in protecting the site and so many of the objects were taken by others and sold to collectors from the West. A British collector took away 29 cases of manuscripts, paintings, and embroideries. A Frenchman took many more. It was not until 1949 that the Chinese government decided to protect and make efforts to restore and care for this cultural inheritance. They established an institute at Dunhuang dedicated to investigation of the Dunhuang caves.

There are now 492 caves covered inside with murals and containing 2,450 colored sculptures from the 4th to the 13th centuries. Many caves have been destroyed by erosion and drifting sand. The caves provide an unbroken historical picture of the Buddhist art of China through almost a thousand years. They contain art from the Northern Wei, Western Wei, Northern Zhou, Sui, and Tang dynasties. The Tang Dynasty cave paintings are particularly magnificent. The murals, rich and varied in color, contain superb figures and faces sensitive and expressive. Here also are the world-famous Tang horses, black, green, or brown, galloping across a rose and mauve desert. Some of the murals from the Tubo period of Tibetan Lamaism depict the daily lives of people on the lower rungs of the social ladder, unusual in Tibetan art. Many manuscripts have been found in recent years in the various caves, some in Sanskrit, some in Tibetan, and some in Chinese.

TIBETAN BUDDHISM

36. Yonghe Lamasery (City of Beijing)

The name of this lamasery means Everlasting Harmony. It was built in 1694 as the residence of the emperor's son, and became a lamasery in 1723. Major renovations were made in 1950, 1952, and 1979. It is a magnificent architectural complex, with five courts, each surrounded by a hall and chambers. Architectural styles of the Han, Manchu, Mongolian, and Tibetan ethnic groups are all found here. The visitor enters through the south gate and follows a path to the first courtyard, which contains the drum and bell towers, as well as two stele pavilions. In the first hall is a magnificent statue of Maitreya, the Buddha of the future, with statues of the four celestial guardians around it. The next hall, the main one, contains three Buddha sculptures. These are the Buddha of the present, the Buddha of the past, and the Buddha of the future. Eighteen arhat statues stand along the east and west walls.

The third hall contains three Buddhas: the Buddha Amitabha, the Buddha of Medicine, and the Buddha of the

Lion's Roar (Buddha's teachings shake the world like the roar of a lion). The fourth hall contains a bronze statue of Tsongkapa and murals telling of his importance. There are also books stored along the walls — Buddhist writings in Tibetan, some written in gold ink. Here also is a famous hill made of sandalwood containing 500 arhats of gold, silver, copper, iron, and tin. The fifth hall is the tallest and is linked to two side halls by "heavenly bridges," or hanging galleries. The hall contains a statue of Maitreya carved from a Tibetan sandalwood tree trunk. It also has a bronze Buddha resting on a pedestal of nanmu wood that is said to have been presented, in 1750, to Emperor Qianlong of the Qing Dynasty by the Seventh Dalai Lama. There are many other significant Buddhist statues and artifacts in this temple, including a stone tablet erected by Emperor Qianlong that is an important source of written material for the study of the lamaist system of Buddhism.

37. Wudang Lamasery (Inner Mongolia Autonomous Region)

This lamasery is called the Lamasery of the White Lotus in Tibetan and the Willow Lamasery in Mongolian. It stands on Huluntu Mountain, about 40 miles northeast of the city of Baotou. It is the best preserved lamasery in Inner Mongolia, and was erected in 1749. At one time there were 1,200 lamas living here. Dong Ko'er Dugong Hall is the oldest and most important hall in the lamasery because of its sculptures. However, the largest one is Suguxin Dugong, where the lamas gather for study and prayer.

38. Labrang Lamasery (Gansu Province)

This is one of the six most important lamaseries of the Yellow Sect, and it was once the most magnificent and powerful one in China. It is located about 80 miles southwest of the city of Lanzhou. It was founded in 1708 and has about 1,000 monks today. In the past there were as many as 4,000. The library has one of the best collections of Buddhist writings in China. Two halls especially attract a visitor's attention. These are the Maitreya Hall, also called the Big Golden Tiled Temple, and the Sakyamuni Hall. In the past, the Labrang Lamasery was famous for its masked dances, which took place on the 14th day of the first lunar month. This and other religious festivals are now being celebrated again. They attract many pilgrims. There are sleeping and eating accommodations in the nearby Labrang Hotel, designed in Tibetan style.

39. Kumbum Lamasery (Qinghai Province)

This lamasery, also known by the name Ta'er, is located about ten miles west of the city of Xining. It is one of the largest lamaseries of the Yellow Sect, and is said to be the birthplace of Tsongkapa (1357-1419), the founder of the Yellow Sect. He entered into a lamasery when he was only two years old. The Kumbum Lamasery was constructed in Tibetan style in 1560. Buildings were added over the centuries and at one time over 4,000 monks lived here. Today there are more than 50. The main building, the Great Golden House, is designed in Han Chinese style. It is supposedly built over the exact place where Tsongkapa was born. South of this building is the Jokhang Maitreya Hall, containing a gilded statue of the 12-year-old Maitreya, the Buddha-to-be. There is also a gold and silver sculpture of Tsongkapa. The Buddha of the Past is in the House of Prayer, north of the main hall. This contains prayer wheels, a statue of Buddha, one of Guanyin, and one of seven-year-old Maitreya. Other halls include the Temple of Dipankara and Great Hall of Meditation. A butter festival, held each year on the 15th day of the first month of the lunar calendar, is a notable event. The lamas and other Tibetans create colorful sculptures of Tibetan butter for use in their sacrificial ceremonies.

40. Potala Palace (Tibet Autonomous Region)

This 13-story wood-and-stone Tibetan Buddhist structure is the central attraction of the city of Lhasa. It stands atop a cliff more than 12,140 feet above sea level. It was first built in the 7th century and its expansions — the White Palace and Red Palace — were completed during the 17th century. At one time the Dalai Lama lived in the White Palace. A wide stairway leads up the mountain to the east gate and Eastern Terrace where ceremonies and dances occasionally take place. The Hall of Sacrifice, the largest building in the Red Palace, has stupas containing the remains of most of the Dalai Lamas. The building has about 1,000 rooms and contains many frescoes, stupas, and Buddhist sculptures. The murals especially will remain unforgettable for the visitor. The Potala Palace is world-renowned for its Tibetan-style architecture.

41. Jokhang Lamasery (Tibet Autonomous Region)

This is the oldest complex in the city of Lhasa. It was built in the 7th century to commemorate the marriage between the Chinese princess Wen Cheng and the Tibetan King Srongtsan Gampo. It is said that Wen Cheng designed the structure and the king's other wife, a princess from Nepal, supervised the construction. In the main hall of this lamasery is the statue of 12-year-old Sakyamuni that Princess Wen Cheng brought with her when she came to Tibet. The building is a combination of Tibetan, Han Chinese, and Nepalese style. An old willow growing at its entrance is said to have been planted there by Princess Wen Cheng. The lamasery is a center of the Yellow Sect.

42. Sera Lamasery (Tibet Autonomous Region)

This lamasery, also one of the largest of the Yellow Sect, was first built in 1418. It is located about 3 miles south of the city of Lhasa. A great number of historical relics are housed here, including the world-famous Tibetan *Tripitaka* written in powdered gold and calligraphy and painted scrolls of the Ming and Qing dynasties.

43. Ganden Lamasery (Tibet Autonomous Region)

This was built in 1409 and is the oldest lamasery of the Yellow Sect in Tibet. It is said to have been built by Tsongkapa, the founder of the Yellow Sect. The lamasery is located about 37 miles east of the city of Lhasa. It was badly damaged during the Cultural Revolution. More than 20 of its halls, including one housing the stupa of Tsongkapa, have been repaired. Buddhist statues and frescoes in the halls have been restored to their original appearance. There are more than 200 lamas in residence.

44. Drepung Lamasery (Tibet Autonomous Region)

This lamasery was constructed in 1416 and is the largest lamasery of the Yellow Sect, as well as the mother temple of Dalai Lamas. It is also the most prominent building in the city of Xigaze. The lamasery holds many Buddhist classics and cultural relics. It became the residence of the Bainqen Lama in 1650. Thanks to extensive restoration during the past few years, the lamasery is in good condition. The oldest remaining buildings are the Great Assembly Hall and the first Dalai Lama's Burial Chapel with excellent murals. The tallest of its building is the Temple of Maitreya, which contains a bronze statue of Maitreya.

45. Tashilhunpo Lamasery (Tibet Autonomous Region)

This lamasery was built by the first Dalai Lama in 1477, and is an important site of the Yellow Sect. It is located in the city of Xigaze. It houses many cultural relics. The most magnificent building is the Great Hall of Maitreya, which contains a seated bronze statue of Maitreya put there in 1914. Another hall contains the stupas of the successive Bainqen Lamas. The lamasery has 750 lamas in residence.

46. Sakya Lamasery (Tibet Autonomous Region)

This is the main lamasery of the Sakya (Flower) Sect and is located about 105 miles southwest of the city of Xigaze. It includes two sections, a northern one built in 1079 but now in ruin, and a southern one built in 1268 that is in good condition. The lamasery has a large collection of precious relics and more than 40,000 volumes of Buddhist classics. In addition, there are many large frescoes and hundreds of scrolls. One is a large mural depicting a scene of Pagba being received by Kublai Khan.

47. Baigoi Lamasery (Tibet Autonomous Region)

This lamasery located west of the town of Zhuangzi, near Xigaze, was originally built by the Sakya (Flower) Sect of Lamaism, but it gradually became a temple embracing various sects. It has an 11-story octagonal pagoda and houses many fine sculptures and murals.

48. Tshurpur Lamasery (Tibet Autonomous Region)

Located in Doilungdeqen County, about 20 miles northwest of Lhasa, this lamasery was built in 1187. It eventually became the leading lamasery of the Karma sub-branch of the Kagyu (White) Sect. Karma Batsong, an abbot during the Ming Dynasty, was titled the "Great Treasure Prince of Dharma" by the Ming emperor. The lamasery houses many cultural relics of the Ming and succeeding dynasties.

PALI BUDDHISM

49. Demenglong Fota Pagoda (Yunnan Province)

The village of Demenglong is near the border of Burma and about 44 miles south of the city of Jinghong. It has three pagodas of Pali Buddhism nearby, the most beautiful of which is this one. The road to this village passes some small settlements, large trees, and a number of temples. The population of the village are mainly people of the Dai and Hani ethnic minorities. This pagoda was built in 1240 and is perhaps the best Burmese-style pagoda in China. Eight small stupas surround a taller, central spire. The entire structure is white in color. There is a Buddhist monastery on the road to this pagoda.

On a hill south of this white one is another pagoda, this one also Burmese in style. It is called the black pagoda, and is somewhat gaudy with inlaid mirrors and bright tiles. There is another Buddhist monastery on the path going up to this pagoda. The third pagoda lies hidden in a rubber plantation across the river southeast of the town, about two and a half miles away.

The visitor may stay at the local hotel, although it is somewhat primitive. It has no restaurant or showers, and the bathroom is behind the building next to a small pond.

Buddhist Tourist Sites

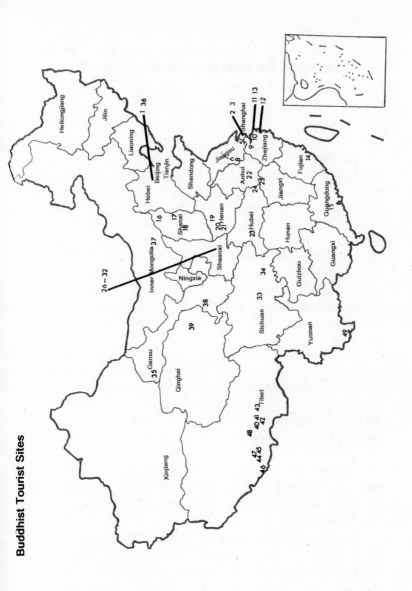

MUSLIMS:

Tightly Bound to Ethnic Cultures

In the thirty-eighth year of the reign of Kangxi (1662-1723), Emperor of the Qing Dynasty, his advisors proposed a ban on Islam. They wanted all Muslims expelled from Beijing. The advisors told the emperor that Muslims were gathering in the mosque at night to plan rebellion. According to a popular Islamic legend, Kangxi decided to investigate the matter personally. He disguised himself as a Muslim and entered the mosque during evening services. Finding nothing to alarm him in the Imam's preaching, the emperor next day issued a protective decree that read, in part, "The crime of bringing serious harm to the Muslim community is punishable by execution."

It is, of course, unlikely that the emperor ever took such a risky trip outside the walls of his Imperial Palace. Kangxi must have relied on other evidence to formulate this decree. Whatever the case, the Muslims of the Libai Mosque in Beijing proudly display the emperor's edict on the wall of their tablet pavilion.

The incident surrounding Kangxi's decree is significant not only because of the emperor's action, but because it points to the kind of discrimination Muslims in China have faced ever since this religion first came to that country during the 7th century.

The long-standing prejudice against Chinese Muslims can be attributed to the fact that almost all these believers in Islam are members of ten minority ethnic groups. They are Huis, Uygurs, Kazaks, Tartars, Kirgizs, Tajiks, Uzbeks, Dongxiangs, Salars, and Bonans. In physical features, dress, and lifestyle many of them are different from the dominant Han Chinese. Some are blonde and blue-eyed. Others have dark hair and Arabic features. Still others, living on China's northern border, are closely related to the Muslim ethnic minorities that live in Russia.

None of the Muslims eat pork, the primary meat consumed by most Chinese. They circumcise their male children, and often write in Arabic script, rather than Chinese characters. Furthermore, they face west toward Mecca for worship, which goes against the traditional Han view of China as the center of all things. The very name for China in the Chinese language is a word composed of two characters meaning "central country."

The Chinese government, since 1949, has done much to try to overcome discrimination against the ethnic minorities within China's borders. The government allows minority families to have as many children as they wish, although it imposes a policy of permitting only one child per family on the Han majority. For the ten Muslim minorities this has resulted in more than doubling their population between 1949 and 1990, the numbers growing from eight million to more than seventeen million.

The government also provides financial subsidies to the minority populations, allows them to have their own schools and hospitals, and gives them other benefits designed to improve their living conditions. As the government views it, such special measures are necessary to overcome centuries of prejudice and economic deprivation to which the minority ethnic peoples were subjected.

In every school, factory, office, or other workplace where there are at least ten Muslims, the government requires that special provisions be made for their dietary needs. One often sees separate tables or even separate dining halls in factory and university canteens. These are specifically designated for the Muslim workers and students. Special mutton dishes are here prepared for their meals instead of the pork dishes that others eat. Where there are less than ten Muslims at a workplace, the government provides financial subsidies so they can afford the Muslim diet.

Some Han workers express resentment at this special

treatment given to members of a minority, but it is the law of the land. And some Muslims point out that these special privileges set them apart from others and thus become the cause for discrimination.

Despite the government's attempts to equalize relationships between the 56 ethnic groups in China, one hears complaints from Muslims about the prejudice they often experience in school and on the job. A friend of mine in Beijing is a member of the Hui Muslim minority. He grew up in a predominantly Han environment. He went to ordinary city schools in Beijing, is fluent in Chinese and English, and has even become somewhat of an expert in deciphering the ancient Chinese written script. He is not religious, and his lifestyle is that of a Han Chinese. Yet colleagues at his workplace refer to him as the Muslim in the office. He also tells me that throughout his school years he was the butt of class jokes because of his Hui ancestry.

The situation for Chinese Muslims was much worse before 1949. Most were then treated with contempt. Those Muslims who lived in cities were often peddlers. They were poor and poorly educated. In some places, such as parts of Fujian Province, local officials of the Nationalist government tried to force all Muslims to eat pork and abandon their religious beliefs. For protection, many of them gathered in Muslim ghettos in the cities and joined to form entire villages in the countryside.

The largest of the ten Muslim ethnic minorities are the Huis. They make up about half of all the Muslims in China. Many of them live in all-Hui villages in Ningxia Hui Autonomous Region, Xinjiang Uygur Autonomous Region, Gansu and Qinghai provinces, and in scattered communities in the city of Beijing. There are also more than 1,000 counties and cities in Hubei, Henan, Shandong, Yunnan, Anhui, Liaoning, and other provinces that have groups of Huis living in them.

Although each of the other Muslim minorities have common roots, the Huis became an ethnic minority through action of Ming Dynasty officials. These officials decided that all followers of Islam in China who could not be identified as

140

members of known ethnic groups should be listed under the category "Hui." Thus some Huis have Arabic ancestors, some have Egyptian ancestors, and some have Persian ancestors. And Jews in the city of Kaifeng were sometimes listed as Huis, mainly because they didn't eat pork.

The other nine Muslim ethnic minorities — Uygur, Kazak, Dongxiang, Kirgiz, Salar, Tajik, Uzbek, Bonan, and Tartar — live mainly in compact communities in the autonomous regions of Xinjiang and Ningxia, the provinces of Gansu, Qinghai, Shaanxi, Yunnan, Henan, Hebei, Shandong, Liaoning, and in the cities of Beijing and Tianjin. There are a few Muslim converts among the Han Chinese, but most of these are persons who became Muslims by marrying someone from one of the ten Muslim minorities.

ARRIVAL IN CHINA

Islam was officially introduced into China in 651 by envoys to the Tang Dynasty emperor, sent by the third successor to Mohammed, Khalifa Uthman ibn Affan (577-656). However, Islam actually entered China earlier through contacts with Arabian merchants and four disciples of Mohammed who were sent to China between the years 618 and 626. Mohammed, the founder of Islam, reportedly took great interest in China and Chinese culture, saying, "Though China is far, far away, we should go there in the quest of knowledge." The first of these four missionaries went to Guangzhou, the second to Yangzhou, and the third and fourth to Quanzhou. The graves of the latter two are preserved today on a hill near Quanzhou.

Throughout the Tang (618-907) and Song (960-1279) dynasties, many Arab and Persian merchants of the Islamic faith came overland to northwest China by way of Middle Asia, and by sea to Quanzhou and other ports in the south and southeast. This promoted the development of trade and cultural exchange with the Arabic countries. Some mosques were erected in China by these merchants.

During the western military expeditions of Genghis

141

Khan, in the early 13th century, many Muslims recruited from Central and West Asia came to China. Later, they were garrisoned with the Mongolian army as farmer soldiers in inland areas. Wherever these mercenaries settled, they brought Islam with them. By the Yuan Dynasty (1206-1368), Islam was thriving in China. The rulers of the Ming (1368-1644) and Qing (1644-1911) dynasties saw advantages in allowing Islam to grow on its own in China and did nothing to discourage it. When the fleet of the famous Ming navigator, Zheng He (1371-1435), reached the Arabian Peninsula, Muslim members among his crew made a pilgrimage to Mecca.

Islamic scholars in China translated many of the classics from the Arabian and Persian languages into Chinese. They promoted Islamic medical knowledge, added to China's knowledge of mathematics and astronomy, and helped to spread new techniques of weaving and cloisonne craftsmanship.

There were sometimes conflicts between Muslims and local government officials, and the imperial army was occasionally called to suppress "Muslim disturbances on China's borders." In the port city of Quanzhou, in the early 1300s, there was an attempt by the Nestorian Bishop Andre to convert all the Muslims in that city to Christianity. The Bishop's campaign led to bloodshed and the destruction of six mosques and probably some of the Nestorian churches, although details are not known. In any case, there are no more Nestorian sites in this city and only one Islamic mosque.

In modern times (shortly before 1949), a campaign was mounted by a Muslim official, employed by the former Nationalist government, to declare independence in an area of what is now Xinjiang Uygur Autonomous Region. He wanted to designate this area a Muslim country named Eastern Turkistan. He convinced enough Muslims to be able to found a small separatist movement. But most of the Muslims of Xinjiang didn't like this proposal, and it never received support from the Imams and other Muslim religious leaders in China. The members of the separatist movement have, from time to time, mounted political independence campaigns with little success. The cause, however, was widely publicized by the Nationalist government after it fled to Taiwan.

BELIEVERS TODAY

The number of Islamic believers in China today totals more than 17,000,000. The statistics represent the combined size of the ten Muslim ethnic minorities. Although there are undoubtedly non-believers within these ten minorities, it is doubtful if there are many because the religion and their ethnic cultures are closely intermixed. Even the ethnic minority members of the Chinese Communist Party tend to observe the religious dietary laws and Muslim customs so as to remain an integral part of their people. In fact, when Muslims decide to join the Communist Party of China, they are never asked if they are religious or not, as are other Chinese who join the Party.

Presently, China has more than 23,000 mosques in which at least 40,000 full-time professionals (Imams and Ahungs) are employed. Most Chinese Muslims are Sunni Muslims, belonging to Ahl al-Sunnah Wa'i-Djama'ah in belief and al-Hanafiyah in doctrine. There are also a few adherents of several other sects of Islam, but all the Muslims of China are united within the Chinese Islamic Association.

China's mosques can be divided into two groups in architectural style: one is Arabic-style architecture, and the other, temple-style *siheyuan* (a compound with houses around a courtyard). The best known mosques include the Sacred Mind (Huaisheng) Mosque in Guangzhou; the Qingjing Mosque in Quanzhou; the Phoenix (Zhenjiao) Mosque in Hangzhou; the Libai Mosque in Yangzhou; the Huajuexiang Mosque in Xi'an; the Libai Mosque in Beijing; and the Aitika Mosque at Kashi, Xinjiang.

All the mosques are built to face west, or at least their worship halls are so built that the worshipers can face west as they pray. West is the direction in which Mecca lies from

China. Muslim graves are also dug so that the head of the deceased will point toward the West. Tradition has it that Mohammed used to stand on a flight of steps to preach while holding a wooden cane in his hand. For this reason many of the mosques have constructed the preaching platform up a flight of stairs and attached a wooden cane to the stairway.

Muslims pray five times daily: at dawn, at noon, in the afternoon, in the evening, and at nightfall. A crier, or muezzin, announces the prayer time. The worshipers ceremonially wash their faces, hands, and feet in the bath area immediately before prayer. The prayers generally consist of reciting passages from the Koran and other phrases of praise to God.

The Libai Mosque (Musjid Niujie) in Beijing, one of 62 mosques in that city, is typical of some of the larger ones in China. It is on Niujie (Ox Street), in an area of the city where 70% of the people (40,000) are Muslims. Near the mosque are Muslim restaurants, bakeries, butcher shops, schools, day-care centers, hospitals, and other Muslim enterprises. The Muslim schools are much like other schools in Beijing, except that they have special courses on the history of Islam and the history of the Islamic nationalities. The teachers are mostly Muslim women. The Muslim hospitals are different from other hospitals only in that all the doctors are Muslims, they provide a Muslim diet, and they primarily service Muslim patients. They are, however, open to non-Muslims as well.

The Libai Mosque has 25 full-time workers, including the Imam (head of religious worship), several Ahungs (assistant religious leaders), bath preparers, and other service personnel. There are, as well, apprentices who study under the Imam. Some Imams in the largest mosques may have as many as 100 apprentices at one time.

There are about 600 persons who regularly worship at this mosque. It has as many as 6,000 visitors on special religious days. The main hall is constructed on the outside in Chinese style, and it can hold as many as 1,000 worshipers. Its interior is Arabic in style. Within the courtyard there is a smaller mosque for the women. Muslim men and women don't usually worship together, and when they do, the women stand behind the men. Muslim women in China, however, do not wear veils as Muslim women do in some of the countries of the Middle East.

Worshipers gather every day in this mosque to offer prayers toward Mecca. They use Arabic in their services. The Friday evening service is set aside for special instruction in the Islamic faith. This is focused toward adults, but it is an occasion where children in attendance can learn verses from the Koran and other aspects of what it means to be a Muslim. Most religious training of children takes place in the home. Muslim families are expected to teach their own children about the faith and dietary laws of Islam. Of course, the ethnic customs and religious beliefs are so interwoven that children as they grow up seldom, if ever, revolt against these beliefs. And even if they refuse to be religious, they keep to the religious dietary practices because these are a part of their ethnic customs and traditions.

Circumcision of all boys is a religious requirement, although there is no special ceremony surrounding this rite. It is generally performed at the Muslim hospitals. And, although the government has a policy of demanding cremation for all deceased persons, Muslims are exempt from this because cremation goes against their religious beliefs.

The mosque organizes no special social service programs, but it is considered the duty for all Muslims to help those in need. The other chief duties for Muslims are daily prayer, almsgiving, fasting during the period called Ramadan, and at least one pilgrimage to Mecca during the lifetime.

The Imam at the Libai Mosque is Haji Dawud Shi Kunbin, a member of the Hui ethnic minority. He was born in Shandong Province, became the apprentice of an Imam there, and then studied at an Islamic training school for many years before he became the Imam at this mosque in the 1950s. Since that time, he has been three times on *hajj*, the Muslim pilgrimage to Mecca, and has visited Muslims in 16 countries as a representative of the Beijing Municipal

145

Islamic Association. He has also welcomed Muslim visitors from 120 countries at this mosque. During the Cultural Revolution the mosque was badly damaged and he was sent to the countryside to be a farmer for eight years.

The closing of the mosques and criticism of Imams during the Cultural Revolution forced all religious activity underground. Muslim families then had to conduct their own worship within the family circle. When the Cultural Revolution ended and mosques reopened, the Imams discovered that the faith of their congregations had been strengthened rather than weakened by the religious persecution of that period. They also found that the number of Muslims had increased. As one Imam put it to me, "The Gang of Four wanted to extinguish all religion, but actually the opposite happened."

Some of the other mosques in China maintain restaurants and even hotels within unused sections of the mosque complex. Such facilities provide income for the mosque. But the Libai Mosque in Beijing derives all its funds from contributions of worshipers and sales at a small gift shop attached to the main gate.

The city of Harbin has 34,000 Muslims and only two mosques. Another one is being renovated and will be open soon. The one in the Daowai District of the city has 500 worshipers, one Imam, and six Ahungs. At the time I visited this mosque, there were a group of women preparing for a funeral. They were wearing white funeral cloths over their heads, a Chinese custom adopted by the Muslims of this area.

The worship area for the Qingjing (Shengyou) Mosque in Quanzhou is small and located behind the remains of what was once a grand mosque built in the style of one of the great mosques at Damascus, Syria. This is one of the oldest mosques in China. At one time half the population of this city was composed of persons from Arab countries. There are only 300 Muslims there today, and the city has only one remaining Muslim restaurant. There is a nearby village that is composed solely of persons of Arabic origin. However, the mosque in that village was so severely damaged during the

146

Cultural Revolution that the villagers have had to use a temporary worship place ever since.

The few remaining Muslims in Quanzhou maintain their dietary rules but no longer circumcise their boys because there is no Muslim hospital in this area. Most of them go to the mosque only on the three major religious festival days. The mosque holds services on Fridays, but the Imam told me very few people come. Both women and men worship together at this mosque, and more men come than women. The services are in Arabic. The mosque charges an entry fee to visitors, receives some contributions from worshipers, and receives additional money from the government for upkeep because it is designated as an historical relic of China. It receives many visitors, 120,000 since 1984.

The mosque has a staff of seven, including the Imam, some Ahungs, and several other staff members. The Imam told us that most Ahungs assigned here dislike the hot southern climate and want to return to their homes in the north, though they can get higher pay and one month's vacation each year by working at this mosque.

CHINESE ISLAMIC ASSOCIATION

In early 1952, the Chinese Islamic leaders Burhan, Depusheng, Makien, and Pang Shiqian began organizing a Chinese Islamic Association. They invited representatives from all the Muslim communities in China to the First Islamic Conference, held in Beijing in May 1953. This marked the birth of the Chinese Islamic Association, the national organization of Chinese Muslims. The members and standing committee members of this body are elected at congresses of representatives from all the Muslim communities of China. A total of 270 local Muslim organizations at various levels were also established, one after another. Haji Ilyas Shen Xiaxi now serves as the chairman of the national body.

The Chinese Islamic Association mainly engages in collecting and collating Islamic books, records, and cultural relics; researching Islamic history and creeds; and organizing pil-

147

grimages to Mecca. The Association publishes *Muslims in China*, a bimonthly founded in 1957. It is published in Chinese and Uygur. Its contents include the results of research into Islamic history and doctrine, recommendations on Islamic classics, and discussions about the implementation of the government's policy on freedom of religious belief. The magazine introduces to its readers the teaching experiences of the Islamic institutes in various parts of the country and the principles of democratic management for the mosques. Furthermore, it reports on Chinese Muslims' contributions to activities designed to safeguard world peace and on their friendly relations with other Muslims in the world. Gong Qingzhi serves as editor-in-chief of the magazine.

Ten Islamic classics, including the Koran, have been translated into Chinese and Uygur and published under the direction of the Chinese Islamic Association. These books are distributed all over China. The Association has also published some Islamic dictionaries. It encourages Muslims to strengthen national unity and take an active part in China's modernization. In addition, it encourages Muslims to carry out family planning, plant trees for beautification and ecological betterment of the country, and take part in public welfare work.

In July 1955, the Chinese Islamic Association set up a national Chinese Islamic Institute in Beijing for the training of specialized Islamic personnel. Here they hold advanced training classes for Ahungs and mullahs (Islamic scholars). The five-year course of study includes classes on the Koran, religious etiquette, creeds, history of Islam, Arabic language, Chinese language, politics, and general history of China and the world. About 70 percent of the curricula are Islamic courses and 30 percent courses for raising the general educational level of the students. The tuition is paid through scholarships provided by various mosques. Since 1982, the Association has sent ten Muslim students of the Hui, Uygur, and Kazak ethnic minorities to Egypt for further studies, three to Libya, and approximately 20 to the International Islamic University at Islamabad, Pakistan.

148

There are also eight other Islamic institutes in China, which together with the main one have more than 400 students attending them. They are in Shenyang, Zhengzhou, Lanzhou, Yinchuan, Qinghai, Urumqi, Kunming, and one more in Beijing. Students can enter these institutes directly after high school graduation. The training course is aimed toward producing Ahungs for the many mosques in China. Such training is considered of primary importance by the Chinese Islamic Association because there are still some senior Imams in rural and grassland areas of China who don't even know how to read and write.

The Ningxia Islamic Culture Institute at Yinchuan opened in 1986 and moved to a new campus in 1989. The Islamic Development Bank in the Middle East donated 1,138,073 RMB *yuan* for the new campus. With arcades, arched window frames and a domed ceiling colored in green and white, the construction gives full expression to Islamic religious themes in its architectural design.

It has graduated more than 100 students. The average age of these students, all of them male, is 24. Eighty percent are married. Before they can enroll in the institute, they must have had at least one year of experience as apprentices at a local mosque. Some have worked under local Imams for more than four years before they apply. The State Education Commission of the Chinese government pays for the students' tuition, as it does for the tuition of students in the public universities. The students also receive from the government a small monthly allowance, free housing, and free medical care.

The students at the Ningxia Islamic Culture Institute attend five classes and five prayer services each day. The training takes three to five years. Many of the students come from rural areas, and this is often their first experience at living in an urban center. They find it exciting and stimulating. Afterwards, some of these rural students are reluctant to return to their home mosques in the rural areas. A few abandon their religious commitment and take jobs in government agencies in order to stay in the city.

Other students, though confident of their religious and general knowledge, believe they are not prepared to become Ahungs or Imams because their lack of social experience may prevent them from winning the support of their congregations. They, too, decide to take jobs outside of the Islamic community. According to the chief administrator of this institute, Zhang Naixing, such students eventually return to the mosques when they become older and have gained broader social experience. The institute directors are now trying to develop new enrollment procedures that will assure them that all applicants are fully committed to remain in their Islamic vocation.

The Chinese Islamic Association has established friendly relationships with Islamic organizations in more than 40 countries, sent delegations to visit these countries many times, and taken part in the Asian-African Islamic Conference and the International Islamic Thought Seminar. Each year there are about 2,000 Chinese Muslims who go to Mecca on pilgrimages. Flights from Beijing alone, in 1989, carried 900 Chinese Muslims to Mecca. The association has also received Islamic delegations from Asian and African countries. During the past ten years, the Huajuexiang Mosque in Xi'an alone received more than 40,000 visitors from 100 countries in Asia, Africa, Latin America, Europe, North America, and Oceania.

RELATIONS WITH THE GOVERNMENT

Since 1949, Muslims have been able to participate fully in national and local affairs of the government as representatives of their Islamic communities. There are 97 deputies for the Muslim communities in the current National People's Congress. This is actually a higher proportion of representatives than the proportion of Muslims in the population as a whole. Muslims account for 3.3 percent of the number of deputies compared to the 1.4 percent of the total population. Their proportion of representatives in local people's congresses has also, in general, surpassed their respective rate in the whole national population. The Chinese People's Political Consultative Congress has 57 members representing the Muslim communities, or 2.6 percent of the total membership of the CPPCC.

The Muslim communities of China have only recently begun to stress the need for women to hold leadership positions. Therefore most of these representatives are men. However, the standing committee of the Chinese Islamic Association has eight women among its 80 elected members.

One often hears Muslim leaders say that their religion calls them to love their country and their religion. They sometimes include elements in their sermons that stimulate an upsurge of patriotic enthusiasm on the part of their congregations. Shen Xiaxi, the chairman of the Chinese Islamic Association, says that patriotism is a part of the fundamental Islamic beliefs, and that the Muslim love for Islam is accordingly based on their love for the country. Likewise, he says, "only patriots can really love Islam and manage its affairs successfully. This is because, on the one hand, patriotism requires them to maintain national unity and work for the socialist economic construction and, on the other hand, only with political stability and continuous economic development of the country and of the local regions will the Islamic cause be expanded. In a word, love for the country and love for Islam is every Muslim's responsibility and duty."

The fact that the government honors persons who make major contributions to the development of the country has been another factor in the fostering of national pride among the Islamic people of China. The Muslims who are so honored are publicly recognized as members of a religious community.

It is interesting to note that Muslim students in Beijing demonstrated against a book published by one of the many government printing houses at exactly the same time that many other students in Beijing were marching in the "Democracy Movement" of Tiananmen Square. The 1989 Tiananmen demonstrations so dominated the world press that the Muslim marchers were ignored outside of China.

151

The issue that motivated them was a book titled *Sexual Customs*, authored by Ke Le and Sang Ya. It was published by the Shanghai Cultural Publishing House in March 1983. The book purported to tell of the sexual practices of the Hui ethnic minority. The Muslim community found it highly insulting to Islam, and many leading Muslims called on the government to ban the book from all bookstores.

Nothing was done about the matter, however, until Muslim students took to the streets on May 12, 1989. Their placards claimed that its publication violated state policies on ethnic minorities and religion. The Muslim student demonstration had the express permission of the Beijing Public Security Bureau, and social order was well maintained by the police. The students handed their petitions to representatives of the Chinese Islamic Association, the Visitors' Bureau of the Standing Committee of the National People's Congress, and the United Front Department of the Central Committee of the Chinese Communist Party.

The students in Beijing not only marched but they collected as many copies of *Sexual Customs* as they could get their hands on and burned them in a public display of their feelings about the matter. After that, the State Administrative Bureau of Press and Publication decided to act on the matter by banning the book.

The Bureau pointed out that the contents were bad, insulting to Islam, seriously hurt the religious feelings of Muslims, and violated the law about protecting the customs of ethnic minorities in China. They said that the book should be banned immediately, and that unsold copies, paper molds, and print films should all be destroyed. They also instructed the Shanghai Cultural Publishing House to halt business. The publisher and distributing units were to be fined and the editors in charge of the book temporarily relieved of their posts for self-examination, and punished according to relevant laws and regulations. In addition, representatives of the Shanghai Press and Publication Bureau went to Beijing to apologize to the Chinese Islamic Association.

Despite this concern over the Chinese book that they

found insulting, Chinese Muslims took little interest in the book controversy that shook much of the Arab world during the late 1980s — the book by Salmon Rushdie called *Satanic Verses*. When I asked some of the Muslim leaders about their attitudes toward Rushdie's book, they told me that they had never seen a copy and all they know about it is what they had read in the newspapers. They further said they would never get involved in calling for a ban on any book unless they had a chance to see the contents for themselves.

One of the stated aims of the Chinese Islamic Association is to work toward the development of world peace and better relations around the world. It was therefore to be expected that Muslims in China would have some response to the Gulf War. They did. The Muslim leaders in Beijing published a public appeal for an end to the war so that all Muslims could go on the annual Islamic pilgrimage to Mecca. The Chinese government had suspended Air China flights to that region after the war began. The Muslim leaders have also expressed concern over the implications of Saddam Hussein's call for *jihad*, a term that translates as "striving" and is often misunderstood as strictly a military call for a "Holy War" against all infidels. It should also be noted that, following the Soviet Union's invasion of Afghanistan, they cited the Koran in an appeal to Chinese Muslims to struggle against "the massacre and repression of our Muslim brothers in Afghanistan."

It would appear that the Chinese Muslims, through the Chinese Islamic Association, are attempting to make themselves into a major force in the worldwide Islamic movement. However, the major power players within the Islamic world are the totally-Muslim countries, nations such as Pakistan, Egypt, and Syria. Chinese Muslims, even though they share in legislative decision making, remain separate representatives of ten ethnic cultures. They are not one united movement of people capable of setting the course for China's future political life.

International events within the Islamic world have only a

peripheral effect on the Chinese Muslims. In the next chapter, we will look at the Chinese Catholics, a religious group that watches closely every action taken by fellow Catholics throughout the world. Yet it is a religious group that survives and grows despite the fact that it is consciously cut off from the center of Catholicism in Rome.

VISITOR'S GUIDE TO MUSLIM SITES

Almost anywhere in China that there is a Muslim community one can find an Islamic mosque. The most interesting ones to visit are below.

1. Libai Mosque (City of Beijing)

The Libai Mosque (Musjid Niujie) on Niujie Street in Beijing was built in 996 during the Northern Song Dynasty. It was designed by Nasurutin, an Arabian scholar who served the emperor of China at that time. The main hall of the mosque is constructed in the style of a Chinese palace, but its interior is typically Arabic in design. The lintel of the gate to the main hall is decorated with words from the Koran written in Arabic, and the door and window frames by the two sides are engraved with eulogies in Arabic. The hall can hold more than a thousand worshipers at a time.

Other halls in this complex include a lecture hall, a tablet pavilion, the building for publicizing etiquette, and a room for baths. The mosque contains two tombs of Islamic elders who came from Arabian countries, a 300-year-old hand-written copy of the Koran, an ancient Ming-Dynasty incense burner, as well as a number of other precious relics. The mosque has over 600 regular worshipers and as many as 6,000 on the Festival of Fast Breaking. The mosque was repaired and renovated in 1955 and 1979.

2. Dongsi Mosque (City of Beijing)

This mosque is located in the East City District and was built in 1447. Its architecture reflects a combination of Chinese and Arabic styles. The rear part of the main hall is a beamless structure in the style of the Ming Dynasty. On the surface of the beams in the central part of the main hall

155

are engraved words from the Koran in Kufic script, a form of Arabic reserved for religious and official purposes. The mosque library contains a copy of the Koran in Arabic that was written in 1318. The mosque has undergone two major renovations since 1949.

3. Harbin Mosque (Heilongjiang Province)

This mosque, though not as famous as the others, is well worth a visit. It is located at 44 South Shisandao Street, Daowai District, in the city of Harbin. It was originally built in 1908 as a structure with five thatched houses, but it was rebuilt on a much grander style in 1935. The construction is in Arabic style. In March 1980 the buildings were renovated and opened once again to the public. The religious services are in Arabic.

4. Libai Mosque (Jiangsu Province)

This mosque in the city of Yangzhou was built during the Yuan Dynasty (1206-1368), although this city was one of the first in China to see Muslim missionaries. One of the four that were sent to China by Mohammed, between the years 618 and 626, came to this city. The mosque displays some of the calligraphy of Shi Kefa, an official and hero of the Ming Dynasty who refused to surrender after the rulers of the Qing Dynasty took power. In the same city, a visitor should see the tomb of Puhaddin, a famous Muslim missionary who came to Yangzhou during the Yuan Dynasty and stayed here for ten years. The tomb is on the east bank of the Grand Canal as it flows through Yangzhou.

5. Phoenix Mosque (Zhejiang Province)

This mosque, also known as the Zhenjiao Mosque, is located in the city of Hangzhou. It was first built during the Tang Dynasty, destroyed during the Song Dynasty, and then rebuilt in 1341 during the Yuan Dynasty. It underwent overall renovations in 1953, 1964, and 1981. The main hall is a brick structure with a dome and without beam frames. Its wall faces are exquisitely carved. The wooden boxes for storing copies of the Koran are carved with Arabic script and are considered an ancient treasure of Chinese Islamic art. There are 19 stelae carved with Chinese, Arabic, and Persian scripts along the mosque's corridor.

6. Qingjing Mosque (Fujian Province)

This mosque, also called the Shengyou Mosque, was built in 1009, during the Northern Song Dynasty, or in the year 400 according to the Islamic calendar. It is located on Tumenjie Street in the city of Quanzhou. The mosque is designed after one built in Damascus, Syria, in the 8th century. It is of a style popular in Arabian countries during the Middle Ages. Although the roof of the original mosque is gone and some of the remainder of the building has partially deteriorated over time, the building is still quite impressive. Worshipers now use a small hall, in the form of a traditional Chinese compound, that is behind this building. There are plans to restore the original structure eventually.

The main gate is the best-preserved part of this old mosque. It was built with blue and white granite and divided into outer, middle, and inner parts, all of which belong to arch-style construction. The shapes of the three arches are all different. One is a star-shaped arch decorated by radiating lines of diabase and traditional Chinese lotus flower designs, symbolizing the holiness, purity, and elegance of Islam. Another is a honeycomb-shaped vault, signifying the 99 beautiful names of Allah. The third is a tapering arched dome that gives the viewer the feeling of standing under a vast and boundless universe. Above this gate of three arches is a "moon-watching platform." When the religious festival of Ramadan approached, the Ahung would climb to the platform and decide on the date for starting the fast.

There are Arabic scriptures of the Koran carved on the stone walls on the lintel of the main hall. There are also seven niches on the stone walls in the western side of the main hall. Some of the historical relics preserved at this mosque include a 1,000-year-old stone fountain resting on carved lotus leaves, a Yuan Dynasty incense burner, and

157

stone tablets from the six mosques that were destroyed during the conflicts between the Nestorians and Muslims in the early 1300s.

7. Lingshan Hill Graves (Fujian Province)

The sacred graves at Lingshan Hill, located east of the city of Quanzhou, is where two disciples sent by Mohammed to China between the years 618 and 626 are buried in two stone sarcophagi surrounded by a stone pavilion. It is said that after their burial, the hill glowed with a strange light every night ("Ling" means spirit and "shan" means mountain in Chinese). Close to the graves of these two disciples is a diabase tablet bearing a ten-line inscription in Arabic, saying that in 1322 a group of Arab Muslims residing in Quanzhou repaired the blessed graves to please Allah and to entreat rewards from him.

On the path up the hill to the disciples' graves, there are two huge rocks, piled one on top of the other. The top one tips a bit if pushed with great effort. This is called the Swaying Rock. It is also said to be sometimes swayed by the wind, and that it was created by Allah. Some Muslims say that it rivals the Swaying Tower of Medina. There are also other stone sarcophagi from the Song, Yuan, and Ming dynasties on this hill, as well as recent graves of Muslim residents of Quanzhou. The older graves have been repaired several times since 1949.

8. Huaisheng (Sacred Mind) Mosque (Guangdong Province)

This mosque, which is located in the city of Guangzhou and also called the Brightness Pagoda, was built in 627 during the Tang Dynasty, making it the oldest mosque in China. It has a main hall, moon pavilion, bath house, guest house, and long corridors along the east and west sides of the courtyard. In the southwest corner is a brick tower on the top of which once stood a gold rooster used to measure the wind direction. It was destroyed during the Ming Dynasty. The light on the top of this tower was once used by sailors as a beacon for navigation. The mosque underwent renovations during the Yuan, Ming, and Qing dynasties. Two large-scale renovations were completed in 1957 and in 1972.

The mosque contains the tomb of Saad bin Waqqas, the maternal uncle of Mohammed and one of the earliest Muslim missionaries to go to China. The mosque is of great significance to the study of China's history of overseas transportation, architecture, and trade and cultural exchanges between China and the Arab countries. It has about 4,000 members.

9. Qingzhen Dasi (Inner Mongolia)

This mosque is located in the city of Hohhot, near the north gate of the Old City. It dates from about 1740, during the reign of Emperor Qianlong. The main hall was restored in 1933. At that time the minaret was also constructed. The mosque contains several valuable editions of the Koran.

10. Huajuexiang (Shaanxi Province)

This mosque in the city of Xi'an was built at the end of the Yuan Dynasty or beginning of the Ming Dynasty. It was later expanded to include five courtyards. The main hall can hold 2,000 worshipers at one time. It has wood carvings of Arabic writings and flowers and leaves that are among the masterpieces of carving of the Ming Dynasty. Stone tablets with writings in Chinese, Arabic, and Persian are preserved along with many horizontal inscribed boards, couplets written on scrolls, incense burners, handwritten copies of the Koran, paintings, and other religious relics.

11. Qingzhen (Sichuan Province)

This mosque on Guiounanjie Street in the city of Chengdu was once a magnificent structure, but it was almost completely destroyed in a bombing raid during the Second World War. It has since been rebuilt. Two gilded columns in the present main hall, or prayer hall, have been preserved from the original structure.

12. Tongxin Mosque (Ningxia Hui Autonomous Region)

This mosque is located in the old city of Tongxin County and was first built during the Ming Dynasty. Its architecture is Chinese traditional style. Its upper part includes a main hall, two libraries, a gate tower, and a bell tower. The lower part includes the mosque gate, outside courtyard, screen walls, well, and bath houses. Between 700 and 800 persons can worship in the main hall at one time. Exquisite Arabic paintings and calligraphy are carved on the walls of the mosque. It has been repaired and renovated since 1980.

13. Aitika Mosque (Xinjiang)

This mosque is in the city of Kashi, and was first built in 1442 during the Ming Dynasty. It has been repaired and expanded many times over the years. It is constructed basically in Arabian style, although it also has some ancient Uygur architectural features. Its eastern section contains the main hall for prayers; the western section is now an Islamic institute. Early in the 20th century, a road was established from north to south that passed in front of this mosque and the Aitika square (in the Uygur language, this means a place for festivals) was then set up.

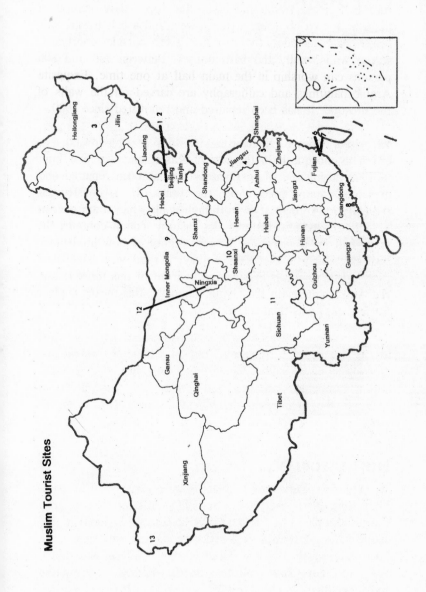

Muslim Tourist Sites

CATHOLICS:

Maintaining Faith Despite Separation

The popes of Rome never understood China. They and their advisors seem to have made every possible mistake in trying to convert the Chinese to Catholicism.

The first Catholic missionaries they sent to China trained no Chinese leadership and so the religion died when the missionaries went home. The next group, the Jesuits, became so Chinese in outlook and manners that the pope restricted their activities. In doing so, he ignited a series of events that resulted, in 1724, in a widespread persecution of Catholics in China. Today, the pope refuses to recognize the Catholics of China because they cooperate with the Communist government. Formal relations between the Chinese Catholics and Rome have been non-existent since 1949.

In other countries such a situation would probably lead to the demise of Catholicism, but in China this religion is growing as never before. China today has more than 3.6 million worshipping Catholics. There were only 2.7 million in 1949, at the time when the Chinese Communists came to power.

THE NESTORIANS

The first Christians to reach China were not Catholics. They were Nestorians, followers of Archbishop Nestorius of Constantinople. The Roman Catholic Church had earlier condemned the Nestorians as heretics because of their teachings. The sect, which still has followers in Ethiopia and India, maintains that Christ had two distinct natures, one human and one divine. They further say that Christ's mother, Mary, was only the mother of his human nature, a mere husk of his divine nature.

Even though this sect was cast out of the Catholic Church, both Chinese Catholics and Chinese Protestants now claim the Nestorians as part of their own heritage. The sect thrived in China for about 800 years. An inscribed stone tablet found at Xi'an, standing over nine feet tall and three feet wide, tells the story of their arrival in China in the year 635 and of some of the progress of this religion in that country. The Nestorians entered China under the auspices of Olopen, a priest or perhaps a pious merchant from Syria, who recruited other Nestorians to join him in spreading this faith among the Chinese. According to the tablet, the Nestorians "spread their religion over ten provinces.... Monasteries occupied every big city."

Until recently, this Xi'an tablet was the only evidence for this religion in China, but now more Nestorian carvings and gravestones have been found at other places. One of these is on the grounds of the Yunju Buddhist temple in Fangshan County, a suburb of Beijing. The stone has the names of four Nestorian monks inscribed on it with the comment "we were here." It is dated to 1438. There is also a Chinese document that tells of a Nestorian Bishop Andre in Quanzhou, who tried, with drastic results, to convert all the Muslims of that city in the early 1300s. Also there is an Arabic record of two Nestorian monks from the city of Beijing in China, one named Mark and the other named Sauma, who arrived in Persia about 1275 on their way to see Jerusalem.

ARRIVAL OF THE CATHOLICS

The first Catholic missionary to reach China was Giovani da Montecorvino, sent by the pope in 1291. He was a Franciscan monk, and he carried with him a letter from the pope to the Yuan Dynasty emperor (Kublai Khan) in Beijing. Giovani remained there for about 30 years, built two churches in that city, baptized about 6,000 persons, and battled with the Nestorians, who apparently charged him with being a spy, magician, and impostor. In a letter he wrote to Rome, Giovani says that were it not for the hostility of the Nestorians, "I should have baptized more than 30,000."

Giovani da Montecorvino also established missions in some other cities in China, and was joined by other Franciscan monks (32 of them) who carried on his work after he died in 1328. The pope even named Giovani the first archbishop of Beijing and sent three bishops to Beijing to consecrate him in this post. Giovani, in turn, assigned one of these bishops to the mission church that was established at Quanzhou.

Only a few years after the death of Giovani da Montecorvino, the Franciscan presence in China disappeared. Despite Giovani's many conversions (40 of them little boys whom he purchased from the Chinese and to whom he taught Greek and Latin), the Franciscans trained no Chinese leadership. So the church died when the Franciscans left. It had to be reinitiated 200 years later by the famous Jesuit, Matteo Ricci.

RICCI AND THE INTELLECTUALS

In 1582 Ricci and his colleague, Michaele Ruggieri, set up a small Catholic mission at Chaocheng, a town west of Guangzhou in what is now Guangdong Province. Their converts were few, but these two Italian priests developed many friends among the officials and intellectuals, primarily because of Ricci's vast knowledge of European science.

Ricci studied Chinese, read the fundamental classics of Chinese literature, and developed an understanding of the Confucian basis of thought and outlook in China. He believed that if Catholicism was to enter deeply into the life of the Chinese, it needed to find points of contact with Confucianism. He expressed admiration for Chinese civilization, pointing out that in economy, technology, literature, and social institutions China was just as advanced as Europe. The only thing in which China was inferior, Ricci believed, was in the matter of religion.

164

After setting up missions in several cities, Ricci moved to Beijing in 1601 where, because of his scientific and mathematical knowledge, he was welcomed at the court of Emperor Wanli of the Ming Dynasty. Ricci built a church in Beijing, and brought other Jesuits skilled in science to the Beijing mission. He converted and trained a number of distinguished Chinese intellectuals in Catholicism, some of whom established Catholic churches in other cities of China. By the year of his death, 1610, it is estimated that there were about 2,500 Catholics in China. The number rose to 13,000 by 1617, 38,200 by 1636, and 150,000 by 1650. Matteo Ricci was buried in Beijing, on land donated for that purpose by Emperor Wanli.

Among the Jesuits who came to China at the request of Ricci were Johann Adam Schall (1591-1666), John Terrentius (1576-1630), and Ferdinand Verbiest (1623-88), all gifted in science. Schall published the first description in Chinese of Galileo's telescope, and Terrentius published a Chinese treatise on the movements of the stars and planets. Verbiest helped the Chinese redesign their observatory on the eastern wall of Beijing and built many of the instruments that were used there. This observatory is now preserved as a museum of Chinese astronomy.

The writings of Galileo that the Jesuits introduced to China caused almost as much controversy in that country as they did in Europe. But in China the emperor approved of this new knowledge. In Europe, Galileo's teachings were condemned by a papal court. The emperor was even more pleased, however, with the cannons that the Jesuits were willing to cast for his army by applying their knowledge of metallurgy. The Jesuits also designed thermometers, atlases of the world, and small steam-powered, paddle-boat toys to delight the emperor.

The success of the Jesuits in China led to a large influx of other Catholic orders — Dominicans, Franciscans, and Lazarites. These Catholics set up missions in almost all of China's provinces. But the arrival of Catholic priests from other orders brought dissension to the Catholic communities in China. The primary disagreement revolved around how Catholics should view the Chinese practice of paying respect to ancestors. The argument, which engulfed many sectors of the Catholic Church all over the world, came to be known as the "rites issue."

The Jesuits, following the advice of Matteo Ricci, gave approval to Chinese ceremonies surrounding the traditional veneration of ancestors. They argued that these were merely "civil" rites and not "religious" ones. The Dominican and Franciscan friars were horrified at this concession to Chinese customs. They accused the Jesuits of participating in pagan rituals and destroying essential matters of faith. After a long struggle, Pope Clement XI gave his support to the Dominican and Franciscan position, and ordered the Jesuits to stop participating in such Chinese rituals.

The rites issue, however, didn't stay within the confines of Catholic discourse. Word of it reached the emperor. The document that the pope issued, *Ex illa die*, said, among other things, that the Chinese worship at family shrines and other allied traditional practices are repugnant to Christianity. Emperor Kangxi, on seeing this document, responded that Europeans had no right to "presume to deliver judgment on the teachings of the Chinese.... It is not advisable to allow the Europeans to proclaim their law in China. They must be forbidden to speak of it, and in this way many difficulties and embarrassments will be avoided."

The emperor continued to allow the Catholic missionaries to work in China with restrictions, but after his death the next emperor outlawed them, in 1724. As a result, the number of Catholics in China sharply declined and the Catholic churches went underground to avoid persecution. Some missionaries remained hidden in China, protected by families that lived on boats and made their living by fishing the rivers and inland waterways of today's Jiangsu and Zhejiang provinces. It is estimated that there were about 300,000 Catholics in China during the latter years of the reign of Emperor Kangxi and only 200,000 at the end of the century.

IMPERIALIST PROTECTION

Catholic missionaries did not gain a foothold in China again until 1842, after the Opium War. At that time Great Britain, the winning power, forced the Chinese government to sign a series of treaties, one provision of which made it possible for foreign religious groups to establish missions in China's interior. From then on, the threat of military intervention by all the major Western powers put Christian missionaries (Catholic, Protestant, and Orthodox) under the protection of foreign embassies. The political and military pressure of Western governments on China also progressively forced China's submission to the demands of these foreign governments for territory and economic privileges.

Because missionaries in China were protected by the imperialist powers, many of the priests and nuns from foreign countries began to adopt the colonialist attitudes of the imperialist governments. Some of these priests and nuns said the Chinese were not suited to become good Catholics. They were fearful of turning church authority over to Chinese because they believed the Chinese Catholics were not yet ready to assume leadership of the church. Yet the training they gave to Chinese was only enough to enable them to fill subordinate positions in the church. At some universities and seminaries the European and American priests sat in segregated fashion at separate tables from the Chinese priests, the head table always occupied by some of the foreign missionaries.

There were other differences from the days of Matteo Ricci. The majority of those joining the Catholic Church were now farmers and fishermen, not the intellectual upper strata of Chinese society. The missionaries kept to their own interests behind walled compounds. And there was little attempt to understand Chinese values and political currents.

Although the Catholics were able to build churches and set up schools, hospitals, and universities in most of the provinces of China, their presence drew forth anger and indignation on the part of many Chinese. This was not so much anti-religious in nature as it was anger directed toward the grievous defeats that China had suffered at the hands of the Western powers. It erupted in the Boxer Rebellion (1900-01), a time in which many Christians were killed.

The Boxer Rebellion was drowned in blood by the forces of eight foreign powers. New unequal treaties, much more oppressive than the old, were forced upon China. A single city, the port of Tianjin in North China, came to have eight foreign-ruled enclaves or "concessions" — British, French, German, Russian, Japanese, Italian, Belgian, and Austro-Hungarian — with troops from most of these countries and the U.S.A. as well. The city of Shanghai was similarly divided into concessions. In the capital, Beijing, the diplomatic corps of envoys of foreign powers maintained a garrisoned and fortified "Legation Quarter" in the heart of the city. No Chinese could enter it without a foreign pass.

By 1949, the number of Catholics in China was 2,700,000. There were about 4,500 Catholic missionaries, both priests and nuns. The number of Chinese priests was 2,700 and Chinese nuns, more than 5,000. Chinese Catholicism was divided into 143 diocese. There were only 20 Chinese among the 143 bishops, and there were three Chinese archbishops, but they had no real power. The power in the church remained securely in the hands of Rome, which maintained its control through the missionaries sent to China. The first six Chinese were appointed bishops in 1926. One of these, Simon Chu, was appointed to the Haimen Diocese (north of Shanghai). Yu Bin was appointed bishop to the Nanjing parish in 1935.

PRESSURES FROM ROME

The response of most of the Catholic missionaries to the victory of the Communists in 1949 was to dig in their heels and refuse to cooperate with the new government. While many Protestant missionaries left China of their own free will after the revolution, the Catholic Church authorities ordered their missionaries to stay. Most of the Catholic missionaries did not leave until after they had been placed under house arrest by the police and eventually expelled from the country in the early 1950s. This caused much ill feeling on both sides.

Several times the pope and other officials in Rome instructed Chinese Catholic clergy persons and believers to boycott all government policies. Rome instructed them not to take part in any activities organized by the government, not to read magazines or newspapers put out by the government, not to join trade unions, not to join the women or youth federations, not to co-operate with the government in any way.

The policy advocated by the Vatican toward the Chinese Communist government was somewhat unique. Catholics in the Communist countries of Eastern Europe were not restrained in this way from participating in public activities. Even in Communist Vietnam, the Vatican consulted with the government before elevating the archbishop of Hanoi, Joseph Trin Nhu Khue, to the position of cardinal. They did the same with his replacement, Joseph-Marie Trinh Van Can, after Cardinal Trin died. But in China the Vatican took a position that amounted to open rebellion against the government and total support for the former Nationalist government. The Church even encouraged the formation of Chinese Catholic organizations that might work underground for the restoration of the Nationalists in China.

In its early years, the Communist government viewed the Catholic Church much as they did all the other religious organizations of China. They tried to bring Catholic leaders into unity with the government's program to develop and modernize China. Premier Zhou Enlai met with the Chinese Catholic bishops on January 17, 1951, and gave his approval to continued Chinese church relations with Rome. Zhou, however, said that such relations might be continued only if the Vatican did not support United States imperialism. He urged the Catholics to become self-supporting and to no longer rely on missionaries and foreign funds to administer their affairs.

The pope's spiritual legitimacy, however, greatly complicated the Chinese government's efforts to limit Vatican influence. Many Catholic leaders maintained their allegiance to the Vatican because they believed that the pope spoke in the name of Christ. For a number of years after the Communist government consolidated its power, the Catholic Church was regarded by most Chinese as one of the few organizations in China that still supported the Nationalists, or Guomindang government in exile in Taiwan.

Yu Bin, the bishop of Nanjing, declared that "the first enemy of Catholicism is the Chinese Communist Party." He took a strong political position in support of the defeated Nationalist government and authored many anti-Communist articles that were published in Catholic and other newspapers around the world.

In Shanghai where there was a large concentration of Catholic families, church members who cooperated with the government were refused the right to communion. Secret lay organizations were established by Catholic officials to oppose government policies. These included catechism groups composed of students who held three-day closed retreats for prayer, reflection, and discussion. There were also small informal groups of businessmen established to "defend the Church against the inroads of the government."

In 1952, Rome appointed Deng Yiming bishop of Guangdong Province. He used this position to spearhead the Catholic opposition to Communism in southeastern China. He refused to cooperate with the government at any time, and urged his fellow Catholics to do the same. I was told that government officials tried to treat him politely and to reason with him, but they finally decided he was unreformable and arrested him, in 1958, as a counterrevolutionary. He left China in 1962.

There were, however, some Catholics who did not agree with the anti-Communist position propounded by Rome. Under the threat of excommunication, they decided to reorganize the Church under Chinese leadership. In November 1951, a "Declaration of Independence and Reform of the Catholic Church," signed by Father Wang Liangzhu in Guangning County, Sichuan Province, and some 500 other Chinese Catholics, gained support from individual Catholics all over China. At a National Congress of Catholics held in Beijing in July 1957, the Chinese Patriotic Catholic Association was founded. This congress adopted a constitution and a policy of independence and self-administration in church affairs. At the same time more than 200 local Catholic patriotic associations were established throughout the country.

Because the Catholic missionaries had been expelled from China and some of the Chinese bishops had gone to Taiwan with the fleeing Nationalist government, the church now had an insufficient number of bishops. The Chinese Catholics, therefore, selected two of their number, in 1958, to be the bishops of Hankou and Wuchang. They reported this to Rome, but the Vatican refused to recognize the new bishops because they had been consecrated without Rome's approval. By 1962, 50 bishops were elected and consecrated by the Chinese Catholics without the approval of Rome.

Between 1952 and 1958, Pope Pius XII issued two encyclicals and an apostolic letter to Chinese Catholics that clearly enunciated his opposition to the new government and exhorted clergy and laity to resist the establishment of a patriotic church. He also excommunicated the newly-appointed Nanjing vicar general, Li Weiguang, for having signed a declaration in support of a patriotic church. The Vatican also secretly appointed 25 bishops to various parishes in China, some of whom, in turn, have secretly ordained priests. The Chinese Patriotic Catholic Association responded to these secret appointments by lodging protests against the Vatican for attempting to restore its colonial control over the Chinese Catholic Church.

No one knows how many Catholics in China still adhere to the policies of the Vatican. Obviously there are some, but it is doubtful if their numbers are nearly as high as reports in the West suggest. (A 1991 article in the *Reader's Digest* puts the number at the ridiculously high figure of ten million, three times as many as all Catholics in China before the revolution.) The leaders of the Chinese Catholic Church call them "dissidents" and express concern over their seeming lack of sound theological training. Most of these "dissidents" worship in private homes because the established churches and cathedrals are all related to the Chinese Patriotic Catholic Association. The leadership of these "dissident" house churches is often held by priests who have had little or no formal education in Catholic seminaries.

I was told by Paul Zhu Shichang, the General Secretary of the Chinese Patriotic Catholic Association that he thought there were only a few persons who still might be classified as "dissidents," i.e., persons who refuse to participate in the activities of the established Chinese Catholic Church. Many former opponents of the Chinese Patriotic Catholic Association are now returning to the churches and cathedrals that have been reopened since the Cultural Revolution. "Some," he said, "may still support the political policies of the Vatican, but they don't demonstrate this openly, and they participate in the activities of the established Chinese Catholic Church. Church members have a tolerant attitude toward such people. They are just confused. For Chinese Catholics, it is just a matter of differences between brothers."

Paul Zhu Shichang said that some of the so-called "dissident" priests have no understanding of the nature of the trinity. Others are married persons with families. One even claimed to be the pope of the Eastern part of the world, on a spiritual par with the pope in Rome. A woman in Jiangsu Province called herself the "living Mary," and a female pope.

Because the Chinese Catholics were cut off from the Vatican when Pope John XXIII called together the worldwide church council on January 25, 1959 (Vatican II), they have not participated in some of the radical changes that other Catholics around the world have experienced. Thus Catholics in China still use Latin in their services rather than the vernacular, or local languages, used by Catholics elsewhere. When I asked members of the Chinese Patriotic Catholic Association why they don't use Chinese instead of Latin in the Mass, they said some priests had experimented with using Chinese but that their congregations didn't think the Mass was meaningful unless it was in Latin.

Chinese Catholics have also missed the ecumenical experience that Catholics elsewhere have had as a result of Vatican II. And they seem to have little or no knowledge of Liberation Theology, discussions of which have consumed Catholics in Latin America, the Philippines, and some other areas of the world. Thus the Chinese Catholics are divorced from many of the Catholic concerns elsewhere, even though they do have contacts with Catholics all over the world, as we will see below.

The position of Rome in terms of China has changed little, perhaps because the present pope doesn't wish to antagonize the Nationalists in Taiwan. His advisors continue to secretly appoint Chinese bishops without consulting the other Chinese Catholic bishops. This happens even though the latest Canon Law of the Roman Catholic Church (1983) requires that the appointment of any bishop be done in consultation with the College of Bishops in that country to which a new bishop is to be appointed.

In 1979, the Vatican appointed Shanghai Bishop Gong Binmei to the position of archbishop. He was in jail at the time because of his anti-government activities. No announcement was made of this appointment until after Gong was released, in 1985, and given permission to visit relatives in the United States. Then the Vatican made public its action. In 1991 the Vatican announced its intention to recognize 20 more Chinese bishops, which the Chinese Catholic community interpreted as yet another attempt to interfere in its independence and self-administration. Chinese Bishop Joseph Zong Huaide, in May 1991, accused some "dissident Catholics" of taking advantage of changes in eastern Europe to "launch illegal activities" in China.

An Italian priest who was given permission to study at a university in Shanghai used his position, I was told by the Religious Affairs Bureau in Shanghai, to make contacts with "dissidents" in the city and to preach to them. The priest also sent regular reports of his activities to Rome and to Catholics in Hong Kong. The Chinese authorities considered such activities to be hostile to China and ordered him to leave the country. I was told that reports of this incident in the foreign press distorted the facts.

CHURCH ADMINISTRATION TODAY

At its second national congress, held in 1962, the Chinese Patriotic Catholic Association reaffirmed its policy of independence and self-administration in church affairs. The congress also outlined the special task of helping each parish to establish a training program for developing new leadership of the church. At the third congress, in 1980, two other national organizations were established — the National Administrative Commission of the Chinese Catholic Church and the Chinese College of Bishops . In addition, a Chinese Catholic Seminary was set up in 1980. Bishop Zong Huaide serves as the President of the Chinese Patriotic Catholic Association, and as acting chairman of both the National Administrative Commission and the Chinese College of Bishops. He is the bishop of the Jinan Diocese in Shandong Province.

The aim of the National Administrative Commission of the Chinese Catholic Church, I was told, is to spread the Gospel of Jesus, to promote the Catholic cause, to guide Catholic priests and lay persons, to scrupulously abide by the commandments of Jesus, to maintain the policy of independence and self-administration in church affairs, to consult and decide important church affairs, and to run the Chinese Patriotic Catholic Association well.

The Chinese College of Bishops is composed of bishops of the various diocese. Its tasks are to study and interpret the Catholic creed and canon, exchange experiences in missionary work, issue important documents and correspondence, and promote friendly ties with Catholics abroad.

All three organizations have stated that they believe the most effective way to carry out missionary work under the socialist system is to encourage Catholics to love their country and to love Catholicism, to serve other people in honor of God, and to participate positively in the on-going state construction.

The Rites Committee and the Theology Research Committee of the Chinese College of Bishops have begun an extensive study of possible church reforms that would make the Chinese Catholic Church more suitable to national conditions and traditional Chinese customs.

The Chinese Patriotic Catholic Association and the National Administrative Commission of the Chinese Catholic Church jointly sponsor a magazine called *Chinese Catholicism*. It was founded in 1980. The magazine reports on the work of the two organizations, explains the Bible, and discusses religious rites and creeds. Some 10,000 copies are printed of each issue, and it is distributed throughout the country's Catholic communities. Some copies are airmailed abroad. Lian Qiuhang acts as its editor-in-chief.

There are 113 diocese in China today under the jurisdiction of 67 bishops. Four of these bishops were consecrated before 1949 or in the early 1950s. The rest were elected and consecrated by the Chinese Catholic Church in 1958 or later. There are more than 900 priests and a total of 1,200 nuns (belonging to the orders of Immaculate Conception, Sacred Heart, St. Joseph, and St. Mary) working in the more than 3,000 cathedrals and chapels under the direction of the National Administrative Commission of the Chinese Catholic Church. Many of the buildings have been repaired and reopened since the Cultural Revolution.

The best-known cathedrals are the Xuanwumen Church of Immaculate Conception and the Xishiku Church of Our Savior in Beijing, the Xujiahui Cathedral to Mary Mother of God in Shanghai, the Shishi Stone Room Cathedral in Guangzhou, the Shanghailu Church in Wuhan, and the Laoxikai Church in Tianjin.

According to Paul Zhu Shichang, membership in the Chinese Catholic Church is growing at a rate of about 50,000 members each year. Many are young persons. The largest concentration of Catholics is in Hebei Province, about one million. Shandong Province has the next largest, 380,000 Catholics. He says that people are joining the Catholic Church today through faith and not because they want to get

175

material benefits from church membership (the so-called "rice Christians"), as often happened when foreign missionaries administered the churches in China. He also told me that the form of preaching is different today. The priests teach believers to do good things, set a good example by working hard, and to help others in difficulties.

The result of this teaching, Mr. Zhu told me, is that many Catholic families have been honored by the government for excellence, and there is one all-Catholic village that has been singled out for praise, again by the government, as a "civilized village." In this village no one ever steals, there is no fighting, and no one smokes, he said. He also told me that local government officials in this area say that the increasing number of Catholics seems to be good for Chinese society. "Before 1949, Chinese saw all Catholics as foreigners, and would say that an increase in the number of Catholics diminished Chinese society. Now they say to have more Catholics is a good thing."

There are more than 3,000 Catholic workers in various factories and enterprises who have been publicly honored for setting an outstanding example for other workers. Mr. Zhu said that non-believers see these people in action and so are attracted to their lifestyle. They then decide to visit the Catholic churches to which these workers belong. Some of the non-believers then decide to join the church.

TRAINING

There are 12 Catholic seminaries in China, of which the Chinese Catholic Seminary in Beijing, founded in 1980, is the central one. The others are at Shenyang in Liaoning Province, Changchun in Jilin Province, Shijiazhuang in Hebei Province, Huhhot in Inner Mongolia Autonomous Region, Taiyuan in Shanxi Province, Jinan in Shandong Province, Wuhan in Hubei Province, Chengdu in Sichuan Province, Xi'an in Shaanxi Province, in the city of Shanghai, and one more in the city of Beijing. These seminaries have altogether 700 male students.

The students are recommended to attend the seminaries from among the religious youth whose educational background is at least of a high school level. They must have the approval of their families to lead single lives in the future, and they must themselves volunteer for Catholic service. They are admitted after a physical check-up and an academic examination. The length of schooling is five or six years. At the central Chinese Catholic Seminary in Beijing, the course of study takes seven years. Here the first year is spent in liberal arts courses, the second and third years in philosophy, and the last four in theology. After graduation, students from these various seminaries may be ordained as priests following approval by fellow church-members and the local bishop.

Women are educated in one or another of the 30 primary convents, run by the parishes. Their length of study is three years. They are accepted as nuns after they forswear property and marriage and agree to devote themselves to the guidance of the Catholic Church. There are 400 nuns presently enrolled in these primary convents.

The theology courses taught at the seminaries and primary convents cover the Bible, doctrinal theology, ethical theology, history of the church, church regulations, missionary methods, and missionary cultivation. The classes in philosophy cover logic, theory of knowledge, ontology, psychology, history of philosophy, and the history of Chinese philosophy. The culture classes include Latin, Chinese, history and geography, politics, music, and sports. A foreign language, other than Latin, is also included.

None of the Catholic churches have schools for children because Chinese laws forbid religious training for children. But most of the churches have classes for children during summer vacation so that they can learn the catechism. These summer classes enroll students between the ages of seven and sixteen.

A SAMPLING OF CATHOLIC COMMUNITIES IN CHINA

In Beijing and the immediate surrounding countryside

there are 14 Catholic churches administered by 23 priests. Five of these churches are in the city proper. There are approximately 40,000 Catholics in this area. The priests average 54 years in age, the oldest being 84 and the youngest 20. There are also two convents, St. Paul Vincent and St. Joseph.

When Michael Fu Tieshan was consecrated Bishop of Beijing, in December 1979, he became only the third Chinese bishop to head this diocese since 1601. He was elected by both clergy and laity at a meeting of the Beijing Chinese Patriotic Catholic Association. At his consecration, he expressed the desire to promote friendship with foreign Catholics "on the basis of equality and mutual respect for each other's independence." He has since traveled to the United States and other countries as a Catholic clergy person and on behalf of the Chinese Committee for Peace and Disarmament.

Prior to his elevation as Bishop of Beijing, he was a priest at the city's oldest cathedral, the Xuanwumen Church of Immaculate Conception. During the Cultural Revolution this was the only Catholic church that was not damaged by the Red Guards, but he was sent with others to a farm to plant fruit trees and grow rice. In response to my question as to how this difficult period affected him, he said, "If people love God, they can get benefits from anything they do."

About 2,000 people attend this cathedral every Sunday, and about 300 people come to services during the week. At the Christmas Eve Mass, in 1991, there were over 10,000 people in attendance. More than 300 confirmations take place in the church every year, and more than 100 couples are married there each year. There are also 1,700 visitors from foreign countries who come to this church each year.

During the week the priests here, as elsewhere, give catechism classes, hear confessions, and receive visitors. The two-hour catechism classes are held two nights each week for teenagers and adults up to 30 years of age. Here students learn about the Ten Commandments, seven sacraments, and canon law. They also learn some church history. There is no Sunday school of any kind, but the priests do conduct special classes for children during the summer vacation time. Bishop Fu Tieshan told me that they expect parents to teach their children about Catholicism, which requires the parents to know more about the Bible than perhaps is true of Catholics in other countries.

The Cathedral has a number of social service programs. They offer free legal counseling and mediation in the case of family problems. They also have teams of youth who provide services for older persons in the community, such as house cleaning, accompanying them to the hospital, etc. They set up a free medical clinic on the street outside the church for those in need. And they have set up booths on the street to cut hair, repair bicycles, repair watches, and do tailoring for those in need.

As part of its social service program, the Cathedral runs a language school that teaches English, French, German, Spanish, Japanese, and Latin. Actually, the bishop said, there is not much interest in the latter, although it is the only Latin class in Beijing. For this reason, the church subsidizes the expenses for this one class. The others are paid for by small tuition fees charged to the students. The main purpose of this school is to prepare students for entrance into college. They also teach classes in Chinese, mathematics, history, and geography. When this part-time school was first opened, about 35 percent of its students were eventually able to enter college. By 1990, 70 percent of the students were able to pass the college entrance exams. The school has trained 7,000 students since 1985.

The Cathedral is particularly proud of its Divine Love Choir, which includes non-Catholic singers. Besides performing regularly in the various church services, this choir has performed for the public at the Beijing Concert Hall and at a number of hospitals for the disabled. The choir director is a former surgeon who retired from his hospital job to work full-time for the church.

In Nanjing, the Immaculate Conception Church on Stone Drum Street was used as an optical factory during the Cultural Revolution. It was reopened in 1981. The building itself had not been damaged, but the furniture inside was destroyed. The factory, however, built some meeting rooms that were turned over to the church when it was returned to the Catholics. It is the largest Catholic church in Nanjing and has more than 300 members. The building was constructed during the 19th century.

The church is the headquarters for the Nanjing diocese and so has a bishop, a priest, and three nuns. These nuns belong to a convent in Shanghai. They are expecting to receive four newly-trained priests during 1992. Both the bishop and the one priest have to travel a great deal to other churches in the province that are presently without clergy leadership. The church holds a Mass every day at 6:30 in the morning. One of its members is Dr. Ma, a Chinese expert on heart disease.

The city of Wuxi is in the same province as Nanjing, but its St. Joseph Catholic Church is unusual in that most of its members are families of river fishermen and women, who once lived on their boats and had no homes on land. Many are descendants of the fishing families that protected the missionaries who remained in hiding in China after 1724, when the emperor banned all Catholic missionaries from China. The Section Chief of the Provincial Department of Culture told me that today some seventy percent of the population of Wuxi County are Catholics.

The boat people no longer have to live on their vessels. Since 1969, the government has provided housing for them on land. Within the Prefecture of Wuxi, 35 out of the 38 villages that have been constructed for these families are composed of Catholics. Three of the fish farms in the area are run by Catholics.

The church is also unusual because, since 1924, it has always had a Chinese pastor. No foreign Catholic missionary resided in Wuxi in 1949, and the city became part of the new Communist government without any fighting in the area. The only damage the church has ever suffered was in 1966 during the Cultural Revolution. At that time it became a warehouse. The rectory became a faculty residence for a local school. The buildings were returned to the church in 1979 and it reopened on Christmas day in 1980 with 6,000 people in attendance at midnight Mass.

The church faces a street that is bordered by a river. Many fishing boats are lined up in the river opposite the church. The people on these boats greet visitors as they go in and out of the church gate. Today there is a prayer service every evening attended by about 100 people. The ordinary Sunday service, administered by two priests, attracts some 1,500 people. On big feast days, they have to invite two priests from out of town to help give the sacrament to over 10,000 people.

During the Qingming Festival (April 5), the traditional Chinese day for sweeping graves, the Catholics of Wuxi are particularly prominent. On this day, often seven to eight thousand people visit the Catholic cemetery there. The streets and public buses are so crowded that the city has to provide extra chartered buses to handle the many cemetery visitors.

The Catholic church in Quanzhou has not yet reopened since the Cultural Revolution, and their property is still occupied by a factory. Most of its members in the past were Filipinos, who returned to the Philippines after 1949. The few remaining Catholics of the city meet in one of the members' homes. The pastor, Father Cai, told me there were no dissident Catholics in the area. They meet in homes only because the church is not yet usable. The Religious Affairs Bureau of Quanzhou is working to find new property into which the factory can move. The city government has ordered the factory to do so, and the national government has allocated 50,000 yuan for the restoration of the church once it is vacated.

Father Cai was labeled a rightist during the Cultural Revolution and suffered somewhat, but now he has returned to pastor the congregation. He is over eighty years old and has the assistance of a younger priest. He told me that before 1949 there were as many as 70 to 80 priests who serviced the Catholics of this area. At one time, he said, there were

100,000 Catholics in this city, but now there are only about 1,500.

The Shishi Stone Room Cathedral on Guangzhou's Yide Road is always packed to standing room only at the Christmas Eve traditional Latin Mass. It holds well over 2,000 people and was closed to worship in April 1966, during the Cultural Revolution. At that time most of the priests serving in the city's five Catholic parishes were sent to work in factories or on state farms. Some were imprisoned. Red Guards ransacked the Stone Room Cathedral and, among other things, completely demolished its polished-marble altar. The building was later turned into a school.

One of the several priests at this Cathedral, Father Andrew Lin, is now Vicar General of Guangzhou. He spent ten years in prison during the Cultural Revolution but seems to bear no outward bitterness. The government provided over 30,000 yuan for the renovation of this church after the Cultural Revolution, a task that took over three months to complete.

BIRTH CONTROL AND PUBLIC SERVICE

When I asked Bishop Fu Tieshan about Chinese Catholic attitudes toward birth control, he said that over-population is a big social problem in China and one that cannot be solved by religion. It is government policy in the cities of China to have only one child and not several. The Catholics in China, he said, do make use of various birth-control methods. "God not only allows people the right to be born, but also wants them to take care of themselves after they are born. People have to eat, have clothes to wear, and to work. Throughout the world there are several millions of people who die of malnutrition and hunger. Humankind is facing a tragedy — not enough food to eat. For these reasons, the church in China is not going to put too much burden on Catholics in the matter of birth control." He said that he has talked about this problem with priests from the United States, Italy, and France and that he believes they all agree that there are no other means to solve the tremendous problem of over-population.

As to women in the church, the bishop told me that they are a great help in church management, but they do not participate in directing church ceremonies. No women are among the Catholic representatives in the national government, but some are representatives in the provincial and city governments. Some are members of the leadership of the Chinese Patriotic Catholic Association. Some are also on the boards of the YMCAs and YWCAs of China, as well, of course, as the board of the Chinese Women's Federation.

Women are particularly active in the various social services that the Catholic Church provides. Bishop Fu Tieshan told me that the church leadership is presently considering how best to raise the status of women in the church.

As to the question of why the Catholic Church is presently growing in China, the bishop said this is due to the will of God as well as the efforts of people in spreading the Gospel. He said that China has a long history of seeking perfection, and so the Catholic Church is attractive to many persons. He also said that, "Jesus Christ says that the Son of God comes to earth to serve people and not to be served. The church, thereby, should encourage its believers to contribute to God, society, and the people."

The Catholics in various centers of China have established a number of social service organizations. One of these is the Shanghai Society for Catholic Intellectuals set up in 1986. This organization has sponsored many advisory sessions to provide information to the public about medicine. The society has also set up a convalescent center in Shanghai and a vocational foreign language school.

In Beijing the church has recently begun to collect money to set up a recovery center for the elderly. In addition, Catholic organizations have set up a retirement center in Nanjing and clinics in Yangzhou, Jiangsu Province, and a convalescent hospital in Wuhan, Hubei Province. For many years, Catholics from various trades and professions have gone to the streets and offered free consultation for the public in such fields as medicine and education. Furthermore, Chinese Catholics have collected much clothing, blankets, and money for the flood victims of 1991.

INTERNATIONAL CONTACTS

While maintaining their policy of independence and self-administration in church affairs, Chinese Catholics say that they still desire friendly exchanges with Catholics in other countries on the basis of equality and mutual respect. They have sent delegations of church leaders to visit Canada, the United States, Belgium, France, Germany, Switzerland, Austria, Hungary, Japan, the Philippines, Hong Kong, and Macao, as well as to attend various international conferences.

And the Catholics have welcomed many distinguished visitors from around the world. After France's Cardinal Etchegaray visited the Chinese Catholics, he issued the following statement: "The history of the relations between China and the Catholic Church has been dotted with a series of unfortunate misunderstandings ...(and) honesty obliges us to recognize our blunders, even mistakes."

Austrian Cardinal Koenig told a journalist, after he returned from China, "Chinese Catholics not only believe in their religion, but they also love their country." He candidly remarked that the Vatican does not really understand China's position and the situation of the Chinese Patriotic Catholic Association, and perhaps this is the source of continued misunderstanding between the Vatican and Beijing.

Every day that Mother Theresa from India was in China, during 1986, she took part in Mass with Chinese Catholics in the various churches she visited. The same has been true of such persons as the Cardinal Sin of the Philippines, the Archbishop of Tokyo, the king and queen of Spain, and the head of the Italian government. When the exiled Chinese Bishop Vitus Chang, now living in Bonn, Germany, returned to his homeland for a visit in 1982, he declared that he had met a whole chain of surprises that were evidence to him "that my country is in the care and love of God."

184

Finally there is the matter of Chinese Catholics in Taiwan and Hong Kong. The latter is being returned by the British to China in 1997. The Chinese government has assured the Catholics in Hong Kong that they can continue to practice their faith and maintain their links with the Vatican. The representatives of the Religious Affairs Bureau in Beijing told me that China will hold to its principle of Three Mutuals in regard to the churches of Hong Kong. These three mutuals are first, not to interfere in each other's affairs; second, to respect each other; and third, no subjugation of one nation (or church) by another. They assured me there could be no such thing as the Hong Kong Catholic Church being forced into the Chinese Catholic community.

Local Hong Kong Catholics, of which there are 260,000, are not as confident of their future under the new relationship. They fear that pressures will be put on them to break their ties with the Vatican. After all, the Vatican is one of the few ruling groups in the world that still maintains full diplomatic relations with the Nationalists in Taiwan and refuses to recognize the government on the mainland as the only legitimate government of China. Only the future will tell whether or not there will be two Catholic Churches in China after 1997, one independent and the other tied to Rome.

Almost all Chinese agree — whether they live on the mainland, in Hong Kong, in Taiwan, or elsewhere — that Taiwan eventually will become a part of China again. When this happens, the Chinese Catholic Church will be faced with the same situation it is facing in the return of Hong Kong to China by the British. One would assume that the way the two Catholic churches work out their relationships in Hong Kong will be the model for the Catholic church in the eventual reuniting of Taiwan with China.

After a look at some special places to visit in China's Catholic community, we will turn to the Chinese Protestants. They are the fastest growing religious group in China today.

185

VISITOR'S GUIDE TO CATHOLIC SITES

There are many rural Catholic churches in China, but the most convenient ones to visit are in the larger cities. Here one can usually find people who speak English so there is no need of having a translator. Some of the most important churches and other sites related to Chinese Catholicism are listed below.

1. Xuanwumen Church of Immaculate Conception (City of Beijing)

This cathedral, the center of the Beijing Diocese, was established in 1294, during Yuan Dynasty. It is on the site where Matteo Ricci lived when he was residing in Beijing. The church was initiated by the Franciscan priest, Giovani da Montecorvino, and later enlarged by the Jesuit Adam Schall, in 1650. It is the oldest Catholic church in China. In 1904 it was rebuilt after a major fire. Beijing residents also sometimes call this the South Church.

The cathedral houses the special relics of Chinese Catholicism found in the city of Beijing, including some noted stone tablets written by emperors of several dynasties on behalf of the Catholic community in China. Visitors to services on Sunday will have a chance to hear the fine and nationally famous Divine Love Choir of the Beijing Diocese.

2. Xishiku Church of Our Savior (City of Beijing)

This cathedral, also known as the North Church, is a stunningly attractive white structure with twin towers. It was originally built in 1703, but the property was so near what is now the Palace Museum (the former residence of the emperors, i.e. the Forbidden City) that it had to be moved, in 1888, when the emperor's residence was enlarged. The emperor gave funds for its reconstruction at its present site.

Many of its beautiful stained-glass windows were broken during the Cultural Revolution and had to be replaced when the cathedral was reopened on Christmas, 1985. The visitor can easily recognize the new panes because they are much brighter than the undamaged ones. Also damaged during the Cultural Revolution were about eight of the stone pillars that hold up its vaulting roof. One part of the church was used for storage and the other for physical exercises during the Cultural Revolution. The sanctuary is illuminated by 33 hanging candelabras, now electrified.

3. Astronomical Museum (City of Beijing)

The observatory on what was once the eastern wall of the city of Beijing is still preserved as a museum, although the rest of the wall no longer stands. Its refitting and redesign was one of the achievements of the Jesuit missionary Ferdinand Verbiest during the 17th century. Many of the instruments he constructed and those of other Jesuit scientists are on display here. The observatory is within walking distance from Beijing's Friendship Store. At one time quite prominent, the observatory is now obscured by many tall buildings and hotels that surround it.

4. Matteo Ricci's Grave (City of Beijing)

The Jesuit cemetery in Beijing contains the grave of Matteo Ricci and more than twenty other early Jesuit missionaries. The tombs of Ricci (d. 1610) and Adam Schall (d. 1666) are the most prominent, but here also are the graves of Ferdinand Verbiest (d. 1688) and lesser-known priests from the period. The arrangement in front of Ricci's and Schall's tombs, including carved steles, altars, and incense burners is typically Chinese. In fact, if the visitor is not aware that this is a Jesuit graveyard, it would appear to be a Chinese one. The inscription on Schall's stele are translated: "He edited many books and his corrections of the Chinese calendar was praised and adopted throughout the empire."

This site is not easy to visit and one must get permission

to see it, but the effort is well worth pursuing. This is because the graveyard, protected by the Chinese government, is at the rear of the Beijing Communist Party Training School and off-limits to non-documented tourists. If you wish to see the graveyard, you can make arrangements to do so through the Xuanwumen Church of Immaculate Conception or by contacting officials of the Chinese Patriotic Catholic Association.

5. Xujiahui Cathedral to Mother Mary of God (City of Shanghai)

This cathedral on Caoxibeilu Street in the Xujiahui District of southwest Shanghai was constructed in 1906. Its two bell towers are over 165 feet tall. It is the seat of the Shanghai Diocese and is one of the largest of the Chinese Catholic churches.

6. Sheshan Catholic Seminary (City of Shanghai)

This seminary is on a beautiful hill in the southeastern suburbs of the city. The property also contains a fine basilica and is a site where more than 30,000 pilgrims go each year to walk through the various Stages of the Cross, arranged down the slope of the hill. The basilica was constructed by French Jesuits in 1925, and the seminary was opened in 1982. Mass at the basilica is conducted in Latin, but the seminary courses are taught in Chinese.

7. Laoxikai Church (City of Tianjin)

This church is the seat for the bishop of Tianjin. It is an old and beautiful church that once serviced the European community of this city.

8. Catholic Church of Shenyang (Liaoning Province)

This huge church, built in European style, looks particularly imposing from a distance because of its elongated structure. Located in the city of Shenyang, it has two towers at the front of the building and long rows of windows on two levels on each side of the building.

9. Hongjialou Church of Jinan (Shandong Province)

The two equal-height octagonal towers of this church in the city of Jinan contain a group of tall windows that are quite spectacular. There is also a fine rose window above the entry door.

10. Shanghailu Church (Hubei Province)

This is the largest and oldest Catholic church in the city of Wuhan and in Hubei Province. It is considered one of the major cathedrals of Chinese Catholicism, partly because of the importance of this river port city.

11. Shishi Stone Room Cathedral (Guangdong Province)

This large cathedral, on Yide Road in the city of Guangzhou, dates from 1888 and was erected according to sketches by the French architect Guillemin. The steeple is more than 190 feet tall. It seats over 2,000 people at the traditional Latin Mass. It is the official residence for the Guangzhou Vicar General, Father Andrew Lin.

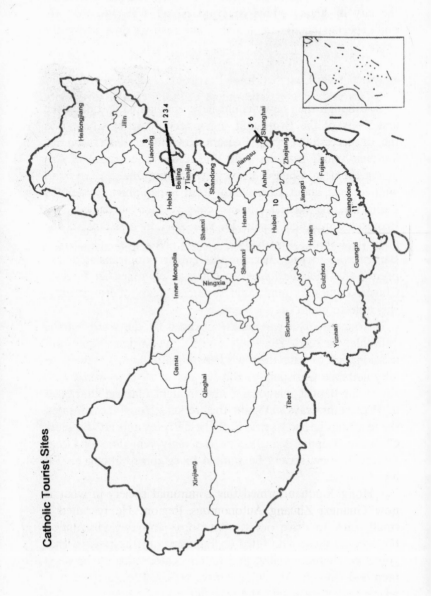

Catholic Tourist Sites

PROTESTANTS:

A Post-Denominational Church

Although they never could have anticipated it, one of the first fruits of the Protestant missionary effort in China was the unsuccessful Taiping Peasant Revolution that raged for fourteen years, between 1850 and 1864. The leader of this major event in Chinese history was Hong Xiuquan, a man who learned about Christianity from a pamphlet written by Liang Fa, the earliest Chinese convert to be ordained as a Protestant minister. Liang Fa was also an assistant to the first Protestant missionary, Robert Morrison, a British Baptist who arrived there in 1807. Morrison translated and printed the *New Testament* in Chinese, compiled an English-Chinese dictionary, and, after seventeen years of evangelizing, was able to claim only ten converts.

Hong Xiuquan was totally changed by the words in the pamphlet he read. He avidly sought out various Protestant missionaries to gain their wisdom. Finally Hong decided to fully embrace Christianity. But he was refused baptism by an American Baptist missionary who thought him yet untrained in Protestant ways. Despite this rebuff, Hong incorporated the teachings he had learned from these Protestants into his semi-Christian Taiping Tianguo, or Heavenly Kingdom of Great Peace, the new society he wanted to establish among his fellow Chinese.

Hong Xiuquan formed this communal society in what is now Guangxi Zhuang Autonomous Region. He recruited a small army to drive out the landlords and then distributed the land to those who tilled it. Furthermore, he insisted that goods be shared equally, and he advocated equality between men and women. All children were required to go to school, where they were taught the *Old* and *New Testaments*. Later,

Hong and his co-workers raised a large army of peasants, many of whom were women fighters, to try to overthrow the feudal Qing Dynasty and set up this new society throughout China.

The red-turbaned, long-haired Taipings fought many successful battles, badly frightening and almost toppling the Qing ruling house. By the time the revolution was finally suppressed, the Taiping army had entered 16 of the then 18 provinces and had captured 600 walled cities. In the areas they conquered, they effected laws based on the Biblical Ten Commandments, forbade slavery, concubinage, foot-binding, arranged marriage, and prostitution. Were it not for inner decay and outside pressures, they eventually might have accomplished their goal.

From the beginning, the Taiping revolutionaries were opposed by most Western missionaries and all of the foreign powers that had imperialistic designs on China's vast territory and potential for wealth. A few American and British soldiers of fortune did join the Taiping army, but their own governments sided with the emperor. The American and British governments sent troops and arms to help the Qing emperor quell the Taiping Revolution.

It was during this period that the Qing government lost the Second Opium War (1858-1860) and was forced to give in to the British by signing a humiliating "Treaty of Nanjing." Through the use of gunboats, the Western Powers (Britain, France, Germany, the United States, and Russia) forced China to submit to many more unequal treaties during the subsequent years of the 19th century. The incompetent Qing government was forced to sign all of them under duress.

Both Catholic and Protestant missionaries benefited from the unequal treaties under a "Toleration Clause." So did their converts, many of whom came from the ranks of the poor, often only to get something to eat (Rice Christians). Some converts were even criminals who fled to the protection of the mission houses in order to evade the authorities. Mission property, according to the unequal treaties, was off-limits to Chinese law enforcement.

MISSIONARY ATTITUDES

The missionaries, for the most part, never reflected on the moral questions raised by the aggression of their own governments. What was important for them was that this foreign intervention gave them a chance to seek converts within this vast nation. The missionaries acted as if they were totally oblivious to the international and economic forces that made their easy access to China possible.

The unequal treaties turned Christianity in China into a hated "foreign religion," and gave rise to a series of church incidents that invariably brought more concessions from the Qing government. Between 1860 and 1899 there were thousands of small incidents and some 200 riots and attacks on foreign missionaries. The hatred of the foreign powers and their religion finally culminated in the Boxer Uprising of 1900. Missionaries and their Chinese converts were prime targets. Thousands of Chinese were killed, as were some 240 Westerners. The Boxers were crushed by a military expedition of about 25,000 men, mounted by the foreign governments operating in China. Frederick Brown, an American Methodist missionary, served as a guide in leading the Eight-Power Allied Expedition Forces from Tianjin to Beijing in order to suppress the Boxers.

Kenneth Scott Latourette, the noted historian, has carefully surveyed the missionary effort in China. In his *A History of Christian Missions in China* (published in 1929), he says that to no other country in the world were so many Christian missionaries sent and was so much effort expended — *with so little result* — as China. Latourette, of course, was including both Catholic and Protestant missionaries in his calculations. But the number is high even when Protestants alone are considered.

By 1869, there were 400 Protestant missionaries in China, and not many more than 5,000 converts. In 1900 there were some 2,800 Protestant missionaries there and only

193

about 100,000 Chinese Protestants. The number of missionaries had doubled by 1913. It reached its peak in 1926'— a total of 8,235 Protestant missionaries representing a variety of Protestant denominations with their headquarters in America and Europe. The number of Chinese Protestants in 1922 was 375,000, and in 1949, 700,000.

During the years following the Boxer Uprising, the reputation of the Protestant missionaries in China improved as they began to build more and more hospitals, schools, orphanages, and other charitable institutions that were open to non-Christians as well as to converts. By 1930, the various Protestant denominations and their missionaries had established well over 6,000 primary schools with 185,000 pupils, and some 265 middle schools with 7,600 students. They also set up many colleges that, in 1947, were consolidated into 14. These colleges had 6,400 students, or one-seventh of all the students in China at that level. The Protestant medical service was centered in 240 hospitals, 600 dispensaries and clinics, and six medical colleges.

Yet the missionaries, despite their contributions to the educational and medical services of China, carried with them the seeds of the colonialist and racist attitudes of their own governments. When the Protestant missionaries working in China held a Centennial of Christianity in China, in 1907, not a single Chinese was invited to attend. And when the First National Christian Conference was held in Shanghai, in 1922, less than half the invited delegates were Chinese.

The Protestant missionaries also put on blinders in regard to the political situation in China. Most of them failed to see the necessity for the overthrow of the corrupt Qing government by revolutionaries under the leadership of Sun Yatsen in 1911, just as they failed to foresee the inevitable victory of the Communists in 1949. In each case, most of the missionaries continued to give verbal support to the decaying and corrupt governments that were soon to be overthrown, long after the majority of the Chinese people were convinced that these governments should be replaced.

At the same time, the missionaries seemed to have no

problem in participating in politics on behalf of their own governments. Peter Parker, one of the first American medical missionaries to go to China, worked for the U.S. government as secretary to the first American political Minister to China. And the last American Ambassador to the Nationalist government, before it fled to Taiwan, was John Leighton Stewart, a missionary who had served as president of the Protestant Yenching University in Beijing. (Stewart, it should be pointed out, was aware of the unique missionary situation in China. He once said that missionaries dominated the Chinese Protestant church because they "have military power to maintain unequal treaties, and the Chinese government can't do anything about it.")

There were a few missionaries who did oppose the imperialism of their own governments, but their numbers can be counted on the fingers of one hand. The American missionary Frank Joseph Rawlinson petitioned the U.S. government to cancel all of the unequal treaties to which it was a signatory, with no success. He later condemned the aggressive war launched by the Japanese against China, and supported the Chinese people's efforts at armed resistance. Dr. Edward Hume, another American and president of the Yale-in-China complex of medical and educational schools in Hunan Province, gave some help to the future Communist leader Mao Zedong during Mao's student days at Hunan Middle School. Mao, in 1919, wrote articles for *The New Hunan*, Yale-in-China's literary magazine, and did so until the Nationalist government suppressed its publication. And the Canadian missionary, James Gareth Endicott, took a public position against the atrocities committed by the Nationalist government and later gave support to the Communist revolution.

Generally speaking, however, the Protestant missionaries were hostile to this revolution. Owing to their educational and cultural backgrounds, they tended to side with the status quo, thus standing unconsciously with the interests of colonialism and imperialism. The success of the Communist revolution caused them great distress, and most returned to their home countries by 1951. A few were jailed because the

Chinese believed they were spies. These were later deported.

THE THREE-SELF MOVEMENT

In the summer of 1950, 40 prominent Chinese Protestants, headed by Wu Yaozong (Y. T. Wu), signed a declaration on "Efforts to Be Made by Chinese Christians for the Building of a New China." The declaration called on both clergy and laity in China to govern their own church, support it with their own financial contributions, do their own evangelistic work, and strive for the "Three-Selfs" (self-administration, self-support, and self-propagation). The declaration received an enthusiastic response from Protestants in many parts of China, and was eventually signed by some 400,000 Chinese Protestants, over half the total.

Wu Yaozong was, at the time, a Protestant layman and head of the YMCA's student division. He had earlier been the editor of the Chinese Protestant weekly *Tian Feng*, but he was relieved of this post in 1948, after he offended the foreign missionaries by writing an editorial titled: "The Tragedy of Contemporary Christianity." In this, he charged that the churches were in no way prepared for the revolution that was about to come to China because they were too interlinked with imperialism — through the support of missionaries — to offer much promise to the future of China. It was a call for a revolution within the Protestant community, a revolution that might "recover the gospel" for the Chinese church.

In an article Wu Yaozong later wrote, he said that too many Christians "are bewildered because they refuse to see God's light that comes through unexpected channels." One such channel, as he saw it, was the Chinese Communist Party. Never a Communist himself, he however believed that "communism can be a vehicle for human betterment and that Christians can learn from other people, even atheists." He was one of the Christians who attended the Chinese People's Consultative Conference in September

196

1949, the meeting at which a Provisional Constitution for China was approved that included a clause on religious freedom.

Another noted Chinese Protestant who shared his views was Zhao Zichen (T. C. Chao), a professor of theology at both Yenching University and Nanjing's Jinling Union Theological Seminary and a former vice-president of the World Council of Churches. Zhao once said of the victorious Communist revolution, "what many missionaries regard as a disaster, we regard as liberation."

In April 1951, more than 150 Protestant church leaders voted to sever all ties with foreign missions. Soon afterward, the Three-Self Patriotic Movement developed widely throughout the country. In July 1954, a National Conference of Chinese Christians was held in Beijing at which there were 232 representatives from 62 churches and Protestant organizations. Never before had this many Chinese Protestants from such diverse backgrounds met together. The conference announced the establishing of the Three-Self Patriotic Movement Committee of the Protestant Churches of China, under the chairmanship of Wu Yaozong. Wu died in 1979, and Ding Guangxun (K. H. Ting) now serves as the chairman.

Soon after the formation of the Three-Self Patriotic Movement, Chinese Protestants turned their attention to the question of how to resolve the denominational differences between them. Such differences were the vestiges of the many different Protestant denominations that had competing missionary programs in China. The Three-Self Patriotic Movement decided that they needed to end the denominational system and become a post-denominational church.

The denominational disagreements were many. Even the most simple things, such as how to translate the word "God" into Chinese, revealed these differences. There were traditionally two versions of such a translation that were preferred by different Protestant denominations. Both had been accepted and used at the China Bible House to satisfy conflicting denominational views. In one version the word

"Shen" (meaning deity or spirit) was used for "God." In the other, the word "Shangdi" (meaning the supreme being above) was used. There were also disagreements over how to conduct baptisms, communions, and ordinations, and whether the Sabbath is on Sunday or Saturday.

In the city of Nanjing alone, in 1949, there were 35 different Protestant churches for only 500 Protestant members. Almost every denomination wanted to have a church in this city because it was the Nationalist government's capital. By 1958 the Three-Self Protestant Patriotic Movement of Nanjing had agreed that they really needed only four of these buildings. There are more in use today. The struggle to achieve consensus among the Protestants consumed most of the energies of the Three-Self Patriotic Movement from 1958 to 1960.

Although it is the uniting organization among Protestants, the Three-Self Patriotic Movement is not a church. There is no Protestant Church of China in the way that there is a Catholic Church. Instead, the Three-Self Patriotic Movement is an organization that assists churches in their development. A national Protestant church, or even a church constitution, has yet to be born. All the Protestant churches carry on their local programs with a great deal of autonomy. They loosely cooperate with one another, but that is all.

The various titles used for church leaders are a carry over from former years — pastor, elder, teacher, brother, and sister. The term bishop is more one of respect than one of authority. There are eight bishops. Two were consecrated before 1949, another two in the early 1950s, two in 1955, and two in 1988. The latter two are Bishops Sun Yanli and Shen Yifan. They were elected at a meeting of the Administrative Commission of the Shanghai Protestant Churches.

Sun Yanli, born in 1914 and baptized in a church of the Methodist denomination, was the head pastor at Shanghai's Muen Memorial Church at the time of his consecration. He was ordained in 1941, and graduated from the Nanjing Theological Seminary in 1944. He is now chairman of the Administrative Commission of the Shanghai Protestant Churches and President of the East China Theological Seminary.

Shen Yifan, born in 1928 and raised an Anglican, was ordained in 1954, after attending the Central College of Theology. He then became pastor of Shanghai's Community Church. His father, Shen Zigao, was a former bishop in the Anglican Church in China and President of the Central College of Theology. Shen Yifan, besides being a bishop, is now vice-chairman of the China Christian Council, established in 1980.

CONTINUING DEVELOPMENT

The Second National Conference of Chinese Christians was held in Shanghai from November 12, 1960, until January 14, 1961. It had 319 delegates from 25 different provinces of China. Its decisions relating to the establishment of the post-denominational church in China were soon put aside by the outbreak of the Cultural Revolution.

This Cultural Revolution lasted from 1966 to 1976. It was a period of trial by fire for Chinese Protestants. It was also a time when all the external attributes of religion (churches, Bibles, hymn books) were taken away from the church goers, and they had to rely on what they had learned in the past from their religious training. Public meetings were not allowed, so people met in house gatherings quietly and in secret. These religious gatherings became a meaningful alternative to a society being wrenched apart by political conflicts.

The experience, I was told, brought Christians together with the Chinese people as never before. With church doors closed, pastors and church workers were put to work in factories and fields, alongside many non-Christian Chinese people. They thus learned how to relate their Christian understanding to other Chinese in a way that no foreign missionary ever did or perhaps could even fully appreciate. I was told that the Protestants came out of the Cultural Revolution experience with a new appreciation of Christian community. Having suffered together, they now know how to better minis-

199

ter to one another.

In October 1980, the Third National Conference of Chinese Christians convened in Shanghai. It focused on the urgency of reopening the churches that were closed during the Cultural Revolution, and on developing a program of theological education. This conference established the China Christian Council to serve the pastoral and ecclesiastical needs of the Protestant churches. Although the China Christian Council works closely with the Three-Self Patriotic Movement, it is distinguished from the Three-Self Movement by the fact that it works directly with and through the ordained pastors, while the Three-Self Movement is an organization of all the Protestant churches and their members in China. Ding Guangxun serves as the China Christian Council chairman, as well holding that post in the Three-Self Patriotic Movement. Provincial Christian Councils have also been established to deal with issues related to the Protestant community within each province. And under these there are some local Christian Councils.

The Fourth National Conference of Chinese Christians met in Beijing in August 1986. All provinces and regions in China were represented, with the exception of Tibet. At least a third of the delegates were women, and each of the Protestant seminaries established since the Cultural Revolution were represented by both faculty and students. The Fifth National Conference was held, also in Beijing, in January 1992. During this meeting, 45 young pastors were ordained. (By this date there were 13 Protestant seminaries training young Christians.)

China now has over 7,000 Protestant churches and 5,500,000 Protestant Christians. That is nearly an eight fold increase over the 1949 figure of 700,000 Christians. During the late 1980s and early 1990s there was a Protestant church in China being built or reopened every two days. All these churches are crowded, and in many of them the congregation is at least 50% under the age of 35. It is often necessary to hold two or more Sunday services in the churches of the larger cities to avoid overcrowding.

In Zhejiang Province, the second smallest province in China, there are 1,600 Protestant churches. Of these, 500 are newly built. The total number of Protestants there is about 800,000-1,000,000 more than all Protestants in China before the Communist revolution. In Wuyang County of Henan Province there were less than 1,000 Protestant Christians in 1949. Now there are 15,000. The church in the county seat had 36 members in 1949, and now has more than 650 baptized members. A survey of Laian County in Anhui Province, made in the early 1950s, showed only 11 Christians. Now there are 989.

Besides the Protestant churches in China, there are about 20,000 self-governing, self-supporting, and self-propagating groups of Protestants meeting in homes or places other than conventional church buildings. These assembly points are mostly scattered in rural areas, but some are also in the cities. Throughout China there are only about 1,000 ordained ministers. Of these, 90 are women, or a little under 10 percent of the total. There are also many volunteer lay preachers, both men and women, to service this large number of churches and meeting places.

Some persons in the West have promoted the belief that the meeting points, sometimes called house churches, that are used by the Protestants are an organized form of resistance to the established Protestant Three-Self Patriotic Movement. But this is hardly the case. There is some opposition to the Three-Self Movement, as we will see below. However it is not found throughout the so-called house church system.

Raymond W. M. Fung, formerly of the Hong Kong Christian Council, made a careful study of 42 such meeting-point gatherings in 11 provinces during the early 1980s and found that few of them could be designated as opposed to the Three-Self Patriotic Movement. He concluded, "nowhere have we discovered the kinds of division that lend support to the theory that there are two Protestant churches in China, the 'Three-Self church' and the 'house churches.'"

Many of the participants in these meeting-point churches

are also members of one or another of the established churches. Some of these people prefer to go to the meeting points because they are smaller and therefore more intimate, and they are nearer to their homes so that the participants don't have to travel far. The mother of Ding Guangxun was the leader of one of these home meeting points until she had passed the age of 97. She died at age 101. She was a strong supporter of the Three-Self Patriotic Movement that her son now heads.

I was told by Reverend Cao Shengjie, the Associate General Secretary of the China Christian Council and a woman pastor of Grace Church in Shanghai, that more than half the members of the churches and meeting points in China are women. As she put it, "although, according to Chairman Mao's famous quote 'women hold up half the sky,' in the Protestant churches, women hold up more than half the sky."

In all my interviews with Protestant leaders, I was told that most of the worshipers in the meeting points and those in the churches work closely together. Some of the meeting-point worshipers hope to be able to construct church buildings someday so as to replace their homes as gathering sites.

THE DISSIDENTS

Many Protestant leaders told me that they are unhappy with the way some church people outside China try to perpetuate the "underground church" theory. They say that such activity cannot help, but can only hurt Christians within China. These leaders believe that those who insist on describing the Chinese church as divided between the Three-Self churches and the house churches are nurturing denominationalism — just what the Chinese Protestants wanted to get rid of when they declared their church post-denominational. They no longer want Protestant Christians divided into Baptists, Methodists, Presbyterians, Lutherans, Anglicans, Seventh-Day Baptists, etc.

The outsiders, waving the banners of "Preaching the

Gospel'' and "China Ministries'' plan strategies in Hong Kong to infiltrate China and set up anti-Three-Self house meetings, I was told. They broadcast from Hong Kong stations to the "people of China'' in an attempt to split the church and destroy Christian unity. They also call, in subtle ways, for the overthrow of the government of China.

Regardless of what the intent of these outsiders may be, their statistics are grossly off the mark. A so-called Chinese Research Center in Hong Kong puts the number of "house church'' members at 30 to 50 million. They describe the movement as "secret, having no set time or place of meeting.'' It is difficult to imagine how such a large underground army of 30 to 50 million Christians could exist without being known to the authorities of the Religious Affairs Bureau or to the members of the Three-Self Patriotic Movement. After all, 50 million is half the number of all religious persons in all of China (Buddhists, Taoists, Muslims, and Christians). Such fabrications can only confuse religious persons living outside of China. The Chinese, themselves, find such statistics amusing.

Outsiders also spread the myth that Chinese Christians are in desperate need of Bibles. Some of these myth spreaders collect large sums of money from eager but naive Christians in the United States and Europe for the purpose of purchasing Bibles for the Chinese. It is probably that only a small portion of this money ever gets used for this purpose, and then it is used illegally — to smuggle the books into China. What these Bibles for China promoters never tell their contributors is the fact that the Bible is openly published and distributed in large quantities throughout China.

One more thing about the Bibles printed in China today is that they are printed in the simplified form of the Chinese written language that was adopted by the government in the 1950s. This is now universally used throughout China. The Bibles printed overseas, as distinguished from those printed in China, still have the traditional form of the language that is used in Taiwan. Many Chinese youth can't read this old form, and so the smuggled Bibles are rather useless in the

Chinese churches.

Because there is so much confusion in the West over this matter of Bible smuggling, it should be pointed out that it isn't illegal for foreigners to bring Bibles into China. Nor is it against the law for any Chinese to own their own copy of the Bible. Bibles are even sometimes used in university classes as a tool for mastering the English language. But government policy says tourists and visitors can't import Bibles "in excess of personal use." The government also rules it illegal to accept mission funds from foreign religious sources whose aim is "infiltration" in an attempt to gain control over Chinese churches, temples, or mosques.

As said earlier, there are Chinese Christians who oppose the Three-Self Patriotic Movement and the established Protestant churches. Some of these are persons who use the language of Christianity to defraud others of money and food by pretending to be preachers. They hate the Three-Self Patriotic Movement because it criticizes such charlatans and exposes their activities.

I was told about one family in a village of Hebei Province that raises fish for a living and has a donkey-cart for transportation. One day the man of the house, a Christian, heard one of the self-appointed preachers saying that Jesus would be coming immediately. After that, the man refused to do any work and the donkey stood idle. The family income ceased. The man spent all his hours in prayer. To make matters worse, he refused to allow his son to continue attending middle school. The son, in desperation, wrote to the civil authorities, saying "Come to the rescue of this family, or we shall all be ruined." The authorities came and eventually convinced the father to take a more rational view of life, thus averting a tragedy.

In Hunan Province there was a man, newly converted to Christianity by a self-appointed preacher, who, I was told, killed his own son in an attempt to reach God through a re-enactment of the story of Abraham and Isaac. The incident saddened the leaders of the Three-Self Movement and was an example to them of the lack of trained leadership in the rural areas. In Anhui Province, seven women drowned themselves in the Cihuaixin River while waiting for the Second Coming of Jesus. They had been told by Sun Yingpeng, a self-appointed preacher from Lixin County, that Jesus would come by a holy boat and that they should go into the water to await its arrival and thus be saved from the impending Day of Judgment.

There are also some properly-ordained evangelists who oppose the position of the Three-Self leaders on grounds of principle. Such a person was the recently-deceased Wang Mingdao, who was lauded by some circles in the West for "opposing the communist control of the Chinese churches." But Wang Mingdao's complaints against the Three-Self Movement had nothing to do with its patriotic stance nor the fact that this movement cooperates with the government. Wang Mingdao advocated an old-fashioned gospel to his Beijing followers, and opposed the Three-Self Movement for being too "modernist" in theology. He opposed most other Protestants around the world for the same reason. In their modernism, he said, they "forsake Christian truth and preach atheism."

Before 1949, Wang Mingdao refused support from any missionary denomination, and after the Communists gained control of China, he refused to cooperate in any way with the new rulers. His obstinacy finally led to his arrest on political charges and not religious ones. A short time afterwards he signed a confession in jail and was released, only to renounce the confession and end up in jail again.

Another opponent of the Three-Self Patriotic Movement was Jing Dianying, leader of the Jesus Family. His followers practiced a communal form of life long before China became a Communist country. But this leader demanded that filial piety be practiced to enforce absolute obedience to himself. He insisted that all the male followers below the age of 70 and all the female followers below the age of 60 be married. These demands brought him into conflict with the government, which was seeking to free women from the traditional bonds of the old patriarchal society. Other leaders of this group were charged with attempts at faith healing, which the health officials allege resulted in some deaths. Most of the leaders of this Jesus Family group were eventually arrested for their refusal to abide by government rules and regulations.

Then there is the Little Flock sect that has been disrupting church services by shouting and yelling as loud as possible during sermons and hymn singing. This group was founded by Watchman Nee, who now resides in Southern California where he produces numerous tracts to be distributed in Taiwan, Hong Kong, and China. There have been times when these "Yellers" were so disruptive that the public security bureau had to intervene and take them in for questioning. Unfortunately such incidents have been publicized overseas as "religious persecution."

Not all the Little Flock members agree that the Three-Self Patriotic Movement should be opposed. Some cooperate with the established churches, but most do not. I was told that in Zhejiang Province, Protestants in the Three-Self Patriotic Movement contributed money to supply Bibles and hymnals to the Little Flock congregations in an attempt to win them over. Some Little Flock leaders accepted the gifts and put them to use, but first cut out the title page that identified them as having been printed by the China Christian Council.

Critics in the West of the Chinese Protestant church sometimes ask, "Why does the established church in China never question the government?" However it only takes a few visits with Chinese Christian leaders to realize that they are constantly in dialogue with the local, provincial, and national leaders of their government. They raise problems with government officials related to government activities and to the policies in regard to religion. And there is ample evidence that the government responds to their requests. The critics in the West might do well to go to China and talk to the Protestant leaders before voicing such criticisms.

SOME CHURCHES

An American visitor attending a worship service in any Chinese Protestant church will find much that is familiar, but also many things that are different. The visitor will find that the order of worship, use of the Lord's Prayer, and many of the hymns are the same. But the session will usually begin with a time for teaching the assembled congregation how to sing the hymns for that day's service. This not only familiarizes the congregation with unknown tunes but gives some of the older persons, who may never have learned how to read, a chance to memorize the words. The sermon will usually last for at least fifty minutes and sometimes for more than an hour. Also the visitor will immediately note that various persons in the congregation are worshipping in individual ways. Some may be kneeling in prayer while others only bow their heads. Some may be reading the Bible while others sing hymns. These differences are remnants of many denominational practices that existed before 1949.

Pastor Kan Xueqing of the Chongwenmen Church in Beijing has the distinction of being the first Protestant pastor to return to preaching after the Cultural Revolution, a time in which he worked in a factory. Besides his church duties, Pastor Kan, who was ordained in 1965, is general secretary of the Beijing Christian Council. He is from the third generation in a family converted by Methodist missionaries. His church is packed every Sunday with more than 1,600 in attendance. The members come from diverse denominational backgrounds. Communion here is offered according to the traditions of five different denominations. As Pastor Kan explains, "We are seeking unity, but are preserving diversity." It is not easy to become a Christian in this church. A person desiring to do so must first attend services for a full year and also take a pre-baptismal training course.

There are now 24 Protestant churches and 57 meeting points in the city of Shanghai proper, and every Sunday there are between 20,000-30,000 people who worship at these churches and meeting points. Each is crowded on Sundays.

Many of the meeting points have more than 1,000 participants. The few pastors in this city have to travel a great deal to care for all these congregations. Bishop Sun Yanli told me that he was trying to convince the members of the largest meeting points to build themselves churches rather than to continue to meet in homes.

Shanghai's Muen Church was occupied by a middle school during the Cultural Revolution. When it was returned to the Protestants in 1979, only the sanctuary was vacated by the school. The church members, with the help of the Religious Affairs Bureau, negotiated with the school to get it to move out of the rest of the building one room at a time. The process took five years to complete. Repairs had to be made to the church tower and every room because most of the windows were broken and the benches had been removed.

The Muen Church has Saturday services as well four Sunday services, and there are church activities (prayer service, Bible study, choir practice) going on at the church every day of the week. I was told that the church has a free medical clinic every Sunday after the main service. Doctors and nurses who are members provide the service. They also have evening classes in English and Japanese that are open to the public. They donate funds from their collection to flood relief, aid to the disabled, and other social services. They are particularly proud of one of their members, a woman chemist named Wang Juzhen, who developed a special material to block nuclear radiation. She won a First Prize from the government for this achievement that is now used not only in China but in many other countries. She is a member of the Shanghai Christian Council and a vice president of the Shanghai YMCA. Many other members of this church and of the Christian community in Shanghai have been honored by the government as model workers.

The Shanghai Community Church, reopened in 1980, has two services every Sunday morning and one on Saturday. During the Cultural Revolution it was used for rehearsals by a Peking Opera troupe. At that time all the church symbols, books, and chairs were lost or destroyed. On the day that the church was reopened, they had to use chairs loaned to them by the local district government.

The sanctuary during worship services is so crowded that many people have to sit in the church hall and chapel on the second and third floors of a side building, where they join in the worship with the help of closed-circuit television. Over one-third of the members are under the age of 40. During the week there are many Bible study classes, prayer meetings, and hymn-singing meetings. There are fellowship programs for retired persons, women, and youth. There are also children's classes for small children during the Sunday worship service. The church has two choirs that together hold a sacred music service once a month. The church also conducts a spare-time class for those who want to learn to speak English, and it has a medical clinic for people in the neighborhood.

The pastor told me about a woman ticket collector, working for the city bus line, who recently joined the church. A passenger got on her bus one day and bought a 15-cent ticket. The passenger then wanted to pay for 30 more such tickets. The collector asked why, and the passenger explained that he had sneaked onto the bus many times in the past and now wanted to make compensation for this behavior, because he had become a Christian. The ticket collector was amazed. It was a common practice for people to sneak onto the buses without paying, and nobody before had ever offered to make up for the losses. Out of curiosity, she decided to visit the church that can produce such behavior in its members. Now the ticket collector is also a regular member of this church.

Grace Church in Shanghai averages more than 5,500 participants in three weekend services, Saturday morning, Sunday morning, and Sunday evening. The Saturday morning service was initiated for those who came from a Seventh-Day Baptist tradition. I was told, however, that most of the former Seventh-Day Baptists now go to one of the other churches. Yet the Saturday service is continued for those who have to work at secular jobs on Sunday.

In the city of Nanjing, in Jiangsu Province, there are

now 10 churches and 21 ordained pastors. Eight of the pastors are over 80 years of age and all but one of the others are over 60. The young one is only 26. There are 50,000 Protestants in the Nanjing area and 10,000 in the city proper. At the Mochou Road Church, constructed in 1936 and used as a factory during the Cultural Revolution, there are about 1,000 people every Sunday at the service. More than half of these are young people. There were 1,000 persons baptized there in 1990 alone. Persons who wish to be baptized into the Protestant faith at this church must have been believers for at least three years and be more than 16 years old.

St. Paul's Church also has an attendance in excess of 1,000. Part of the church property (the pastor's residence) is still occupied by an optical factory that controlled the whole structure during the Cultural Revolution. They have two services on Sunday, one at 7:30 a.m. and the other at 9 a.m. They also have an adult Bible class on Friday, but no class for children on Sunday because there is no space for this.

The city of Wenzhou, in Zhejiang Province, has almost 400,000 Protestants, who meet in more than 2,000 churches and meeting points. There are so many Christians here that the city is sometimes referred to as China's Jerusalem. Yet there are only 133 full-time clergy and church workers, including 23 newly graduated seminarians. So a great deal depends on help from voluntary church members. There are 3,000 lay men and women who act as voluntary church workers within this city. They teach Bible classes, organize church meetings, do construction and renovation work in the church buildings, and keep the finances.

Chengxi Church is the oldest and largest church in the city. It was formerly an English Methodist church, and was founded 100 years ago (it is marked for historic preservation by the municipal government). Half of the property has yet to be returned to the church, because it is still being used as a factory. When this portion is returned, Chengxi Church will be the largest Protestant church building in China. It has a membership of 3,000.

Pastor Li, the senior pastor of this church, says that they have three Sunday services and two afternoon choir practices. On Wednesday there is a Bible class for young people; on Thursday afternoon, a women's Bible class; and on Thursday evening, a men's Bible class. Friday evenings are devoted to a prayer meeting. A young adults fellowship is held Saturday evenings. There is also a Saturday morning prayer service beginning at 8 a.m.

I was told that churches in Wenzhou and the surrounding counties all have children's classes on Sunday, known as *xiaozi ban*. The government permits these, it is said, because otherwise the "children would disturb the church services." Wenzhou has its own regional hymnal with selections chosen by each of the six Protestant denominations that were present before 1949. Surplus church funds are pooled for building new churches in the region.

In Quanzhou in Fujian Province I visited two churches that have factories attached to them. One, the Seventh-Day Church, makes ceramic statues that are sold all over the world. The other, South Church, makes shoes that are sold throughout the province. Both factories support the attached churches and employ church members and non-church members in the production lines.

Factories attached the churches in China are not unique to Quanzhou. At Zhengzhou, in Henan Province, a Protestant church is supported by the Zhengzhou New Life Chemical Industrial Association, a factory that makes skin cream and powdered shampoo. All the workers in this factory are Protestants and members of this church.

THEOLOGICAL EDUCATION

Theological education is a high priority of the Three-Self Patriotic Movement because of the grave shortage of preachers. At present there are only about 6,000 pastors in the whole country. The Jinling Union Theological Seminary, in Nanjing, after being closed for 15 years, was reopened in February, 1981. The 51 students in the first class when it

211

reopened were chosen by examination from 308 final applicants (drawn from several thousand) recommended by their local churches. They came from 22 different provinces and included 22 women and 29 men, ranging in age from 19 to 35. About two-fifths of them came from non-Christian families. They were financially supported by their local churches and some seminary scholarships. The course of study takes four years, and the seminary is headed by Ding Guangxun.

The course of study at this seminary is divided into four basic areas: Biblical, Pastoral, Theological, and Historical. The students are expected to read the Bible in its entirety during the first year of study. Courses in Chinese language and culture, world and church history, political affairs, and languages (English, German, Greek, and Hebrew) are taught. Music and art are highlighted, and the seminary choir is well known throughout the province for its ability. The seminary publishes twice a year the *Jinling Theological Review*, which covers a wide range of topics from Biblical studies to hymns and notes from seminary alumni and local pastors. Eleven graduates have been sent to the United States, Canada, Great Britain, and Germany for advanced study.

One of the graduates of this seminary is a woman who was the daughter of two Communist leaders. Before the Cultural Revolution she was educated in a special school for the children of Communist leaders in Beijing, and during the Cultural Revolution she went to the countryside to work in a factory. She was very lonely and eventually developed a friendship with another factory worker, a Protestant. She visited a Protestant church where she found the kind of care and friendship that was missing in her life. This convinced her to become a Christian, and she did so against the wishes of her parents. The struggle between her parents and herself was not resolved until many years later. The church she joined promoted her candidacy for seminary training, and she is now an ordained minister serving a church in a large city.

Since the opening of the seminary in Nanjing, 12 more theological institutes have been established. They are located in the cities of Beijing, Tianjin, Shenyang, Shanghai, Wuhan,

Chengdu, Fuzhou, Hangzhou, Hefei, Guangzhou, Jinan, and Kaifeng. The curriculum at these institutes is similar to that used at the Jinling Seminary, although theirs is only a two-year course. Together with Jinling, they have about 700 students, and they have graduated 1,300 students so far. Fifty per cent of these are women, all of them planning for ordination. The students return to their local churches after graduation.

In some cities, graduates become ordained only after about three years experience in church work, but elsewhere ordination can take up to four or more years. The veneration of age over youth is a major factor in Chinese society, and so young graduates have to prove their ability in church work for some years before they will be accepted for ordination.

Short-term courses are held in many provinces for voluntary lay leaders, and a monthly syllabus is sent from the Nanjing theological school to approximately 45,000 lay leaders. The Nanjing theological school also sponsors a correspondence course in the Bible that takes three to four years to complete. There are about 3,000 students presently enrolled in this course.

PUBLICATIONS

The Three-Self Patriotic Movement together with the China Christian Council sponsor the journal, *Tian Feng* (*Heavenly Breezes*) that is edited by Shen Chengen. It has a circulation of 40,000 copies. They have printed more than five million copies of the Bible, including copies printed in five other languages used by ethnic minorities in China. They furthermore publish a number of religious books. Twice a year they print and distribute *Sermon Collections*, a collection of about twenty of the best sermons preached by Chinese pastors.

They have produced a new Chinese hymnal that is widely used. About 2.3 million copies of this have been printed. One of the editors of this hymnal was Cao Shengjie, a woman pastor in Shanghai. It has 400 hymns of which 106 have been written by Chinese. Half of these were composed after 1981.

SOCIAL SERVICE AND THE AMITY FOUNDATION

Almost all the Protestant churches have their own programs of social service and they raise funds for such national government campaigns as support of the handicapped and flood relief. Some churches have established homes for senior citizens and visitation programs for the elderly and those with disabilities. Many also on certain days set up public medical clinics in front of their churches, as well as stalls to provide free haircuts, do mending, and serve tea without charge. The largest churches contribute significant funds to the Amity Foundation, established in Nanjing in April 1985, which is one of the most unusual service-oriented organizations in the world.

While designed to contribute to humanitarian needs in a socialist country, the Amity Foundation is not run by the government as are most other such institutions in socialist countries. It is a non-governmental organization that was initiated by individual Chinese Protestants. Its board of directors includes religious and non-religious persons, and it is neither a religious organization nor a division of the Chinese Protestant Church.

The purpose of the Amity Foundation is to contribute to China's social development through the fields of education, public health and welfare, and printing and publishing. It also desires to make Christian involvement and participation more widely known to the Chinese people, and serves as an international channel for resources and people-to-people relationships.

In regard to education, by 1990 the Amity Foundation had invited 312 foreign teachers to China to teach English, German, and Japanese in over 60 institutions of higher learning throughout the country. Priority in the placement of these teachers was given to small, local teachers colleges and other institutions with low funding. The Amity Foundation also organizes lecture trips for specialists from overseas and helps to arrange for opportunities for Chinese students to engage in overseas study.

In the field of public health and social welfare, the Amity Foundation sponsors more than 50 projects in eight provinces. It provides advanced medical equipment for departments of internal medicine, ophthalmology, gynecology and obstetrics, and pediatrics in Jiangsu, Zhejiang, Hunan, Henan, and Sichuan provinces, and in the cities of Beijing and Shanghai. It holds training classes on children's nutrition, recovery of disabled children, and ways to assist retarded adults and children. Amity has initiated a center for the rehabilitation of hearing impaired children. The computerized artificial limbs project that it jointly sponsors with a university in Jiangsu Province won a gold medal at the Beijing International Fair in 1989.

The Amity Foundation has organized a number of rural development projects aimed at improving irrigation systems, reclaiming wasteland, and popularizing advanced farming techniques in rural areas where the standard of living is not as high as it is in other parts of China. The Foundation has also contributed emergency relief to areas affected by forest fires, hurricanes, earthquakes, and floods. In 1991, monsoon rains caused the worst flooding that China has experienced during the 20th century. Eighteen provinces were affected and over 35,000 villages were covered with water. Nearly ten million people were made homeless. The Amity Foundation immediately launched a program to build 10,000 shelters and homes for families in some of the affected counties. They also provided funds to purchase cotton-padded overcoats for the flooded-out farmers during the cold winter, and helped the farmers to erect temporary structures for primary schools.

In printing and publishing, under a joint venture with the United Bible Societies, the Amity Printing Company has set up modern facilities for the printing of Bibles and other Christian literature. It also serves the general public by printing books, magazines, and pictures in the areas of culture, education, and public health.

There are eight criteria used by the Amity Foundation to select a project to which they will commit people and resources. These include many assurances: that the receiving institution has competent leadership; that the projects are of a pioneering nature with a multiplying effect that can reach large numbers of people; that the project will have basic facilities, adequate personnel, and careful planning; and that support will be present for the development of local communities where the help is most needed. For each project, Amity insists that structures be established to enable decision making at the local level.

The Amity Foundation receives donations from many individuals and organizations outside of China as well as from churches and individuals within that country. Although funds from within China accounted for one-third of Amity's 1985 budget, in subsequent years over 90 percent of the funds have come from overseas. The foundation cooperates with and welcomes support from various Chinese government agencies in meeting humanitarian needs. As the general secretary of this agency, Han Wenzao, puts it, "As long as the government ensures religious freedom and effectively serves the people, we have no reason not to be cooperative."

THE YMCA AND YWCA

When the Communists took power in 1949, the YMCA and YWCA were in a different position from other Protestant organizations in China. They were completely independent of foreign control and were staffed and supported by Chinese. Both organizations were well known throughout the country for having popularized modern sports and for their welfare work. Their membership was open to all youth, both Christians and non-Christians. Some of the leaders — Wu Yaozong, Liu Liangmo, and Deng Yuzhi (Cora Deng) — were among the first Protestants to give support to the Communist cause. Also many of the Communist leaders, persons such as Zhou Enlai and Deng Yingchao, had been members of these organizations when they were university students and so gave them support when other religious groups were being criticized.

When the Communist government established the Chinese Youth Federation, it included both the YMCA and YWCA among the member organizations. Other members included the Young Communist League, and the Student Union. Thus the YMCA and YWCA fared better than did the churches during the Cultural Revolution, even though they were primarily Protestant organizations, although the activities of the Ys were suspended at that time.

The YMCA was founded in China in 1885 and the YWCA was founded in 1890, both originally in schools run by missionaries. Only later did city units become organized in Tianjin, Beijing, and Hangzhou. The YMCA building that was erected in Shanghai in the 1920s is still standing and being used by both the YMCA and the YWCA in that city today.

The purpose of the YMCA, when established, was to confront the youth of China with the Christian message. However, the movement spread throughout China because of its sports program. It was the YMCA that introduced modern sports — volleyball, basketball, gymnastics — to the Chinese people. It initiated the first National Athletic Meet ever held in China. This took place in Shanghai. The YMCA also introduced a series of popular science lectures in the 1920s that attracted a wide following.

The YWCA became famous throughout China for its evening education classes directed toward young women factory workers and for providing scholarships and living expenses to many poor students prior to 1949. The YWCA also established the first kindergarten in China, in the city of Shanghai, and the first physical education program for women in China. Today the organization works to improve the educational level of women and to enrich their leisure-time life.

Before 1949 there were about 2,000 cities and towns in China that had either a branch of the YMCA or YWCA, or both. The two organizations, at the time, were then receiving about eighty percent of their funding from the United States and other foreign sources. Today they are both self-supporting and there are YMCA and YWCA chapters only in Shanghai, Beijing, Tianjin, Xi'an, Wuhan, Nanjing, Guangzhou, Hangzhou, Chengdu, and Xiamen. However the membership is growing rapidly in these cities, and the leadership of both organizations consider this a good time for the growth of this movement in China.

The National Associations of both organizations are in Shanghai. The head of the YMCA is Li Shoubao. It has an elected 19-member board that includes some women. The head of the YWCA is Shi Ruzhang (Phoebe Shi), and it has a 21-member board, all women. One-third of the YWCA board is by tradition non-Christians. The two organizations are unique in that they cooperate with one another in their programs. The Ys in other parts of the world do not usually do this. Also the Chinese Catholics have a good working relationship with these two Protestant organizations, which does not often happen elsewhere.

The YMCA provides cultural, educational, and sports activities for young men and women. The YWCA holds similar activities for women, as well as operating nurseries and kindergartens. Sometimes they jointly sponsor activities. For example, in some cities they have opened training courses in foreign languages, tailoring, Chinese and English typewriting, repair of typewriters, computers, traditional Chinese painting, gymnastics, violin classes for pre-school children, garment designing, and Peking opera. They raise money for children's welfare and conduct international activities designed to enhance friendly contacts and visits.

With some financial support from the YMCA in the United States, the Chinese YMCA is in the process of constructing a large educational and medical complex in the ethnic minority area of Yunnan Province. When completed, this will include a school and hospital.

RELATIONS WITH OTHER CHURCHES AROUND THE WORLD

The principle of "Three-Selfs" doesn't mean that the

Chinese Protestants want to exist in isolation. On the contrary, Chinese Protestants hold that an independent and self-supporting church in China can contribute more to strengthening relations between churches around the world than a church dependent on support from others.

Chinese Protestants send delegations every year to visit churches in other countries and to participate in international conferences, such as the World Conference on Religion and Race. They have also invited many religious leaders and scholars of foreign countries to visit China. On February 18, 1991, at the Seventh Assembly of the World Council of Churches, held in Canberra, Australia, the China Christian Council was welcomed into membership in this organization.

THEOLOGY IN CHINA TODAY

Prior to 1949 there was hardly any theology that Protestants in China could claim to be characteristically their own. The churches merely reflected the theologies that were brought to China by the various missionary societies. But this is no longer the case. Although the sermons one hears on Sunday morning are generally conservative-evangelical in tone, the leading theologians in China are breaking new ground in Protestant Christian understandings.

Part of this new theology grows out of the experience of being Chinese and part of it out of the experience of living in a socialist society. Ever since at least the Song Dynasty, the prevailing view of human nature among the Chinese has been that persons are born good. It is an optimistic view, and is in direct contrast to the traditional European Christian view of human beings as bearers of original sin. Thus Chinese theology puts its stress on the image of God in all human beings and the indwelling of the Holy Spirit in the world.

The foremost proponent of Chinese theology is Ding Guangxun (K. H. Ting), who studied at the Union Theological Seminary in New York City, was secretary of the Student Christian Movement in Canada, and worked for the World Student Christian Federation in Geneva, Switzerland, before he returned to China in 1951. Speaking on the matter of sin, at Riverside Church in New York City in 1979, he said, "What is new … is the awareness that man is not only the sinner but also the sinned against, not only the violator of God's laws but also the violated against, and the realization that the task of evangelism is not just to convict man of sin but to stand alongside man the sinned against our society, to feel with him, to be for him. Just to convict man of sin is not yet evangelism proper. It doesn't necessarily move man to repentance and to acceptance of Christ as Savior."

The Chinese believe that they have entered into a new stage in human history — that of breaking away from exploitive capitalist systems and of building socialism in a country that was previously semi-colonial and semi-feudal in its structure. The Chinese Christians' response to this transition may be as significant as was the European Protestant response to the Reformation at the time when feudalism in Europe was changing into capitalism.

They readily admit the dangers in working closely with the Communists in building the new China, but again as Ding Guangxun puts it, "if we must err, I would prefer to err on the side of naivete rather than cynicism. The cynic bangs the door of opportunity himself and lands himself in nothing but spiritual frustration and greater cynicism. But the naive Christian worker sticks to his job. Doors banged against him will eventually give him the needed corrective to make him a true realist. There seem to be some redeeming possibilities in naivete that cynicism lacks."

The experiences of the Cultural Revolution have given the Chinese theologians an insight into the role of the broad masses of the people in revolutionary situations. Although they express appreciation for the way that Liberation Theology developed by Christians in Latin America mobilizes Christians in the struggle for more humane socio-economic systems, they do not think it fit to deify the poor and make economic justice the main content of Christian teaching. As Ding Guangxun puts it, we "would hesitate to think that the poor, just because they are poor, are necessarily the bearers

220

of truth and that the mandate of history is necessarily in the hands of the poor in their struggle against the rich. To be poor is miserable. The poor deserve justice. But poverty is no virtue, unless voluntary, and it does not always bring wisdom. To make a messiah of the poor just because they are poor, and to pit the poor against the rich without the guidance provided by correct theory is neither Marxist nor Christian. We saw its harm all the more clearly during the Cultural Revolution, which turned out to be very anticultural and not in any sense a revolution.''

Finally on the role of evangelism, Ding writes, ''A certain amount of religious freedom must exist for evangelism to happen. But religious freedom is not everything. There must be an enthusiasm and an inner drive to witness to Christ on the part of the church and its members. This enthusiasm comes from a spirituality in which Christ means everything to the believers rather than from a formal teaching on the Great Commission. When Christ means everything to the believers, they cannot but tell others of Him, and that is evangelism. Only then the question of methodology comes in. We in China do not have any overall plan for the evangelization of China, either in this generation or in a number of generations' time. I am inclined to think that a large part of the evangelistic work is being carried on by many Christians who are spreading the good news spontaneously, naturally, and perhaps unpurposively.''

VISITOR'S GUIDE TO PROTESTANT SITES

Almost every city in China has a Protestant church, and so do many villages. A visitor can usually find the address of one of the local churches by asking at the information desk in a hotel or by contacting the local Religious Affairs Bureau. The churches and other significant points of interest for Protestants that are listed below are ones that I have found to be the most interesting.

I would advise the visitor not to try to attend or participate in one of the Protestant meeting points. These are considered highly private affairs (like family gatherings) and the members do not generally welcome intruders. Don't be surprised if Chinese Christians tend to be suspicious of your motives in desiring to visit some meeting points. It is most difficult to arrange such visits and it usually takes several days to do so. Such arrangements can be made through the local Religious Affairs Bureau or at one of the Protestant churches.

1. Chongwenmen Church (City of Beijing)

This church, in the Xiaoshun Hutong area that is near the main train station, was the first Protestant church in the city of Beijing to be reopened after the Cultural Revolution. The Gothic-style building was erected by the Methodist Episcopal denomination in the 1870s. It was badly damaged during the Boxer Rebellion in 1900, and rebuilt in 1903. It is partly surrounded by a low-lying wall. The church is now somewhat difficult to locate because a large European-style hotel was recently built nearby, and this obstructs the view of the church from the street. However the desk clerk at the hotel will be able to direct the visitor to the small street at the rear and thence to the church gate.

2. Shanghai Community Church (City of Shanghai)

Located at 53 Hengshan Road (corner of South Urumqi Road), this church was built in 1925 and has a solemn neo-Gothic edifice. Even though the church is large, it is always crowded at its two Sunday morning services and the overflow crowd has to be seated in the hall and upstairs chapel where they can listen to the service over closed-circuit television.

3. Muen Church (City of Shanghai)

This church, formerly known as the Moore Memorial Methodist Church, is the largest Protestant church in Shanghai. It holds four church services on Sunday as well as one on Saturday. If you decide to attend a service here, plan to arrive early, as the church is always crowded. It has a fine choir that will make for a memorable visit.

4. Shanghai YMCA (City of Shanghai)

Both the headquarters of the YMCA and YWCA are in this ten-story building in traditional Chinese style located at 123 South Xizang Road. It was originally constructed as the YMCA building in Shanghai in the late 1920s and opened in 1929. It has since been completely renovated. The fourth to ninth stories of the building are used for a YMCA hotel that is open to both Chinese and foreign guests.

5. St. Paul's Church (Jiangsu Province)

This church in the city of Nanjing is located at 365 Taiping Road. It was formerly an Anglican church and resembles many that can be found in English villages. The church has two services on Sunday, one at 7:30 a.m. and the other at 9 a.m. Many of the foreign residents of Nanjing go to this church along with the more than 1,000 Chinese who attend every Sunday. The attached building, formerly the pastor's residence, is still occupied by an optical factory and so it cannot be visited.

6. Jinling Union Theological Seminary (Jiangsu Province)

The theological school in Nanjing is the leading Protes-

223

tant training institution in China. It is located on the campus of Nanjing University. It has a well-trained staff, fine library, and other facilities that are worth seeing. If school is in session, the visitor may want to talk with some of the students or professors. Most of them speak English.

7. Amity Offices (Jiangsu Province)

The Amity Foundation offices are located next to the Jinling Union Theological Seminary in Nanjing. This foundation was created on the initiative of Chinese Protestants for the purpose of promoting health, education, social service, and rural development in China. Its staff is involved in designing and handling a multitude of projects throughout the country. As an organization it is unique, and it represents a new form of Christian involvement in Chinese society. The visitor should plan to also see the Amity printing plant where many Bibles, books, and magazines are produced. Transportation will need to be arranged, since the printing plant is some distance from the offices.

8. Museum of the Taiping Revolution (Jiangsu Province)

Located in the rooms of a former palace (that of the founder of the Ming Dynasty), this was the residence of Hong Xiuquan, the leader of the Taiping Revolution, after his troops occupied the city of Nanjing. In 1958, it was opened as a museum of the Taiping Revolution. The museum tells of the ideals of this would-be Christian society. It also shows diagrams of the battles fought, describes personalities involved (including American and British mercenary soldiers who assisted the Taipings), and displays some of their weapons and uniforms. There are beautiful gardens in which the visitor can relax while visiting this museum.

9. Sishengci Church (Sichuan Province)

This church in the city of Chengdu has been completely rebuilt on the foundations of an old church that was badly damaged during the Cultural Revolution. It is used not only for church services (the chapel seats about 1,000 persons), but also as the site of the Sichuan Theological School.

10. Seventh-Day Baptist Church in Quanzhou (Fujian Province)

This church is in the fourth-story loft of a ceramics factory in Quanzhou. Income from the factory supports the work of the congregation. It employs several hundred Christians and non-Christians in production and design. The ceramic objects (dogs, cats, people, houses) are sold all over the world in gift shops. It is best to visit this church during the week so that you can see the factory in operation. It is closed on Saturdays because that is the day of worship. The visitor will find it impossible to attend a worship service because the church is so crowded. Because this site looks like any city factory, the visitor will need to get directions from the local Religious Affairs Bureau in order to find it.

Protestant Tourist Sites

ORTHODOX:

Remnants of a Dying Tradition

The Chinese Orthodox Church, formerly the Russian Orthodox Church, is rapidly disappearing from the religious landscape of China. It is the only worshipping group in China that is not growing. It is disappearing.

Two Chinese Orthodox churches have been reopened since the end of the Cultural Revolution, but their congregations are small because many of the Russians who once lived in China and were members of the various Russian Orthodox churches have returned to their home country. Some have emigrated elsewhere, to places such as the United States.

The first Orthodox Christians from Russia went to China in 1685. These included a priest and 31 prisoners of the Qing Dynasty, captured during the Battle of Albazin. After the prisoners were released, they stayed in China where they became paid soldiers in the army of the Qing emperor, Kangxi. In later years, the Orthodox Church in Russia assigned one priest and then another to go to China to minister to this small group of army recruits.

The Russian government sent an official Orthodox mission to the Qing emperor in 1715. And in 1727, with the signing of the Treaty of Kiatka, this mission became a permanent one in Beijing. By the 19th century, there were Russian Orthodox clergymen heading churches in Xinjiang, in Inner Mongolia, and in the cities of Harbin, Shanghai, Tianjin, Qingdao, and some other places.

It was not until about 1900, however, that the church began to try to evangelize among the non-Russian Chinese. Prior to that, all members of this church were either Russian citizens working temporarily in China or Chinese who were members of the Russian ethnic minority in China. It is reported that by 1916 there were 5,000 members of the Russian Orthodox Church in this country (most from the Russian ethnic minority), as well as 61 churches and 20 Russian missionaries who had been assigned there by the Primate in Moscow.

The Russian Revolution, in 1917, ended all mission support for the Orthodox Church in China. However, membership in the church increased with the influx of White Russian refugees, who settled in urban centers such as Harbin and Shanghai. Harbin was the end point of the Trans-Siberian Railroad and so there were many Russian railway workers living in this Chinese city at the time.

The city of Harbin still had 23 Russian Orthodox Churches with 140,000 members in 1949. These were mostly members of the Russian ethnic minority, but also included Russian citizens remaining in Harbin after Chinese Communists took over the country. The close working relationship that China now had with Russia brought many Soviet advisors to the city, some of whom worshiped in its Orthodox churches.

But in 1959, relations between the two countries began to deteriorate. Khrushchev publicly · criticized "certain" Chinese leaders and privately aimed his barbs at Chairman Mao Zedong. The Chinese retaliated by questioning some of the policies of Khrushchev and the Soviet Communist Party. In July 1960, the Soviet Party served notice on China that it would withdraw 1,390 Soviet experts from China within a month and would suspend 343 development contracts and close the 257 industrial projects they had established in China. All the Soviet advisors went home and many of the other Russians living in China went with them.

By the start of the Cultural Revolution, in 1966, there were only six Orthodox churches in Harbin and less than 2,000 members. Ten years later, there were only 50 Russians left in the city, and today it has just one church with about 200 members. These include 20 remaining Russians, more than 100 persons from the Russian ethnic minority in China, and the rest Chinese converts.

Debates began, as early as 1950, among Orthodox Church members as to whether or not they should maintain their formal relationship with the Russian Orthodox Church. By 1956, those advocating separation had won the day. The church members from various places in China held a conference and formally disassociated themselves from the Russian Orthodox Church, changing their name to that of the Chinese Orthodox Church. They decided, however, to continue to use the Russian language in their services because that was the language to which the membership was accustomed to use in their worship. It was a decision that would prevent further church growth and lead to an inevitable decline in membership.

Ten years later the Cultural Revolution put an end to Orthodox church services. The churches were closed and the various Red Guard units began their destructive campaigns against church property. The six Orthodox churches in Harbin were badly damaged. One of them was reopened in October 1984, after extensive repairs to the outside of the building.

There was no need to open any others. Harbin no longer had enough Orthodox members to merit any other churches. One of the former Orthodox churches in this city was leased to the Catholics, who renamed it the Virgin Mary Church. The others have been turned into office buildings or torn down to make room for housing.

The Bishop of the Chinese Orthodox Church died during the Cultural Revolution and no one has been named to replace him. Most of the former priests in Harbin were Russians, and they have since left China. The Chinese priests in that area of China have, for the most part, become so old that they can no longer take care of any congregation. The one priest who remains active is Zhu Shipu, who came to Harbin originally from Shanghai. He is now 68 years of age. He was trained for about nine years at the Russian Orthodox Training School in Beijing, and before 1949, was assigned to the Harbin area. The school in Beijing was closed after 1949.

When Zhu Shipu first came to the city, he was assigned

to be an assistant to one of the Russian priests. Over the years he served in five different churches in this city, usually as an assistant to the head Russian priest. During the Cultural Revolution he became a typesetter for a government printing office that produced materials in Russian and in English.

The church in Harbin is open every Sunday from 9 to 11:30 a.m. and also on church holidays (Christmas, Easter, Three Kings Day, and the other nine special holidays of the Orthodox calendar). The average age of the members is between 40 and 50 years, with the oldest being 86 and the youngest 30. More of the members are women than men. The service is conducted in Russian, and all the participants stand throughout it, just as they do in other Orthodox churches around the world.

The priest conducts baptisms, marriages, and funerals for members of the congregation. He gets assistance in this from three or four members of the congregation, both male and female. He told me that the members talk of the need to train some new priests, but no course of study has yet been designed for this purpose. When it is, he will be the person who will have to do most of the teaching, since he is the only active priest in the Harbin area.

The church appears to have no outreach program and stands empty much of the week. Part of its property, once used for a Russian Orthodox school, is now an office complex for a computer firm. The rent from this office building provides the main income for the church. They also maintain an Orthodox cemetery in the suburbs of the city.

There have been no formal exchanges between the Chinese Orthodox Church and the Russian or other Orthodox churches in the world, although this church in Harbin has welcomed some foreign visitors, particularly Russian tourists, to its Sunday services.

The priest, Zhu Shipu, is member of the provincial People's Political Consultative Conference, a post he holds as the representative of the Orthodox Community in Heilongjiang Province. He told me that this allows him to voice criticisms of the government and make suggestions to it.

I asked him what he saw as the future for the Chinese Orthodox Church. Zhu Shipu replied, "It is hard to say whether the church has a future or not. As far as I am concerned, I will continue to serve the church in this life, and God in the next."

There is one other Chinese Orthodox Church that has opened since the end of the Cultural Revolution. This one is in Urumqi, the capital of northwest China's Xinjiang Uygur Autonomous Region, an area with about 2,600 inhabitants who belong to the Russian ethnic minority. This church reopened in 1985. The head of the Orthodox community in this city is reportedly a woman by the name of Seyniya. She is over 80 years in age and has a daughter living in the former Soviet Union and a son living in Australia. The church was badly damaged during the Cultural Revolution, and the government provided a large sum for its renovation.

In the next chapter we will look at the history of a religious group no longer represented in China, the Jewish community of Kaifeng. We include it because there is wide interest in the West in this particular community.

VISITOR'S GUIDE TO ORTHODOX SITES

There are only three places that a person interested in the Chinese Orthodox Church can visit, and one of these is not open for worship. However, this church in Shanghai is well worth seeing because of its beauty. Just after World War II, it was a bustling center of Russian Orthodox activities in China.

1. Closed Orthodox Church (City of Shanghai)

This church is at the corner of Xinle Road and North Xiangyang Road. It is a structure of Byzantine architecture with four beautiful towers crowned with blue and gold roofs. It is closed to visitors and empty inside, but the outside is well maintained by the city of Shanghai. Perhaps someday it will be refurnished and turned into a museum. The number of Orthodox believers in Shanghai is too small to support any religious congregation.

2. Church of the China Orthodox Community (Heilongjiang Province)

Located at 54 East Dazhi Street in Harbin, Nan'gang District, this church was built in 1930, opened in 1936, and closed in 1958. This was several years before the start of the Cultural Revolution, in which the exterior of the building was badly damaged. In 1984 the church was renovated by the government and it is now open again. The adjoining building, which was once used as a Russian Orthodox training school, is now rented by the church for the offices of a computer company. The Orthodox priest also lives there. Services are in Russian and begin at 9 a.m. each Sunday morning. Most of the rest of the week it is closed, and so the visitor may have to find the church janitor, who lives on the property, to get permission to enter.

It is a small church, but quite attractive. The architecture is Byzantine. Another church on the same street and only a few doors away is a Protestant structure of Gothic architecture. The visitor to Harbin may also see the Orthodox cemetery that the Orthodox church maintains, which is in the suburbs. Directions and permission to visit this site can be obtained from the priest at the church.

3. Orthodox Church (Xinjiang Uygur Autonomous Region)

The Chinese Orthodox Church in Urumqi, the capital of northeast China's Xinjiang Uygur Autonomous Region, reopened in 1985 after having been closed for twenty years. The building was badly damaged during the Cultural Revolution. It is located in the southwestern part of the city and has been completely renovated. Services are held on Sunday morning.

Orthodox Tourist Sites

HISTORICAL NOTES ON THE JEWS

There is no worshipping community of Jews anymore in China, and there hasn't been one for a long time. However, there remain several hundred residents of the city of Kaifeng, in Henan Province, who consider themselves ethnic Jews in spite of the fact that they have had no rabbi for nearly 200 years, no synagogue for more than 100 years, and no Jewish communal organizations for generations. They remember nothing of their faith or the traditions of their ancestors. The only visible remnant of this community is a sign identifying the street on which many of them once lived. It reads: "Lane of the People Who Teach the Scriptures."

That the Kaifeng colony of worshipping Jews, isolated from the rest of the Jewish world, should persist in the heart of China for almost eight hundred years is one of the remarkable facts of the religious history of China. It points to the strength of religious traditions. It also demonstrates the tolerance of the Chinese toward all religions, so long as they never threaten the well-ordering of society. As the American historian Michael Pollack has pointed out in his book *Mandarins, Jews, and Missionaries*, the "Jews were at no time singled out for maltreatment by the bulk of Kaifeng's residents or subjected to the kind of governmentally inspired persecutions that their brethren in other lands knew only too well."

The earliest Jewish settlers in China apparently came from Persia, for it is known that they spoke a dialect of Judeo-Persian. They were traders who followed the ancient Silk Road through Central Asia until they reached the city of Kaifeng, where they settled in relatively large numbers. Some Western writers say that this was the farthest outpost of Judaism, but there were undoubtedly other Jews who settled in other parts of China that are even further out. There are direct and indirect references to Jews in ancient times living at Luoyang, Dunhuang, Guangzhou, Ganpu, Hangzhou, Ningbo, Beijing, Quanzhou, Ningxia, Yangzhou, and Nanjing.

The first Chinese record of the Kaifeng Jews dates to the year 950 when there were a number of Jewish families in Kaifeng working as merchants, peddlers, restauranteurs, teachers, physicians, and butchers. They had a rabbi with them and built their first synagogue in 1163 on land granted to them by the Song Dynasty (960-1279) emperor. They named the synagogue the Temple of Purity and Truth. Three hundred years after the emperor gave them the land, they recorded his words on a stone tablet: "Respect and preserve the customs of your ancestors, and hand them down here in Kaifeng." This tablet was carved in 1489, and is now preserved in the city museum.

The tablet lists their 17 family names as Yen, Ai, Gao, Mu, Shi, Huang, Nie, Zuo, Bai, two different families named Li, two different Zhaos, two different Jins, and two different Zhangs. By the 13th century there were more than 4,000 members of these 17 families in Kaifeng. In the 16th century there were still more than 2,000 of them. Intermarriage with the Chinese and migration of individuals to other places in China gradually reduced this number. Only seven families can be identified today in a Jewish population of about 200. Their surnames are Li, Ai, Gao, Zhao, Jin, Zhang, and Shi.

In the year 1279, the Jews of Kaifeng rebuilt and enlarged their synagogue, which may have been damaged during the Mongol Conquest. Some of the Kaifeng Jews at this time held military and administrative positions in the government. This was also the period when Marco Polo visited China and returned to Europe to report that there were several prosperous Jewish communities in that country. The synagogue was again repaired in 1421.

In 1605 Ai Tian, an elderly Kaifeng scholar and minor official, made a trip to Beijing to apply for a promotion in the imperial civil service. Ai Tian visited Matteo Ricci's Catholic community there, thinking it must be Jewish because he had heard that its members were not Muslims and worshipped only one God, as his own people did. Ricci invited Ai Tian into the Catholic chapel where they were celebrating the festival of Saint John the Baptist. When Ricci bowed at the altar before two paintings, one of the Madonna and Child and the other of Saint John, Ai Tian did the same out of politeness. He remarked to the host, however, that people in Kaifeng never worshipped images.

Ai Tian assumed that the paintings represented Rebecca and her sons, Jacob and Esau. Seeing portraits of four evangelists on the wall, Ai Tian asked Ricci if they were four of the twelve sons, which Ricci understood to mean the twelve Christian apostles. Ai Tian, of course, didn't mean this at all. He was referring to the sons of Jacob. After much discussion, Ricci finally realized that this man belonged to a "lost" colony of Jews living in China. To Ricci's amazement, the man from Kaifeng had never even heard of Christianity. Ai Tian, on his part, never understood that these Christians were not a Jewish sect. He considered them a somewhat degenerated branch of Judaism, but Jews nonetheless.

Ai Tian told Ricci that the Jews of Kaifeng found it difficult to keep their laws because circumcision, purification rites, and not eating pork put barriers between them and the Chinese. This was especially true for Jews wishing to become officials, as Ai Tian had done. Meanwhile Ricci demonstrated to the man from Kaifeng that he was familiar with the scriptural passages found in the *Old Testament*. Ricci could read Hebrew, which Ai Tian could not. And Ricci knew all about the early history of the Jewish people.

After Ai Tian returned to Kaifeng, he wrote to Ricci proposing that the Jesuit come to that city to succeed the ailing rabbi. Ai Tian was still under the impression that the Jesuits were a branch of Judaism. He also requested of Ricci, should he accept this post, that he renounce his disgusting habit of eating pork.

Matteo Ricci never found the time to travel to Kaifeng,

but in later years various members of the Jesuit mission did go there. The Jesuits also eventually set up a mission house at Kaifeng. They held many discussions with the Jews on the distinctions between Judaism and Catholicism, and they sent reports about the synagogue and its members to their colleagues in Europe.

Civil war destroyed the city of Kaifeng in 1642, and left many thousands of its residents dead. The defenders of the city, in order to stave off the invaders, opened the Yellow River dikes to flood it. The water surged into the city, completely burying it in so much silt that its 30-foot-high city wall was completely covered. The Jews lost their homes and their synagogue, including their Torah scrolls and prayer books. The Jesuit mission was also destroyed.

By 1653, the Jewish survivors began rebuilding the synagogue on its original foundations. They also gathered what fragments of the Torah scrolls they could find and pieced them together to form a new Torah, their only copy. Within ten years the synagogue was completed, along with a ritual bath, slaughter house, and school. A stone was erected to memorialize the rebuilding. It lists 241 members of the synagogue, 21 of whom were synagogue leaders and 38 who were Jewish civil and military officials in the imperial government.

When a Jesuit named Jean-Paul Gozani visited the Kaifeng synagogue in 1712, he wrote that the Jews "start learning how to read Hebrew from childhood, and many of them also know how to write it." Another Jesuit, Jean Domenge, visiting in 1722, described the synagogue as built in the style of a Chinese temple with many gates and inner courtyards and having pagoda-style roofs. The size was particularly impressive — 400 feet by 150 feet. This is considerably larger than the largest Jewish synagogue in the world today — Temple Emanu-El in New York City.

The Jesuits continued to visit the community occasionally until 1723. That was the last visit by anyone from the West until 1866, when the Jews of Kaifeng were seen by an American Protestant missionary, W. A. P. Martin. By then the community no longer had a rabbi and consisted mainly of shopkeepers and poor families. Their dilapidated and long-unrepaired synagogue, further damaged by a flood in 1849, had been torn down. The last rabbi of Kaifeng died in about 1800, and with him any understanding of the Hebrew manuscripts.

In 1910, Bishop William Charles White of the Canadian Church of England established a Protestant church in Kaifeng. He wanted to build this church, for symbolic reasons, on the property of the torn-down synagogue, but was unable to purchase the land from the Jewish owners. After he established his church elsewhere in the city, however, they did entrust the two stone tablets to his care, under an agreement that he would protect and display the tablets properly.

In 1914 they agreed to sell the synagogue site to White. He converted it into a YMCA-sponsored playground, after he had unsuccessfully tried to persuade persons in Shanghai to provide funds for the construction of a hospital there. When Bishop White returned to Canada, he took a number of artifacts from the synagogue with him. These he gave to the Royal Ontario Museum in Toronto. The Chinese government, in recent years, has erected the hospital that White dreamed of on this site that once held the Kaifeng synagogue.

Several Jews from America visited Kaifeng during the 1930s. One of these, a physician named David A. Brown, recorded the pleas of a community spokesman. According to Brown, the man named Ali said, "We need a school for our children, that they may learn who they are and in what respects they are different from the other Chinese. We know we are Jews, and that our people came here many centuries ago; that we once had a synagogue and a rabbi, but we have lost all knowledge of this; and we are anxious that our children shall walk in the footsteps of those ancient people from whom we have sprung."

The Chinese have often mistaken Jews for Muslims. In Chinese writings they are frequently referred to as Huis (the largest of the ten Muslim ethnic minorities in China). Their neighbors in Kaifeng also called them the blue-capped Muslims because of the headgear the Jews wore at prayer. The mistake should not be surprising. After all, the Jews share with Muslims the practices of circumcision and ban on eating pork.

The Muslims of Kaifeng, however, sometimes displayed an anti-Jewish bias that was quite contrary to Chinese attitudes. They apparently wanted to prove to others that the Jews were in no way affiliated with Islam. An English writer, Oliver Bainbridge, visited Kaifeng in 1906. He stopped at a Muslim mosque there to request information about the Jews. His questions about the Jewish community raised suspicions among the several mullahs that he might be a "Jewish rabbi in disguise." Soon a mob of several thousand irate Muslims had gathered wielding clubs and shouting anti-Semitic slogans at him.

Today the Muslim Dongda (East) Mosque in Kaifeng has a collection of tiles from the demolished synagogue, as well as two stone basins from there and some other artifacts. The two stone tablets that formerly stood in front of the Canadian Anglican church were removed during the Cultural Revolution and are now in the city museum. Other artifacts of the Kaifeng Jewish community were taken from that city by various foreign visitors and are now in museums in England, the United States, and Canada.

Wang Yisha, the curator of the city museum, says that there are still 140 families in China that bear Jewish surnames. Of these, 79 live in Kaifeng (166 persons in all) and 61 have moved away to other parts of China. A survey conducted in 1949 indicated that many of the Jews in Kaifeng worked as shop keepers. One was a silversmith, another a carpenter, another a salt maker, another a bookkeeper, and four were teachers. There were also two mailmen, and one who had become a Buddhist monk.

There is yet another facet to the story of Jews in China, and this is a modern one. Soon after the signing of the Treaty of Nanjing (1842), the city of Shanghai became a haven for Jewish refugees fleeing from persecution in Europe and elsewhere. Sephardic Jews arrived there in large numbers in 1843. Later Ashkenazi Jews came from Russia and Great

Britain. They set up synagogues in Shanghai and Tianjin.

There were also Polish Jews who fled to China from Tsarist Russia and settled in the city of Harbin, in what was then Manchuria. They also established a synagogue. The Russian Revolution brought another surge of Jewish immigrants, fleeing from Communist Russia to China. Most of these settled in Harbin, as well. It seemed a particularly good area because it already had a large Russian population and was the end point to the Trans-Siberian Railroad. But the Japanese occupation of Manchuria in 1931 proved constrictive to the Jewish population there. All but 5,000 of the 19,000 Jews in Harbin soon moved to Shanghai and Tianjin.

The final wave of Jews entered China because of Nazi persecution during World War II. More than 19,000 German Jews went to China at that time. They settled mostly in the cities of Shanghai and Tianjin. After the war almost all of these Jewish refugees moved to the United States or to Israel.

In 1955 all books and Torah scrolls from these modern Chinese synagogues were sent to Israel. The buildings were sold, with most of the proceeds going to the Israeli government at the request of the remaining German, Russian, and Polish Jews. There were only 84 of these immigrant Jews still in Shanghai in 1958. In Tianjin there were 32 and in Harbin, 178. The Polish synagogue in Harbin is now used as an office building.

And what of the Kaifeng Jews? In 1980 a United Press correspondent, Aline Mosby, visited Kaifeng with the intention of tracing the remaining Jews there. She reported that one of them, Ai Feng Ming, told her that the Japanese came to Kaifeng during World War II, at the instigation of their Nazi allies, to search for the Jews of China. They, however, didn't identify themselves as Jews to the soldiers. It is probable that other Chinese, when asked, would have said they were members of the Hui minority.

In 1984 a young woman scholar, named Qu Yinan, went from China to the United States to study English and

American Culture. Her mother, Jin Zhaojing, is descended from one of the Jewish families of Kaifeng. She studied in Portland, Oregon, where she met some Jewish families and eventually asked Rabbi Joshua Stampfer to teach her to read Hebrew. After that she began to attend Sabbath services at Mr. Stampfer's synagogue in Portland (the Congregation Neveh Shalom), where she helped with the Sabbath school and was sometimes called upon to recite the Torah blessing at religious services. Later she received a full scholarship to attend the University of Judaism in Los Angeles.

She is now the only Kaifeng Jew who can read Hebrew and participate in basic Jewish rituals. Although she is still studying in the United States, she is planning to write a book about Judaic traditions for her relatives in China.

QUANZHOU, 1991

Quanzhou, the departure point for Marco Polo's home-ward return, in 1292, was also my last stop in China, in 1991. I wanted to see this historic city because I knew it was once a center of religious diversity. Its reputation is well deserved. I saw remnants of many ancient religions there, and there I discovered new things about religion in China today.

Non-Chinese visitors from the West seldom go to Quanzhou because it is not listed on usual tourist routes. It has no airline, passenger ship, or train service. The only way to get to this city is by bus or taxi from Xiamen, 68 miles away. Yet many Chinese from Taiwan and Southeast Asia do go there to visit relatives and friends. Hopefully, in time, so will tourists from outside the Asian community.

My route to this city was by plane from Nanjing to Xiamen and then by car to Quanzhou. In Xiamen, I was wel-comed by two officials from Quanzhou, one from the Reli-gious Affairs Bureau and the other from the Cultural Affairs Bureau. It was pouring rain that night, and as we drove north I wondered how the driver could find his way through the impenetrable dark on those slippery, rutted roads. The trip took more than two hours. The driver wove left and right trying to avoid the worst ruts. Many times I was sure we would get stuck in the muddy holes left behind by large and heavily-loaded trucks. But eventually we reached the hotel in Quanzhou, exhausted and hungry.

Since it was late and the hotel kitchen was closed, Ms. Wu, the staff member of the Cultural Affairs Bureau, sug-gested that we go to a small restaurant across the road from the hotel. The staff member of Religious Affairs Bureau decid-ed to go home to sleep, instead. My fatigue did not blunt my appreciation of the local sea food delicacies. Ms. Wu told me that the next day would begin with an orientation to the city and its many religious communities. Afterward, we would be able to visit its churches, temples, a mosque, and other religious sites.

We met next morning at the offices of the Cultural Affairs Bureau because, I was told, the offices of the Religious Affairs Bureau were too small. The head of the Cultural Affairs Bureau, Mr. Zhuang, gave the orientation. He began by saying that Quanzhou is one of 24 cities designated by the national government as "famous for historical culture," in this case because it was the ancient starting point for the "silk road on the sea."

He went on to say that the city was established in the year 711 and given the name "Zaitung," according to the *Quanzhou Prefecture Annals*. At one time the city's shape was somewhat like that of a fish, and so it was popularly known as the "Carp City." It was here that trading ships from Arabia and Egypt came to exchange their perfume, pearls, and jewels for highly prized Chinese products such as porcelain, tea, and silk. And it was from here that Zheng He, the great Chinese navigator of the Ming Dynasty, sailed to India and Africa.

Some of the traders who came from foreign countries remained in Quanzhou after their ships docked. And today there are still more than 30,000 descendants of these Arab travelers living in and around the Quanzhou. The Arabs built several mosques, only one of which is still standing. There were also Persian and Indian merchants living here, as evidenced by Manichaen, Hindu, and Brahman remnants, and Nestorian and Roman Catholic Christians, whose grave stones are preserved in the Quanzhou Museum of Overseas Communication History. Their temples and churches stood near the many Taoist and Buddhist structures that once dotted the Quanzhou skyline.

There were undoubtedly also some Jews living in Quanzhou, but only one reference to them has so far been uncovered. This is in the letters of a Franciscan Bishop,

Andrew of Perugia, who wrote to Rome from this city, in 1326, that he was unable to convert any of the Jews to Christianity.

"The many diverse religions existed side by side at relative peace with one another," Mr. Zhuang said. It was clear from his orientation and various things I have since read about this city that, during the 11th and 12th centuries, Quanzhou not only was one of the largest ports in the world but it also was the world's most interfaith community.

Today the Manichaen religion no longer exists in China nor anywhere in the world, and the Hindus and Nestorians departed from China long ago, but most of the other religions still have a presence in Quanzhou. Mr. Zhuang said that today there are within the city or in its surrounding counties 54 Buddhist temples and monasteries, 88 Protestant churches, two Catholic churches, and one Muslim mosque.

I was given other information about the city as well, information not related to religion. Quanzhou is a center for marionette and puppet design and construction, and has been famous for this since the Song Dynasty. The marionette troupe from here performs all over China. Their repertoire includes more than 400 plays. In the past, the marionettes were manipulated by sixteen strings, but today some of them have twenty to thirty strings. This enables the handler to make them perform all sorts of subtle and complex movements. The city also boasts professional opera troupes that produce Liyuan, Gaojia, and Xiangju styles of Chinese opera, and there is a city orchestra that performs Nanyin music, an ancient form closely related to the southern operas.

TWO FACTORY CHURCHES

The first Protestant church I visited in Quanzhou was the most unusual one I saw in all China. It is located on a narrow street, more like an alley than a road, and sits atop a ceramics factory. I would never have known this was a church had the translator not pointed to a small sign inside the doorway, written in Chinese characters. This said the

245

building was the "home of the true church."

The factory's founder, Liao Gengde, met us at the door. He is also the pastor of this former Seventh-Day Baptist church. He established the factory in 1980 with an investment of 300 *yuan*. At first he employed only his family members. But the enterprise grew phenomenally. It now employs about 300 persons and ships its products to Italy, Malaysia, Singapore, England, Sweden, France, Australia, and Hong Kong. The yearly profits are about two million *yuan*. The factory is called the Art and Art Craft Company of the Seventh-Day Church.

Pastor Liao conducted us through the work shops to a stairway leading up to the second floor, where there were many more factory work rooms. He also introduced us to his son, now the general manager and designer of all the ceramic objects they make (miniature dogs, cats, human figures, etc.). Over the years the factory has produced more than 1,000 different kinds of ceramic objects, none of them religious in nature.

We climbed more stairs and finally reached the small room that serves as Seventh-Day church. Here, in this chapel on top of the factory building, we were served tea. The pastor then told us about his life and the church congregation.

During the Cultural Revolution, Pastor Liao told us, the original Seventh-Day Baptist Church was destroyed. He, as pastor, was put out of work. He began to seek new ways to support his family. Many years before he had been apprenticed to a pottery maker. It thus seemed logical to once again turn to this trade. The items he manufactured he placed for display on a little mat rolled out on the sidewalk. During the ten-year Cultural Revolution period he was able to sell enough of them to purchase food and other needs for his family. He told us this time was the most difficult in his life.

When the government reaffirmed its policy on freedom of religion, Pastor Liao began to search for ways to re-establish his church. His son suggested that he found a ceramics factory to raise money for its building. The preacher did so, and the business thrived. It has done so well that they now have sufficient money to rebuild the church, but the factory takes up all the intended space. Pastor Liao is now looking for a place in the suburbs to which they can move the factory so that they can demolish the workshops and erect the new church.

Most of the workers in this factory are not members of the church. But all of them take their day of rest on Saturday, because that is the day the factory closes for worship services. Most of the profits, after taxes, are put aside for building the new church, although one percent is allocated for support of the Protestant Three-Self Patriotic Movement. The pastor said there are about 100 people who attend his church, more than can fit into its small chapel room. Those who cannot get inside stand on the porch outside and listen at the windows.

Despite his age, 79, Pastor Liao is still youthful in appearance and seems quite energetic. He devotes all his energies to the church, letting others handle the ceramics business. He is a member of the standing committee of the Quanzhou Three-Self Movement, and he acts as interim pastor for four home meeting points, as well as handling the affairs of his own church. On Saturdays and Sundays he goes from one point to the next to lead the assembled congregations. At this Seventh-Day church he is assisted by four lay persons, one of whom is a woman. He said that he is presently training his successor, should he ever decide to retire.

We visited another Protestant church in Quanzhou that same day, this one about three blocks away from the first. It is also centered around a factory, and is called the South Street Christian Church. The senior pastor, Rev. Zhang, was away at the time helping in the work of one of the smaller churches in another part of the county. Wu Jingyuan, the head of the factory, and Mrs. Zhong, the leader of their lay Christian training course, gave us a tour of the factory work shops and church.

Most of the 100 workers here are women and members

of the church. They make shoes for children and adults, hats, and various other types of garments. The items are mainly sold in the local markets, although some are shipped to Hong Kong and to Germany. This factory is called the Quanzhou Three-Self Patriotic Hat and Garment Factory. It was founded in 1981 by the pastor as a source of income for church development. One percent of its income (about 20,000 *yuan*) now goes to the church in the form of rent for the use of the church property. The rest goes into salaries for the work force, improvements in machinery, and taxes to the government. The 10,000 *yuan* capital to start this enterprise was contributed by members of the church.

This is the largest Protestant church in Quanzhou. Its sanctuary seats about 2,000 persons at a time. The church has some 6,000 members. I was told that about a third of them are young people, and a third of them are old. They hold two services every Sunday, one in the morning and one in the afternoon. Besides the senior pastor, there are two assistant pastors (one over 90 years of age and the other over 60). The church has paid for the education of five younger pastors, but all of these are now working in other churches in Fujian Province.

There is a youth meeting on Saturday evening, a Sunday school for about 100 children, a 25-member choir, Bible study on Sunday, Monday, and Thursday evenings, and a special service on Wednesday afternoons. The church is also the headquarters for the Quanzhou Patriotic Three-Self Movement.

Before 1949, this church was controlled by the Anglican denomination. At that time it sponsored a middle school and had an extensive program run by missionaries from England. It was closed during the Cultural Revolution, but not destroyed, and the old cross still stands on top of its sanctuary. Its bell tower, however, was badly damaged and has since been rebuilt.

BUDDHIST AND MANICHAEN TEMPLES

The first Buddhist temple we visited was the Kaiyuan Temple, built in 682. It was crowded because this was a day of celebration— the 26th day of the lunar calendar. According to the host monk, they expected 10,000 people to visit the temple on that day. He said they hold such a celebration every month on the 26th day of the lunar calendar.

Many people carried incense, candles, and baskets of fruit as they entered the temple gates. They burned the incense and candles before Buddhist images and left the fruit there as a gift. Some of the bundles of fruit in front of the Buddhist statues were still in the shopping bags in which the fruit was purchased.

At one time there was a Brahman temple near the site of the Kaiyuan Temple, and some of the pillars used in later renovations of the Buddhist Temple were moved there from the Brahman structure. One can still see the original Brahman symbols on them. The monk pointed with pride to a mulberry tree that he said was planted about the year 1300. It still produces flowers in the spring, although it no longer yields any fruit.

There are today 48 monks assigned to this temple, about a third of them under age 40. Every morning at 8:30 they hold a worship ceremony here that is attended by many believers. The monks play musical instruments as they march and chant, followed in their marching by the faithful. They maintain a vegetarian restaurant at which, the monk told me, visitors are allowed to pay whatever they wish for the food they eat.

Next to the Kaiyuan Temple is an exhibition hall that preserves the remains of an ancient sailing ship from the 11th century. It was discovered in 1973, buried under sand that was once part of the ancient port. Some of the wood from this ship became exposed after a storm, and the local fishermen who found it tried to use the wood for firewood, but it wouldn't burn. Apparently it was so water-logged from centuries of sitting under the bay that it could no longer be ignited. Thus the ship was saved from destruction until archaeologists could excavate the rest of it and place it in this museum.

The ship originally had three sails made of bamboo rather than cloth, and was large enough to have several dozen sailors in its crew. It had 13 separate cabins and a deadweight capacity of over 200 tons. The archaeologists were able to date it by the more than 500 coins, spice barrels, and other items found in its cargo. They speculate that the ship sank during a sea battle. Another such ship was discovered in 1982, but this has yet to be excavated.

I visited other Buddhist sites in and around Quanzhou, but none as unusual as the Cao'an Temple built on the side of Huabiao Hill in nearby Jinjiang County. This temple was established in 1922 at the site of a Manichaen temple destroyed long ago. The Buddhist nuns who inhabit this temple preserve a stone representation of Mani that once stood in that Manichaen temple.

The Manichaen religion was a mixture of Christianity, Parseeism, and Buddhism. It was founded by a Persian, Mani (216-276), who was banished from his own country because of his teachings. Mani subsequently traveled to the Far East where his doctrines flourished for many centuries. When Mani returned to his home country, around 270, he was arrested and later executed by the ruler, Brahram I.

The religion gained followers in China from the 7th century to the 14th century. The worshipers eventually offended the emperor of the Ming Dynasty, Emperor Taizu, who ordered them banished from China. The representation of Mani at the Cao'an Temple is one of the few physical remnants of this religion that still exist. When a world conference on this religion was held in Sweden several years ago, this stone replica was adopted as the symbol of the conference.

The Buddhist nuns at the Cao'an Temple have adopted the Mani stone as one of their own, and use it as a point for their worship. They call it the "Buddha of Light." The figure carved into the stone has a beard and hair that are so different from the other Buddhist statues in the temple that it is obvious it comes from a foreign tradition. The figure also has the rays of the sun radiating from its head, something not found in Buddhist statues elsewhere. I was told that during the Cultural Revolution a Red Guard unit came to this temple and tried to destroy this image of Mani. However, the rock is so hard that they could not do much damage to it. The nuns keep a flame permanently burning before this image of Mani.

There are twenty nuns at this temple, and their special temple day is June 13, considered to be the birthday of Mani. On this date each year they receive as many as five or six thousand visitors. The nuns here specialize in taking care of abandoned female children. Some of the nuns at this temple have shaved heads, as do nuns in most other Buddhist temples, but some do not. The guide told us that it is the custom in this area of China to allow Buddhist nuns to keep their hair, if they so wish.

MUSLIM AND TAOIST SITES

The Qingjing Mosque in Tumenjie Street in Quanzhou is under the protection of the central government because it is one of the oldest mosques in China. When it was originally built in 1009, it was a magnificent granite structure designed in the style of one of the Islamic mosques in Damascus, Syria. This style is not found elsewhere in China. Although the mosque has deteriorated with age, it is still quite impressive. Its main gate is the best preserved part of the building.

Toward the rear of the property is a small worship hall built in the form of a traditional Chinese compound. Here is where the Muslims of Quanzhou worship today. They have made plans to restore the large ancient structure, but they now do not have the funds to do so and the congregation is too small to support a worship site of such size.

The Imam at this mosque told me that Islam spread to Brunei (a country on the northern coast of Borneo) from Quanzhou. It was introduced there by a Chinese of Arabian descent named Pu. He was originally a member of this mosque. The Chinese names of other well-known Arabian

251

families in this area are Ding and Gao. Their ancestors are all buried at the Muslim graveyard on Lingshan Hill, in the eastern suburbs of Quanzhou.

The Muslims of Quanzhou take care of this graveyard and all the deceased members of this mosque are buried there. Here are also the sacred graves of two followers of Mohammed, who came to China in 622. There are several old Arabian inscriptions behind these two tombs, one of which dates to 1322. The graveyard also contains stone sarcophagi of other Muslim notables from the Song, Yuan, and Ming dynasties, as well as many modern graves.

The Taoist temples that once dotted the Quanzhou landscape have mostly disappeared, but there is one Taoist statue that still stands out prominently. This is the Laojun Crag at the foot of Qingyuan Hill, about two miles north of the city. This statue of Laozi was carved in one solid piece of rock during the early Song Dynasty, and is a fine example of Song era sculpture. It is the oldest and largest Taoist statue of its kind in China, being more than 16 feet tall and 23 feet wide. It depicts Laozi sitting on the ground. His long ears, bushy eyebrows, beard, and folds of his clothing look as vivid today as they must have when the statue was first carved more than a thousand years ago.

There used to be many Taoist monasteries on Qingyuan Hill, and it is known that the Laojun sculpture was originally located inside such a monastery. However, nothing remains of the building today. Further up the hill are several Buddhist temples that attract many visitors.

The collection of religious artifacts that have been uncovered over the years in Quanzhou is housed at the Museum of Overseas Communication History. Here they have Islamic stone inscriptions from the various mosques that once existed in the city. There are also Hindu statues of the god Krishna and carvings of elephants embracing Lingam trees with their trunks. There are 30 Nestorian gravestones with a variety of Syrian inscriptions and Christian crosses and cherubs on them, and Catholic Franciscan gravestones inscribed in Latin from a slightly later period. Included among the latter is the headstone for Bishop Andrew, the man who wrote the letter to Rome concerning the Jews. The museum also preserves a black glazed bowl from one of the Manichaen temples. It is marked with Chinese characters that say "sect of fire worship."

Other parts of this museum, which is in a new building in the suburbs, include rooms dedicated to the maritime history of Quanzhou, the types of porcelains that were exported from here over the centuries, and the folk customs and genealogical documents relating to overseas immigration. This is the headquarters for China's Research Association of Overseas Communications History and for the Fujian Provincial Research Society into the Maritime Silk Route.

AN INTERFAITH MEETING

Toward the end of our visit in Quanzhou, the head of the Religious Affairs Bureau suggested that my interviews with the local religious leaders might be best expedited if I had the chance to meet with them all at one time. The suggestion was an excellent one because it allowed me to participate in one of their regular interfaith gatherings. These, I was told, take place about once or twice a month. They are organized by the Religious Affairs Bureau with the intention of coordinating the work of the religious groups in Quanzhou. As far as I could learn, such cooperation among the religions is unique to this area.

At the meeting were Abdola Huang Qiurun, the President of the Islamic Association of Quanzhou and head of the mosque; Mr. Wu Zexun, the Deputy President of the Quanzhou Buddhist Association; Rev. Wei Shouren, the Deputy Director of the Quanzhou branch of the China Christian Council: Rev. Zhang Chunquan, the President of the Protestant Three-Self Patriotic Movement and senior pastor of the South Street Christian Church; Father Cai Yizhong, a Catholic priest and leader of the Quanzhou Patriotic Catholic Committee; and Mr. Lin Cunyi of the Taoist Cultural Research Society. Several of them are also elected members of

253

the Provincial People's Political Consultative Congress.

Abdola Huang was the first to speak. He began by describing how Islam came to Quanzhou through the arrival of the two missionaries sent to China by Mohammed in 622. He also described the discrimination against Muslim believers before 1949, and how the officials of the former Nationalist government had criticized their beliefs and tried to force them to eat pork. He said there are now 300 Muslims of Arabic ancestry in the city plus about 30,000 people of similar ancestry living in the surrounding areas, or altogether 30,300 persons considered to be Muslims. Most of them, he said, are not religious. However, they do not eat pork and they do participate in the major festivals of the Muslim religion. He further said that on special festival days they always invite representatives of the other religions to come to the mosque to celebrate with them.

The Buddhist spoke next. He said there are 80,000 Buddhist monks and nuns in the Quanzhou area, and described how the Buddhist temples of the city were closed and damaged during the Cultural Revolution. But now "these have been restored and many are more beautiful than ever before," he said. He also told how a delegation of Buddhists from Japan had recently visited the Kaiyuan Temple and seen the way Buddhism is flourishing there. The Japanese, he said, attributed this to the support that the government is now giving to the Buddhists of Quanzhou.

Rev. Zhang spoke on behalf of the Protestants. He said there are 88 Protestant churches in the Quanzhou area, with about 80,000 members. Before 1949 there were only 20,000 Protestants here. The Patriotic Three-Self Movement and the Christian Council were established in this city in 1987, and there are now 30 people assigned to working for these two organizations. Their major problem is the shortage of trained clergy. They have sent 20 persons to be trained at the theological schools in Fujian Province and in Nanjing, and about 140 persons have been trained for church leadership in the 16-day short courses for elders that the Three-Self Movement offers here. They have choirs in the five major Protestant churches in Quanzhou, and some of these churches have children's classes on Sunday morning.

Father Cai spoke next for the Catholics. He said that there are 1,500 Catholics in Quanzhou. There were more here before 1949, but many of them were Filipinos who returned to the Philippines after the Communist revolution. The Catholic church was occupied by a factory during the Cultural Revolution and the factory still uses the property. Thus there have been no formal church activities within that building for many years. However, the Catholics do meet in another building and there is another Catholic church operating in one of the surrounding counties. With the help of the Religious Affairs Bureau, they are trying to regain the Quanzhou property so that they can again hold services within the church. The government has promised to give the Catholics 50,000 *yuan* for restoration after the factory moves out. He said he knew of no dissident Catholic activities in this area, although there were such groups in other parts of the province. In the past there were 70 to 80 Catholic priests in Quanzhou for a Catholic population of over 100,000. Now there are only two other priests, one who is quite old and the other who is 33 years of age.

Finally the Taoist told of the situation with his religion in the Quanzhou area. He said it is a difficult time for Taoists here because there are so few left and there are only three places of worship in the surrounding area, none of which have any priests or nuns to take care of them. The three Taoist temples are the Flower Bridge Temple, the Huxiu Temple, and the Fumei Temple. These worship sites receive 2,000 to 3,000 visitors a year from other parts of Asia. Although he is the representative of the Taoist Cultural Society in Quanzhou, set up to preserve Taoist cultural relics here, he hopes that this organization will eventually evolve into a branch of the Taoist Association of China. This has not yet happened because there are so few Taoists in Quanzhou. They are looking for leadership to head this Association once it is established.

On the final evening in Quanzhou, the leaders of the

Cultural Affairs Bureau and the Religious Affairs Bureau invited me to a banquet. During the many toasts, I interjected that I was surprised that these two bureaus in Quanzhou seem to work so closely together. Mr. Chen of the Cultural Affairs Bureau and Mr. Cai of the Religious Affairs Bureau both laughed. They told me that this was because they had been classmates during their middle school days. I naturally asked them what school they had attended. To my surprise I learned that these two Communist leaders both studied at the middle school that was once operated by the Anglican church. This, they said, was the best school in Quanzhou before 1949.

The several days stay in Quanzhou allowed me to reflect on what I had seen on this trip to China and on my many interviews with the various religious personages. My thoughts turned on three basic questions: How is it possible for religion to thrive in a country where the leaders of the government advocate atheism? Is the practice of religion truly free in China? Why is religious interest growing in China today?

RELIGION VS. ATHEISM

It is my belief that the common Western idea that there must be conflict between religion and atheism is a fallacy. What I have seen in other countries suggests that the relationship between religion and atheism throughout the world is much like it is in China today. That is, all shades of atheism and agnosticism co-exist with the established religions.

Some Westerners would like to make this issue the central one in their opposition to socialism in China. But I am sure they will be no more successful in attacking atheism in China than the Cultural Revolution propagandists were in trying to block religion.

Far better would it be to heed the words of China's Premier Zhou Enlai, who in a 1956 interview with a reporter from India said, "I must frankly tell you that we have no scientific basis for foretelling the future of religion in China. Religion may continue for all time, or it may fade out.... It may last forever, or it may disappear.''

Many governments in the world have tried to control the religious thinking of their citizens, but none have been successful. In China, the attempt to do this during the Cultural Revolution proved a disastrous failure. Political campaigns, political repression, war? None of these ever change an atheist into a theist, or vice versa. Religion and atheism are matters of personal faith, not matters of state.

The Chinese Communists reject religion partly because they are Marxists. They also reject it because, in their experience, most religions — particularly the various Christian religions — have usually been on the side of imperialism and reaction. After all, it was the so-called Christian nations of the West that entered China with imperialist armies to impose unequal treaties on the government and to set up foreign enclaves within that nation.

In 1949, when the People's Liberation Army was about to cross the Yangtze River in pursuit of the Nationalist forces, there were Christians who prayed that God might perform a miracle and drown the soldiers of the People's Liberation Army in the river waters. After the Communist victory of 1949, Christians outside of China and most of the Christian missionaries who tried to remain in China continued to support Chiang Kai-shek, the leader who most of the Chinese people considered to be their enemy. Thus for many patriotic Chinese, the Christian religion became one of the many problems that China faced in trying to reorganize their country rather than any kind of solution to those problems.

Any consideration of ideological commitments to atheism or a particular religion need to be seen in the broader context of history — the ongoing events that shape a person's ideology. Here, for China, the primary historical event of modern times is the Chinese Communist revolution. For Westerners it is important to understand this, not only so as to understand China but also to understand many of the other events that have taken place in the Third World in recent years — the Vietnam War, hostilities in Central and South America, and Arab-Israeli conflict in the Middle East.

257

Many of the forces that led to the Chinese revolution can also be found in the revolutionary movements throughout the Third World. These include a deep desire to overcome poverty, resentment against white racism, opposition to Western imperialism, and the determination to establish a free, self-respecting society.

It is interesting to note that atheism and religion often play complimentary roles in history, a fact that proponents of either side tend to forget. Consider, for example, the contribution of the various educational institutions that the Christian missionaries established in China during the early part of the 20th century. They were a vehicle for Western influence, of course. But they also provided models for the future socialist society and were a training ground for atheist revolutionaries.

These religious institutions fostered the idea of conversion, that is changing the individual. The Chinese Communists call this *fanshen*, or turning over.

Also these Christian institutions promoted the ideas of reaching out to the common people, opposing the rigid class distinctions espoused by the Confucian elite, and bringing literacy to everyone. These were concepts finally brought to fruition by Chairman Mao and the Chinese Communist Party. The list could go on — rural reconstruction, hospital care, famine relief. Many of these programs, now part of everyday life in China, were initiated and tested by religious pioneers long before China's revolution fully developed.

The destiny of the Chinese people, who for thousands of years were at the very bottom of society, has been changed for the better by the revolution. The whole society is more united now than ever before, and the Chinese people are working for a common goal. The religious people of China have experienced these changes and express their approval through their support of the government. In fact the revolution has provided Chinese Christians, particularly, with an opportunity to think anew about the meaning of religion and the role of the church. As Ding Guangxun (K. H. Ting) puts it "Today...there is in China a Christianity to which revolution is no longer a stranger, and a revolution to which

Christianity is not such a stranger either."

Religious people all over the world generally shrink from what is called "the terrible cost in lives of a revolution." But they do not always shrink from the terrible cost of not having a revolution. In China the revolutionaries developed a deep sense of history. Not only did they reflect on the centuries of famine, poverty, and peasant revolts against unbearable conditions that cost many tens of millions of lives, but they also reflected on the hundred years of imperialist wars that tore China apart and forced the disaster of opium on the country. The long revolutionary struggle led by Mao Zedong has now created a strong, independent, and socially equitable China where the Chinese are confident that such things can no longer happen.

The founder of the Three-Self Patriotic Movement, Wu Yaozong (Y. T. Wu), put it well when he said "Since Communism is practicing what Christianity merely professes, Christians have no right to stress the points on which they differ from Communists, until they are similarly practicing their beliefs."

Finally, is it really Marxist atheism that is the enemy of religion? Just as one can define religion in many ways, one can define atheism in many ways too. The German theologian Paul Tillich defined atheism in his book, *The Shaking of the Foundations* (1948), as a view of life that has no depth— a view that is shallow. If one defines atheism in this way, then it is the narrow-minded cold warrior of the West who is the atheist, and not the Communists. Certainly much of contemporary commercialism in the West is far more shallow in outlook than are the Chinese Marxists.

RELIGIOUS FREEDOM

The very fact that religious freedom appears to be a universal concept, easily measured against objective criteria, leads us into the trap of cultural misunderstandings. We forget that every country has its own set of values regarding what constitutes religion and how religious believers should behave. These are built of historical conditions peculiar to that culture, and they are universally accepted by members of that culture. It is all too easy, for example, for people in the Unites States to point the finger of religious intolerance at other cultures, while forgetting our own long history of religious intolerance against Catholics, Mormons, and the indigenous religions of the native Americans.

China has just as long a history of struggle for human rights and freedom as do most of the countries of the West. The Communist revolution in China itself was part of this striving for human rights, and it achieved certain freedoms that are only partially honored in the West, such as the right of every person to a livelihood and equal medical care. The emphasis on individual rights that is so important in the United States, however, takes secondary importance in this country where, for many centuries, the welfare of the community as a whole has always preceded that of the individual.

Many of the comments by Westerners on freedom fall flat in the Chinese context. Consider this paragraph from a 1980 speech made by Rev. Shen Yifan, now Bishop but then pastor of the Shanghai Community Church, to an audience of Protestants in Hong Kong. He said, "In the 1950s, one foreign churchman visiting China made a comment that Chinese Christians found incongruous. He said, 'China has no freedom because she has no prostitutes.' To us, to take the existence of prostitution as a symbol of freedom is utter mockery of real freedom. Only in a society where prostitution and other social evils are abolished are human liberty and dignity truly respected. How could it be that to oppose social evils is to interfere with personal freedom? How could it be that voluntary dedication to the cause of righteousness of mankind is the road to bondage?"

Every religious leader I spoke with in China emphasized the fact that their government guarantees them freedom of religion. During the ten-year period of the Cultural Revolution this constitutional guarantee was suspended, but they assured me that such an event could never happen again because every Chinese had learned a lesson from it. Before China be-

260

came a socialist country, they told me, China's religions were somewhat curtailed and religious persons were often discriminated against because such freedom of religion was not a part of the national law.

On my return to the United States, I received a copy of a report published by Asia Watch, titled "Freedom of Religion in China Today." This organization monitors human rights issues throughout Southeast Asia, and its reports on human rights abuses in South Korea and the Philippines have been widely acclaimed. I do not think this report on China, however, was written with the same objectivity or evenhandedness as some of their earlier papers.

Much of the data included in the Asia Watch report comes from unverified Hong Kong and Taiwan sources that have a history of manufacturing "horror stories" to support their opposition to the Chinese government. Some of the data appears to be out of date and coming from the days of the Cultural Revolution. The report lists the arrests of certain persons "for religious reasons," none of which are so categorized by the Chinese civil authorities. In every case I have been able to verify, the persons so listed were arrested for anti-government activities that had nothing to do with their religious beliefs.

The rest of the report contains data similar to what I have included in this book, but it is written with a dark twist that makes Chinese officials seem devious and evil. For example, the Asia Watch report says, as I do, that there are about 20,000 Protestant meeting points in China. I found that most of these meeting points are part of the established Protestant Three-Self Patriotic Movement. Asia Watch, however, implies that they are all underground churches, opposed to the Three-Self Movement.

Asia Watch says that the Religious Affairs Bureau maintains administrative control over all places of worship, which must meet official standards. In terms of the Protestants and Catholics, they say, "espousing those parts of the Bible that deal with eschatology...are considered propaganda and cannot be mentioned in a sermon." Obviously the authors of this report have not listened to many sermons or hymns in the churches of China, or they would never make such a ridiculous statement. (For those not familiar with the term, "eschatology" has to do with the doctrine of last or final things, such as death, heaven, hell, and the second coming.)

The Asia Watch report also says that the Chinese authorities have branded *qigong*, the ancient Taoist exercise and healing art as "superstitious and, therefore, illegal." Again one suspects that the authors have never been to China to investigate the matter. Any visitor will see *qigong* being practiced every day by individuals and groups in the public parks. The visitor will also find many books on the subject in government bookstores, including the recently published *Believe It or Not: Ancient and Mysterious Chinese Qigong*, a laudatory book about this healing art that was published in both Chinese and English by one of the government printing offices.

THE GROWTH OF RELIGIONS

All the religions of China are today experiencing growth, except for the Chinese Orthodox Church. And, of all the religions of China, the most phenomenal growth has been experienced by the Protestants — from 700,000 in 1949 to 5.5 million in 1991 — an increase of nearly eight fold in a little over forty years. Many of the new converts are young people and many are college graduates, including professors, writers, doctors, and engineers. Of the more than 6,000 Protestants in the city of Shenyang, for instance, young people make up 26 percent.

In the case of the Muslims, some of this growth can be attributed to the growth in their population. But that hardly accounts for the increase in Buddhist, Taoist, Catholic, and Protestant membership. In all my interviews, therefore, I asked for reasons why religious interest seems to be increasing so rapidly in this atheist country.

One youth told me that after the turmoil of the Cultural Revolution the churches and temples represented a kind of peace and stability that she had not experienced before. Others say that people are turning to religion to seek help from God to be rid of an illness or to overcome difficulties. Others are seeking a way to end their loneliness or to have their sins forgiven. But perhaps the most important reason for the religious resurgence in China is a search for emotional and spiritual fulfillment.

Protestant Bishop Ding Guangxun put it this way, "All young people today are curious about religion. They also feel an emptiness in their lives, an emptiness that is not dealt with in their schools or by television or the news media. Their curiosity brings them into contact with churches. Many of the young people in church on any Sunday morning are there only out of curiosity, and will attend church only a few times. Others are there searching for love and human care that they miss in their own families and in the work place. They find this in the church. Later some of these same people find that the church can't give them everything that they are seeking, and they then leave. But many do stay and become active church members."

Disenchantment and loss of Communist idealism due to past mistakes of the Communist Party has also been a factor in the turn to religion on the part of youth and intellectuals. They find in religion a new source of ideals. The Religious Affairs Bureau officials readily admit that this is a factor in the growth of Protestantism and say that the Communist Party needs to take this as a challenge to do a better job in ideological education.

A writer in the March 20, 1989 issue of *Beijing Review* reported the following statement made by a young Protestant doctor in Wenzhou. He said, "The Party's work style and many social practices are in a mess. Abuse of power, bribery, cheating, and prostitution are widespread. I'm tired of all this. It's a relief to step inside a church and sing 'Holy, Holy, Holy.' Then I can hear heaven calling me."

The same writer points out that another reason for the popularity of Protestantism is that while rapidly expanding production has helped the Chinese people realize many of

263

their material aspirations, it does nothing to fill a spiritual void. Many educated young people have little to do in their spare time. For this reason, they often turn to religious activity. The writer told of a young Protestant from Anhui Province who said, "We've had no shows or cinemas in our township during the last one or two years. The cultural center and the militia club have closed. The Communist Youth League is no longer active. What else can we do but join the religious people."

It was interesting to me how often religious leaders cited moral values as a factor in the attraction of religion for people in China. Many times they cited persons in their churches or temples who had been honored as model citizens. They told me that these values came directly from the teachings of their religion rather than from values taught in schools or in the community. They said that their religion — Taoism, Buddhism, Islam, Catholicism, and Protestantism — taught its members to do good for society and for the religion.

But perhaps the most important reason for the growth of the Protestant and Catholic churches in China is the fact that they are now truly Chinese churches and not branches of the Western missionary movement. Before the revolution, any Chinese who joined a Protestant or Catholic church was viewed as a loss to China. Many Chinese condemned Christianity with the phrase: "Win a convert, lose a citizen." But now the Chinese Christians control their own destiny and there is no longer the cloud of "foreign religion" preventing natural church growth.

I left Quanzhou not by boat, as did Marco Polo seven hundred years earlier, but by car to Xiamen and then by airplane to Hong Kong. Whereas twenty years ago when going from mainland China to Hong Kong one experienced the culture shock of leaving the austerity of life in China to enter the glitter and commercialism of Hong Kong, I found this no longer so. China is changing. It is wise for us to change along with her. We can only do this if we strive to better understand that country of over one billion people, one fifth of the world's population.

CHRONOLOGY
OF CHINESE HISTORY

Xia Dynasty	c. 21st – 17th century B.C.
Shang Dynasty	c. 17th – 11th century B.C.
Zhou Dynasty	c. 11th century – 256 B.C.
Western Zhou	c. 11th century – 771 B.C.
Eastern Zhou	770 – 256 B.C.
Spring and Autumn Period	770 – 476 B.C.
Warring States Period	475 – 221 B.C.
Qin Dynasty	221 – 206 B.C.
Han Dynasty	206 B.C. – A.D. 220
Western Han	206 B.C. – A.D. 25
Eastern Han	A.D. 25 – 220
Three Kingdoms	220 – 280
Jin Dynasty	265 – 420
Western Jin	265 – 317
Eastern Jin	317 – 420
Southern and Northern Dynasties	420 – 589
Sui Dynasty	581 – 618
Tang Dynasty	618 – 907
Five Dynasties	907 – 960
Song Dynasty	960 – 1279
Northern Song	960 – 1127
Southern Song	1127 – 1279
Liao Dynasty	907 – 1125
Jin Dynasty	1115 – 1234
Yuan Dynasty	1206 – 1368
Ming Dynasty	1368 – 1644
Qing Dynasty	1644 – 1911
Republic of China	1912 – 1949
People's Republic of China	1949 – present

BIBLIOGRAPHY

Bai Shouyi. *An Outline History of China*. Beijing: Foreign Languages Press, 1982.

Blofeld, John Eaton Calthorpe. *Beyond the Gods: Taoist and Buddhist Mysticism*. New York: Dutton, 1974.

Bonsall, Bramwell Seaton. *Confucianism and Taoism*. London: Epworth Press, 1934.

Brown, C. Thompson. *Christianity in the People's Republic of China*. Atlanta: John Knox Press, 1983.

Cameron, Nigel. *Barbarians and Mandarins*. New York: John Weatherhill, Inc., 1970.

Carino, Theresa C. *Christianity in China: Three Lectures by Zhao Fusan*. Manila: De La Salle University, 1986.

Chu, Theresa and Christoper Lind. *A New Beginning*. Toronto: Canada China Programme, 1983.

Ellis, Jane. *The Russian Orthodox Church: A Contemporary History*. Bloomington: Indiana University Press, 1986.

Fairbank, John K. *The Missionary Enterprise in China and America*. Cambridge: Harvard University Press, 1974.

Fung, Raymond. *Households of God on China's Soil*. New York: Orbis Books, 1982.

Gladney, Dru C. *Muslim Chinese*. Cambridge: Harvard University Press, 1991.

Hanson, Eric O. *Catholic Politics in China and Korea*. New York: Orbis Books, 1980.

Heyu. *Tibet: A General Survey*. Beijing: New World Press, 1988.

Hsu, F. C. *On the Theory of Pure Consciousness*. Beijing: New World Press, 1990.

Jones, Francis Price. *The Church in Communist China: A Protestant Appraisal*. New York: Friendship Press, 1962.

Lai, T. C. *The Eight Immortals*. Hong Kong: Swindon Book Company, 1972.

Lu Yun. *Religion in China — 100 Questions and Answers*. Beijing: New Star Publishers, 1991.

Lutheran World Federation. *Theological Implications of the New China*. Geneva: Lutheran World Federation/Pro Mundi Vita, 1974.

Luo Zhufeng. *Religion Under Socialism in China*. Armonk: M. E. Sharpe, Inc., 1991.

MacInnis, Donald E. *Religion in China Today: Policy and Practice*. New York: Orbis Books, 1989.

Meisner, Maurice. *Mao's China: A History of the People's Republic*. New York: Free Press, 1977.

Needham, Joseph. *Science and Civilization in China, Vol. 2*. Cambridge: Cambridge University Press, 1956.

Orr, Robert G. *Religion in China*. New York: Friendship Press, 1980.

Pollack, Michael. *Mandarins, Jews, and Missionaries*. Philadelphia: The Jewish Publication Society, 1980.

Polo, Marco. *The Travels of Marco Polo the Venetian*. London: Everyman's Library, 1903.

Shapiro, Sidney. *Jews in Old China*. New York: Hippocrene, 1984.

Smith, D. Howard. *Chinese Religions*. New York: Holt, Rinehart and Winston, 1968.

Su Kaiming. *Modern China: A Topical History*. Beijing, New World Press, 1985.

Suyin, Han. *Lhasa, The Open City*. London: Jonathan Cape Ltd., 1977.

Ting, K. H. *Chinese Christians Speak Out*. Beijing: New World Press, 1984.

Towery, Britt E., Jr. *The Churches of China*. Waco: Long Dragon Books, 1987.

Waddell, L. Austine. *Tibetan Buddhism, with Its Mystic Cults, Symbolism and Mythology*. Mineola: Dover Publications, 1972.

Welch, Holmes. *Buddhism Under Mao*. Cambridge: Harvard University Press 1973.

Whitehead, Raymond L. *No Longer Strangers: Selected Writings of K. H. Ting*. New York: Orbis Books, 1989.

Wicker i, Philip L. *Seeking the Common Ground*. New York: Orbis Books, 1988.

Yu Hanzhang. *The Biographies of the Dalai Lamas*. Beijing: Foreign Languages Press, 1991.

Also the following journals (all published in English):

Beijing Review, Beijing
China Daily, Beijing
China News Update, Louisville, KY
China Notes, New York
China Talk, Hong Kong
China Today, Beijing
China' s Tibet, Beijing
Chinese Theological Review, Holland, MI
Eastern Horizon, Hong Kong

INDEX

中国宗教概览

Foster   stockwell   著

*

新世界出版社出版

（北京百万庄路 24 号）

北京大学印刷厂印刷

中国国际图书贸易总公司发行

（中国北京车公庄西路 35 号）

北京邮政信箱第 399 号   邮政编码 100044

1993 年（英文）第一版

ISBN 7-80005-184-6

02800

2-E-2840P